STRONGMAN'S HIS NAME... II

by Drs.
Jerry & Carol
Robeson

Whitaker House

Unless otherwise indicated, all Scripture quotations are taken from the King James Version (KJV) of the Holy Bible. Scripture quotations marked (AMP) are taken from the *Amplified® Bible*, © 1954, 1958, 1962, 1964, 1965, 1987 by The Lockman Foundation. Used by permission. (www.Lockman.org)

STRONGMAN'S HIS NAME...II

Dr. Carol Robeson
Shiloh Publishing House
P.O. Box 100
Woodburn, OR 97071
1.800.607.6195

ISBN-13: 978-0-88368-603-4
ISBN-10: 0-88368-603-1
Printed in the United States of America
© 1994 by Dr. Carol Robeson

Whitaker House
1030 Hunt Valley Circle
New Kensington, PA 15068
www.whitakerhouse.com

Library of Congress Cataloging-in-Publication Data

Robeson, Jerry, 1938–1999.
Strongman's his name—II / by Jerry and Carol Robeson.
p.   cm.
Originally published: Woodburn, OR : Shiloh Pub., 1994.
ISBN 0-88368-603-1 (pbk. : alk. paper)
1. Spiritual warfare—Biblical teaching. I. Title: Strongman's his name ... two.
II. Robeson, Carol, 1939– III. Title.
BS680.S73 R63 2000
235'.4—dc21
00-020281

5 6 7 8 9 10 11 12 13 14 15 **UJ** 14 13 12 11 10 09 08 07 06

TABLE OF CONTENTS

PREFACE

When we left the mission field after 20 years in the 1980's to teach spiritual warfare in the U.S., many of our friends and pastors, who had supported and encouraged us for years, thought we were either crazy or out of touch with reality. Their attitude suggested that all that "stuff" about demons only happens on the mission field so why bother them with it here in the U.S.?

We knew we had clearly heard from God so we took a gigantic step of faith, left people's attitudes to the Lord and began teaching the people who were willing to listen to what we had to say about the subject.

We sent our STRONGMAN'S HIS NAME WHAT'S HIS GAME manuscript off to various publishing houses, but they seemed to be afraid of it. Spiritual warfare had been abused in so many ways over the years that there was a natural tendency for them to shy away from it.

One day the Holy Spirit spoke to my spirit as clearly as I've ever heard Him. He said, "Why don't you publish the book yourself?"

The thought had never crossed my mind because we didn't know anything about publishing, but the thought immediately excited me. "Hey, that's a great idea!" I answered and that is how Shiloh Publishing House came into existence. God has led us every step of the way since then and we give Him all the glory.

Now, a number of years later the atmosphere has changed considerably. No one asks us anymore why we are teaching about things that only happen on the mission field—the mission field problems have come to our own cities and communities. Spiritual warfare and binding the strongman are now common terms that we hear all the time.

Everywhere we go people thank us for being obedient to the Lord in making the Strongman book available to the Body of Christ. The truth is, we are honored and thankful that the Lord entrusted us with this message and our greatest desire is to get it out to all the world—something which is happening now!

Introduction

The response to our book, *Strongman's His Name What's His Game*, has been phenomenal. We have received letters and phone calls from all over the world and talked with thousands of people in our seminars about the subject of spiritual warfare.

Most people asked questions about how to deal with their particular problems. From those questions we observed certain patterns developing which we could see needed to be addressed in a more formal context. So that is what we will do in this book.

The major discovery we made was that many Christians feel they are not adequately prepared to deal personally with the devil and their spiritual problems in an effective manner.

Our principle ministry for twenty years on the mission field was to take the new converts from the open-air crusades we had been involved with and mold them into the new church body that would carry on the ministry of the new church under the leadership of the new pastor. We quickly learned that we didn't have time to baby along 2000 to 3000 new converts. As the Holy Spirit led us, we developed methods of teaching the new ones to fend for themselves in spiritual matters much sooner than had been the pattern in the past.

For instance, after giving them thorough instruction concerning Divine healing, we would instruct them, "If you get sick, don't call the pastor—you pray for yourselves. Your faith is as effective as ours so just believe what God's Word says and receive it by faith." They were new converts and didn't know any different—so they did it—

1

and were healed! When they realized the power and authority they had in God's Word they started looking for other sick people to pray for and God was faithful to heal them also as they believed and received by faith in God's Word.

That lifted a large load from our shoulders and we were freed to concentrate on other areas of ministry. Eventually the new converts were leading souls to Jesus, praying for the sick and doing spiritual warfare instead of expecting the pastor and other leaders to do it for them.

When we returned to the U.S., we felt led of the Holy Spirit to use that same approach in sharing the spiritual warfare principles He had given us with the rest of the world. So we wrote our Strongman's His Name What's His Game book from the perspective of giving people a simple, effective tool to help them pinpoint their own spiritual needs, deal with them according to God's Word and find freedom in their life without having to rely on other people to do for them what they should be doing for themselves to receive their deliverance.

Great numbers of our readers used our book that way and reported tremendous victories in their lives for which we thank the Lord. That encouraged us to continue believing that this was what the Holy Spirit wanted to accomplish in His Body. It was time for the Laity to share the battle with the enemy instead of depending on pastors and spiritual leaders to do it for them. Should the day ever come in America that Christians are persecuted to the point that they cannot openly worship God according to the dictates of their conscience and convictions, these teachings will also serve to help them do battle in the spirit realm so they can accomplish God's Will in their lives and live the overcoming life of a conqueror that Romans 8:37 promises believers, no matter what the situation may be.

But we were troubled by the small percentage of people who felt they could not break through to victory in their life without the help of others.

We understand that there are those who are so bound or even demon possessed that they are incapable of receiving freedom without assistance—their need for in-depth deliverance is understandable.

The underlying problem, we discovered for those who are overly dependent on others to receive deliverance, is a faith problem. For various reasons they find it difficult to make a step of faith on their

Introduction

own and do what they know they should do. The Holy Spirit and the Word of God have usually spoken to them about it, but they either (1) don't recognize it as the Holy Spirit, (2) are fearful of the reactions of people around them if they follow the Holy Spirit's and the Word's direction, (3) feel unqualified to confront the devil, take authority over him in the Name of Jesus and boot him out of their lives, (4) really don't want to give up what has caused the problem to begin with and are looking for someone to tell them it is alright to continue living as they are, (5) have given in to discouragement and believe what the devil tells them about the situation, (6) or any number of other reasons which eventually reduce down to the simple fact that **they have not put into practice in their lives what God has to say about the situation.** The fact is that God has provided for our every need, but it is our responsibility to meet whatever conditions He demands in His Word so that we can receive His Promises.

For instance, God has provided Salvation for every individual on this earth. But in order for them to be saved, (1) they **have** to be told that Salvation is necessary and possible, (2) they **must** repent of their sins and confess with their mouth the Lord Jesus, (3) they **must** believe in their heart that God raised Jesus from the dead, (4) and they **must** receive the salvation from their sins by an act of faith in God's Word. (Romans 10:9)

We all know of people who feel those steps aren't necessary and as a result are not able to **receive** Salvation. God wants them to receive and so do we, but until **they** actually **believe God** and **do** what is necessary to be saved, they will not be saved.

So the bottom line for Christians who have spiritual problem areas in their life is to understand that they must believe God's Word more than anything else if they truly desire to have victory in their lives. The problems will not disappear until they symbolically grab the "horns" of their problems by faith in God's Word and deal with them correctly. If they continue (1) wishing their problems would go away, (2) blaming others for them, (3) getting angry with God or people in the Body of Christ, (4) or making excuses for them, etc., they will only get worse.

This is crunch time in world history. The devil is running loose in a last desperate attempt to deceive the inhabitants of this earth. The powers of heaven are being shaken. There is distress of nations, earthquakes, hurricanes, drought, famines, wars and rumors of wars, men's hearts failing them for fear. (Luke 21:25,26)

We must stop playing games and get serious about serving God. When we do, God will do everything He has promised in His Word. We will be the more than conquerors that Romans 8:37 says we are. We will use these last, perilous days (II Timothy 3:1-17) to show the Power of God as it has never been shown before in history.

Don't be impatient like the people of this push-button generation. Spiritual warfare is just that—warfare conducted in the **spirit** realm. We would all rather see it happen instantly in the **physical** realm, but it usually takes time to manifest itself from the spirit realm so that it can be seen with our natural eyes. That involves faith in God and **that** is usually where the breakdown occurs when people have difficulty in spiritual warfare.

When a lifetime of faulty habit patterns collide with the way God says we must live, guess what has to change? That process of getting our habit patterns straightened out takes time. God does His part in the situation and then we must walk it out with the help of the Holy Spirit on a day-by-day basis, applying the Word of God **consistently** to the problem area of our life until the walls of our spiritual defense system are strong enough to withstand the battering ram of the devil's deception.

There is no place in spiritual warfare for laziness. We've had people call or write us about some major problem area in their life, who have either just skimmed through our book or else haven't even read it, although they have a copy in their possession. They expect us to wave a magic wand by praying a prayer over them that will change their life. That just doesn't happen. Each one of us must be faithful to do **our** part in the situation; pray, read our Bible, believe, resist the devil in the Name of Jesus, loose or allow the Holy Spirit to do His Will in our lives, live in obedience to the Word of God and receive His Promises by faith, among other things. When we do, we will experience all the freedom, joy and power God has for His children.

Is that what you want? Read on because that is exactly what God wants you to have!

4

Chapter 1

QUESTION: "Why does it seem like my prayers are not accomplishing anything? I pray and believe, but it doesn't seem to work. It seems like heaven is welded shut and my prayers are not getting through to God.**

In natural warfare the soldier must have absolute confidence in his rifle and the manufacture's handbook with the instructions on how to use and care for it, if he is going to confront and defeat the enemy.

When the soldier enters into combat, his rifle is the most important item in his life. It protects him, helps him drive back the enemy and actually becomes an extension of his body as he lives and even sleeps with it in his hands.

Your "rifle" in spiritual warfare is your faith in God's Word, the Bible, *"the sword of the Spirit."* (Ephesians 6:17)

To conduct successful spiritual warfare you must have **absolute, unshakable, unwavering faith in the Word's ability to stop the devil's activities in your life whenever you use it on him correctly.**

One of the major differences between physical and spiritual warfare is that when you shoot a physical rifle you can usually see the damage that has been inflicted by the bullet. In spiritual warfare you must depend entirely on what the manufacturer's handbook says the resulting damage will be when you shoot your spiritual rifle.

For instance, James 4:7 tells you, *"Resist the devil, and he will flee from you."* But because you can't physically see the devil in the act of fleeing, you have to **believe with total faith and confidence** that when you resist the devil in the spirit realm, that is **exactly** what is taking place.

"But it doesn't **feel** like he is fleeing," you say. "The symptoms are still there, the problem is even worse now, my husband is drinking more than ever, my finances are in worse shape than before I prayed. How can the devil be fleeing if the circumstances are worse than before?"

The answer to your question is found in the manufacturer's handbook—the Bible. Does it say you have to **feel** good, better or different to prove that your rifle worked and the devil is running away from you? No, it doesn't say that.

The only condition James 4:7 emphasizes is that you have to be submitted to God when you resist the devil. *"Submit yourselves therefore to God."* That condition **must** be met in your life if you ever expect the devil to flee from you.

Are you submitted to God? Are you staying free from sin and keeping your fleshly desires that aren't pleasing to God under control by the Power of the Holy Spirit? Is Jesus the Lord of your life? Are you living according to His will, in humility and obedience?

If not, you have given the devil a foothold or open door in your life which gives the devil a right to not only hang around, but to also continue hassling you. *"Neither give place to the devil."* (Ephesians 4:27) You must repent of the sin in your life and get the door closed **first, before** you begin shooting your rifle again, or you are just wasting ammunition.

If you are submitted to God and your heart doesn't condemn you, then you will have total confidence in your rifle and know that the bullet hit the target **exactly where you aimed** it and that the enemy is on the run. *"Beloved, if our heart condemn us not, then have we confidence toward God. And whatsoever we ask, we receive of him, because we keep his commandments, and do those things that are pleasing in his sight."* (I John 3:21,22)

The devil will try to trick you because you are shooting blind physically. He will tell you that you missed, God's Word didn't work for you this time, God doesn't really like you so He gave you a rifle that misfired, your ammunition was all wet, you are too fanatical, **anything to make you doubt God and His promises in His Word.**

Who Will You Believe?

What you decide at this critical moment will determine whether you experience victory or defeat in your life. Are you going to believe the circumstances and tricks of the devil or are you going to believe God's Word?

Ephesians 6:11 says that the armour of the Lord is for just such an occasion as this. *"Put on the whole armour of God, that ye may be able to stand against the **wiles** (tricks, deception, schemes, illusions) of the devil."*

People who are victorious in God's family live by faith in what God's Word tells them. *"The just shall live by faith."* (Galatians 3:11, Habakkuk 2:4, Romans 1:17 and Hebrews 10:38)

If your faith is weak, then you must get God's Word so deeply implanted in your heart or spirit, by listening to what it says about the situation, that you can **override** whatever your mind or flesh tells you when the battle is raging in your life.

The devil will use your mind and body to trick you into doubting God, so Paul tells you in Romans 12:1 & 2 that you must make your body a living sacrifice, or actually take away its "vote" in any spiritual matter. Then you transform or change the way your mind thinks by filling it with the Word of God. ***"So then faith cometh by hearing and hearing by the word of God."*** (Romans 10:17)

As faith floods your heart, the instruction handbook (God's Word) becomes so engraved on your heart that you **know without a doubt** that when you follow its instructions, your rifle will work perfectly and will do **exactly** what the manufacturer (God) says it is capable of doing. After that you follow what God tells you in your **spirit** instead of following your body, mind and emotions. You **know** that what God says about the situation is absolutely true no matter how out-of-control it may appear in the physical, natural realm. ***"for we walk by faith, not by sight:"*** (II Corinthians 5:7)

It doesn't matter if you are in the middle of an earthquake or forest fire or financial depression or divorce or medical crisis or an atomic bomb attack, **first establish what God's Word says about the situation,** then make **that** your point-of-reference as to what you truly believe and how you will act or react from that point on.

Paul assures us after a life filled with spiritual warfare, "Who shall separate us from the love of Christ? Shall tribulation, or distress, or persecution, or famine, or nakedness, or peril, or sword?...No, in all these things we are more than conquerors through him that loved us." (Romans 8:35 & 37) Nothing can defeat you if you truly put God and His Word first in your life!

It is important also for you to note that **God wants the devil to be powerless over you** or Jesus would never have defeated the devil and then given you a rifle and handbook to keep the devil in that continued state of defeat as you use them correctly.

Neither are you to become overly concerned with the devil or what he tries to do. You simply have a quiet confidence in your rifle and manufacturer. *"...and having done all, to stand."* (Ephesians 6:13) You are not moved by the physical realm, but by what God says.

Your attention and thoughts are on Jesus—you live for Jesus—then when the devil starts doing things he has no right to do to a child of God, you command him to stop in the Name of Jesus, just as Jesus commanded the wind and waves. Then you go on living for Jesus.

Let me warn you though, one of the great signs of the end-time is a lack of faith (even in Christians) in God and His Word. *"Nevertheless when the Son of man cometh, shall he find faith on the earth?"*(Luke 18:8)

A Huge Key To Successful Spiritual Warfare

So a huge key to successful spiritual warfare in your life is this important scripture: *"Have faith in God."* (Mark 11:22) Do not, under any circumstances allow this world, the flesh, the devil or even certain Christians to rob you of your faith in God and His Word in these last, perilous days!!!

Whether the heavens seem welded shut has nothing to do with the situation. What God's Word has to say about it and whether you believe and act on what He says is what is important.

Let us look at a physical example of warfare to illustrate what we are talking about. The Israelites had just been delivered from Egypt by a stunning display of God's Power. They had been freed from the enemy just as we have been freed from the devil when we accept Jesus as our personal Savior.

God had a beautiful future prepared for the Israelites, complete with their own land that flowed with milk and honey. All they had to do was **believe** God's promise that the land was theirs. *"...for I have given you the land to possess it."* (Numbers 33:53)

It is true that *"possessing the land"* meant that they had to fight for it, but as long as they obeyed God and believed what He said, they were promised total victory over the giants who lived in the Promised Land. That is our situation today in the spirit realm. After we accept Christ as our Savior we are promised total victory over the devil if we **believe** God's Promise, *"...in all these things we are more than conquerors through him that loved us."* (Romans 8:37)

So why do we have problems keeping the devil under our heel? For the same reason the Israelites had problems—we believe the enemy when he pulls his tricks on us and we let him wriggle away from the total dominion God has given us over him.

The Israelites did it by second-guessing God. They saw the circumstances that faced them, the giants that were in the promised land, and believed the devil's lies that God had apparently not taken the giants into consideration when He promised them the land.

We do the same thing. When the giants in our life loom up on the horizon we think, "Why did God save me to let this happen in my life? These giants are too big for me to defeat." (which is true) **We** don't have to defeat them because Jesus has already done it for us, and now we simple believe **that** more than what the giants say.

When we begin doubting God's promises we fall into fear and fear causes us to forget who we are—the **conqueror** over the giants or problems. We stop thinking sensibly and become immobilized on the border of the Promised Land, paralyzed with fear.

A Giant Surprise

Do you want to know something that will surprise you about all of this? **The enemy we are afraid of is actually afraid of us!** That's right! The very people the Israelites were supposed to defeat in the Promised Land were **terrified** of the Israelites. Doesn't James tell us that if we resist the devil he will flee from us, which alludes to the terror the devil feels when he realizes we aren't tricked by his wiles anymore? (James 4:7)

Rahab, who lived in Jericho, the first walled city the Israelites encountered, shared this little tidbit with the spies she hid in her house when they were spying out the land. *"And she said unto the men, I know that the Lord hath given you the land, and that **your terror is fallen upon us**, and that **all the inhabitants of the land faint be-***

cause of you...as soon as we heard these things, (The Red Sea incident and battles Israel had won enroute) *our hearts did melt, neither did there remain any more courage in any man, because of you;"* (Joshua 2:9 & 11)

Isn't that about the most ridiculous thing you've ever heard? Christians who are afraid of demons and the devil must really look pitiful in the spirit realm. All they have to do is believe God and stand on his Word and the enemy will run like a whipped cur. Instead, because they doubt God, **they** are the ones who run from a defeated, cowering foe!

Rahab reveals, with this brief glance into the kingdom of Satan, what the enemy feels when we wheel up to his borders with all the Firepower of God at our disposal to drive him out of the land (victory over problems in our life) God has promised us.

How Long Will It Take?

The forces of evil **know** they are defeated in our life if we truly **believe** God and do what He says we can do in the Name of Jesus. The amazing thing is that it took the Israelites 40 years of wandering in the desert to finally realize that fact. The question is, **how long will it take us**?

How do you perceive yourself? The devil tells you that you are weak; that you have just had bad luck in your life and will have to live with it; that you aren't important to God; that everyone else will receive from God except you and on and on. But that isn't what God thinks about you. He says, *"The Spirit itself beareth witness with our spirit, that we are the children of God: And if children, then heirs; heirs of God, and joint heirs with Christ;"* (Romans 8:16 & 17)

So we must stop listening to the enemy's lies and deception. We must stop looking at our failures and begin looking at God's victory. *"The weapons of our warfare are not carnal, but mighty before God to the pulling down of strongholds and every high thing that exalts itself against the knowledge of God."* (II Corinthians 10:4)

When we really get this down in our heart and believe it, we'll wonder why we ever put up with the sand, dust and heat of the "desert" when we could have been enjoying our privileges as a child of God in the Promised Land of Victory that flows with milk and honey!

Instead of letting the devil beat on us, we beat on him now. We see the fear in his eyes when he feels the Power of the Sword of the Spirit which is the Word of God, flashing in our hand.

When the enemy attacks, use the Word of God like Jesus did. Live according to God's Word and believe God instead of the devil.

"Have not I commanded thee? Be strong and of good courage; be not afraid, neither be thou dismayed: for the Lord thy God is with thee whithersoever thou goest." (Joshua 1:9)

General Jonathan Wainwright's Victory

On August 14, 1945 news didn't travel in seconds around the world as it does today by satellite communication. That was the date the Japanese emperor ordered a cease-fire of all military activity after Japan surrendered to the Allied armies.

The war was over—the enemy had been defeated. But because it took time for the order to reach isolated areas, thousands of Allied soldiers continued to suffer at the hands of the Japanese even though Japan had been defeated.

General Jonathan Wainwright was one of those cases. He suffered terrible hardships as a prisoner at a prison camp near Mukden, Manchuria along with other allied prisoners of war. Because of a lack of knowledge, they continued to obey authority figures who no longer had any authority. They obeyed rules that were no longer in force. They gave respect to a system that didn't exist anymore. They were prisoners of a foe who had been conquered.

Isn't that a picture of many Christians today? The devil was defeated by Jesus Christ 2000 years ago, but for a variety of reasons some of God's people are still prisoners of war, caving in to a satanic system that has no right to exert authority over them.

They look at the sinners around them and think they must pattern their life after that ungodly lifestyle. They believe they have to be fearful because everyone else is fearful in this world. **Not true**! We were set free from the bondage of fear when Jesus destroyed the works of the devil. (1 John 3:8)

They think they have to dread death because everyone else does. **Not true**! Paul says that death can't get its stinger into us because Jesus rose from the dead and has the keys of hell and death. (Revelation 1:18)

They believe they must worry and fret about what the future holds for them like the sinners do. **Not true**! Jesus promises that if God takes care of the birds and the lilies He will surely provide for us if we put His kingdom first in our life. (Matthew 6:25-34)

One day a paratrooper handed a letter through the fence to one of the prisoners of war and told him to deliver it quickly to General Wainwright. That letter from General MacArthur forever broke the power of the Japanese over the Allied prisoners in that camp because it carried the good news that the Japanese army had been defeated.

General Wainwright took the letter to the commanding officer of the prison and demanded that the Japanese officer surrender his sword in a sign of surrender. The officer could do nothing but obey. What a great feeling that must have been for the hero of Corregidor! **The captive became the captor and immediately began exercising his authority over the defeated Japanese officer** on the authority of the letter from headquarters.

Have **you** read your letter (Bible) yet? Did you notice that paragraph in the letter that says, *"Behold, I give unto you power (authority in original Greek) to tread on serpents and scorpions, and over* **all** *the power of the enemy: and* **nothing** *shall by any means hurt you."* (Luke 10:19)

I suppose some of the prisoners doubted that the contents of the letter were really true. Perhaps they should just be quiet and not rile up the enemy by talking about how badly he was defeated. We've had Christians tell us that when we teach our seminar.

No! General Wainwright was tired of being in prison and having his rights violated. It was much more satisfying to be the victor instead of the victim.

When the devil comes around trying to intimidate you with fear, temptation, physical symptoms of sickness and unbelief, just point out to him some of the choice paragraphs in your "letter" from your Commanding General, Jesus Christ.

Demand the devil's sword in the Name of Jesus! Treat him as the loser that he is. We are more than conquerors because of the victory Jesus won for us 2000 years ago.

Now, live like a conqueror instead of a prisoner of war!

Chapter 2

QUESTION: "If God won the victory over the devil when Jesus died and rose from the dead, why do I have so much trouble with the devil today?"

It is true that Jesus defeated and, in fact, utterly humiliated the devil. Colossians 2:15 reveals that the devil was completely disarmed, *"[God] disarmed the principalities and powers ranged against us and made a bold display and public example of them, in triumphing over them in Him and in it [the cross]."* (Amplified Bible) God took **all** the devil's weapons away from him and has **never given them back!**

Then Jesus **destroyed** the devil's weapons of sin, sickness, fear, death, depression, poverty, murder, lust, rebellion, discord, stealing and cruelty, etc. so that even if the devil could get them back, they wouldn't work. *"For this purpose the Son of God was manifested, that he might destroy the **works** of the devil."* (I John 3:8)

But Paul also tells us that Satan is still the "god" or ruler of this world's system. *"In whom the god of this world hath blinded the minds of them which believe not, lest the light of the glorious gospel of Christ, who is the image of God, should shine unto them."* (II Corinthians 4:4)

He is still the prince of the power of the air. *"Wherein in time past ye walked according to the course of this world, according to the prince of the power of the air, the spirit that now worketh in the children of disobedience;"* (Ephesians 2:2)

And there is still spiritual combat, which Paul calls "wrestling", that we engage in with the devil. *"For we are not wrestling with flesh and blood—contending only with physical opponents—but against the despotisms, against powers, against [the master spirits who are] the world rulers of this present darkness, against the spirit forces of wickedness in the heavenly (supernatural) sphere."* (Amplified Bible Ephesians 6:12) Could these "master spirits" be the 16 Strongmen mentioned by name in the Bible?

Someone says, "But if the devil has no weapons then why do we still have to resist him so that he will flee from us as James 4:7 instructs us? What is there left to resist?"

Ephesians 6:11 says that we must put on spiritual "armour" to be able to resist or *"stand against the wiles of the devil."* The word, "wiles," means "tricks, deceptions, schemes, illusions or sleight-of-hand gimmickry." **Now he can only gain power over us if we gullibly believe his lies and trickery. If he can make us believe he still has his weapons and can do what he threatens to do to us, it is just as good as if he really did have his weapons back.** We hear all the time of people who rob banks by threatening that they have a gun when, in reality, they have no weapon at all. The bottom line of this trickery is that the devil has gotten us to disobey God and pushed us into doubt and sin. This strategy of trickery has worked so well for the devil that he has subjugated the greater part of the human race with it!

Why do we still have problems with sin, sickness, fear, death and depression if God took those weapons away from the devil and Jesus destroyed them? The answer is simply that we believe what the devil says about sin, sickness, fear, death and depression **more** than what God says about them.

Jesus **did** win a total victory over the devil, but the truth is that **we** must **enforce** or **apply** that victory to our lives on a personal, daily basis until Jesus returns by using all the power and authority over the devil which Jesus has given us in Luke 10:19.

Jesus' victory has only been manifested to this point in the spirit realm. The physical world is still under the influence of the devil because of Adam's and Eve's decision in the Garden of Eden and the fact that the majority of people in the world have continued to fall for the devil's lies and deception.

God's children must be aware of this fact and use the knowledge, power and authority God has given them to limit the devil's influence in this world and free the prisoners of sin from the devil's strongholds. Jesus said, *"...how can one enter into a strong man's house, and spoil his goods, except he first bind the strong man? and then he will spoil his house."* (Matthew 12:29)

We live in enemy territory in this world. Jesus has commanded us to apply the victory He won for us over the devil by "occupying" this world until He comes back. (Luke 19:13) The word used here for "occupy" in the original language means "to dominate conquered troops or territory in a spiritual sense." God wants us to keep the devil in a defeated, controlled and subjugated state so that he cannot continue his program of deception on this earth.

Using the Word of God as our basis of authority, we treat the devil as we would a misbehaving dog. When he tries to do something in our life that he has no right to do, we tell him, "Stop that right now in the Name of Jesus. You can't do that according to this scripture in God's Word," and we quote the scripture which gives us our legal right to act in Jesus' Name. Then we tell the devil, "I 'bind' you according to Matthew 16:19 and 18:18 in the Name of Jesus and I agree with or 'loose' the Holy Spirit to do His perfect will in this situation according to Matthew 16:19 and 18:18."

Bring The Devil Back To God's Word!

We continually bring the devil back to what God's Word says our rights are as children of God and what his limitations are in the situation and force the devil to bow his knees to God's Will in the situation.

The devil will try every trick in the book to distract us from God's Will through the lust of the flesh, intimidation, pride, fear, sickness, bondage and all the rest of the Strongmen. That is the reason we must **know** what God has to say about it and then BACK UP what we pray or command with the appropriate scripture and verse. That gives us our legal authority to act correctly without fear of retaliation from the devil.

Jesus said, *"I give you power (authority) to tread on serpents and scorpions, and over **all** the power of the enemy: and **nothing** shall by any means hurt you."* (Luke 10:19)

An integral part of God's plan for the human race is that we take this kind of dominant stance over the devil. If we don't, we will live beneath our rights as children of God and the lost souls of this world, under strong delusion and deception from the devil, may be lost forever because we must stand in the gap for them in the spirit realm. We intercede on the sinner's behalf, using the power and authority God has given us according to His Word, until they see and believe the

Truth which the Holy Spirit has been showing them through His conviction in their life.

In our own lives, we make God's Word **our point of reference in everything** we say, do or think. God's Word and our relationship with God are the most important things in our lives. When we put God's Kingdom first in our lives, all the rest will be added unto us. (Matthew 6:33)

Ultimately, we will inherit final power over this world and its devilish system through Jesus Christ when He returns to establish His spiritual kingdom on this physical earth. Until then we must expose the illegal activities of the devil with the Light and Truth of God's Word and command him to suspend his deception in people's lives.

The Mafia is an illustration in the physical realm of how the devil operates. The Mafia has no legal right or authority to exist or operate in the United States. It is an evil, vile system that seeks to undermine every good law and statute of our country.

Why does it succeed? Because people are either ignorant of their rights as citizens of the United States or else they are afraid that if they stand up for their rights the Mafia will harm them. So people treat the Mafia as many Christians treat the devil—they try to stay out of their way and hope they never have to actually have a confrontation.

But **someone** has to stop them or anarchy will result. Law enforcement must use the Law to prosecute the Mafia for the crimes they have committed and cause them to be "bound" or thrown into prison so that they cannot do what they want to do. Thankfully we are seeing the Mafia greatly hindered these days because brave law enforcement men and women are bringing them to justice.

So it is in the spirit realm. The devil has no right to operate in the Christian's life unless the Christian has forfeited his rights through ignorance of the Law—God's Word—or because the Christian has gotten into sin, doubt and fear which automatically open him up to the harassment of the devil. (the Mafia feeds on people's fears and once they get something of a damaging nature on them, they blackmail them into obedience.)

We're Not Devil Conscious

If we stand for righteousness and live according to God's Law, He will back us up every step of the way and we will be able to bring

16

the devil to justice and keep him from carrying out his agenda in our lives and this world.

This does not mean that we become devil conscious—always thinking about the devil, rebuking the devil, worrying about what he is trying to do to us. No. We are **Jesus conscious**. We live for Jesus, think about Jesus, worship Jesus. But when the devil steps out of line, we nail him with the Word, bind him in the Name of Jesus, agree and cooperate with what the Holy Spirit wants to do in the situation and then we go on living for Jesus.

There is a lost world out there waiting for God's people to be used by the Holy Spirit to deliver them by the Power of God from the strongholds of sin, bondage and the devil. We are part of God's Law-enforcement program to keep the devil behind the bars of Truth where he belongs.

"For the weapons of our warfare are not carnal, but mighty through God to the pulling down of strongholds;" (II Corinthians 10:4)

The Difference Between "Victory" and "Triumphing"

There is a distinct difference between the two words "victory" and "triumphing" in God's Word that helps us understand what the situation really is in all of this.

Victory is when one opponent wins the battle over the other. The loser surrenders to the winner, the conflict is terminated and the loser agrees to abide by the rules which the winner decrees.

Triumphing is what **follows** the victory. For instance, every 4th of July, as citizens of the USA, we celebrate our independence from the English. We don't have to fight the war all over again because the war is over. Since we won, we have the right to celebrate or triumph because of that victory.

God Won The War Over The Devil

In the area of spiritual warfare it is absolutely essential to understand the difference between "victory" and "triumphing" if we are going to live as God has planned for us to live.

When Jesus died on the cross and rose from the dead, He won the victory over the devil once-and-for-all. The **completeness** of what

17

Jesus accomplished for us is not clearly understood by many Christians today and as a result they spend an excessive amount of their life fighting a war that has already been won for them.

God isn't asking us to win the war again over the devil—that is ancient history. He wants us to **believe** what truly happened 2000 years ago and use that victory in our daily lives to keep the devil in a bound condition as far as we are concerned. That is what triumphing is all about. Now we can celebrate or triumph over the devil every day because we know what the Truth is about the victory Jesus won for us. *"Thanks be unto God, which <u>always</u> causeth us to triumph in Christ."* (II Corinthians 2:14)

Let's look at God's version of what really took place at Calvary. *"[God] disarmed the principalities and powers ranged against us and made a bold display and public example of them, triumphing over them in Him and in it [the cross]."* (Colossians 2:15 Amplified Bible)

Speaking in modern terms, God "disarmed" or took the devil's "guns" away from him and stripped him of his ability to do what he had formerly done to the human race. Then God boldly and publicly showed that Satan is no longer allowed to ravage mankind, provided we will accept Christ and His finished Work in our lives and live on God's terms.

Paul takes his language here from the Roman customs of that time. When a Roman general defeated his opponent in war, the Roman Senate arranged a triumph for him upon his victorious return to Rome. A giant procession was organized—led by the conquering general. He was dressed in all his finery and placed in a magnificent chariot pulled by two beautiful white horses.

The defeated general and all his underlings who had survived the war were stripped naked, bound and **chained** to the back of the conquering generals chariot. This was purposely done to show the people they had nothing to fear from this defeated enemy from that time on.

The procession then advanced through the streets of Rome as the citizens cheered the winning general. After his chariot passed by, however, the cheers turned to shouts of derision for the conquered foe who followed. The people insulted them, spit upon them and hit them with rocks; absolutely humiliating this enemy who had had the gall to believe he could defeat the mighty Roman empire.

Applying this scenario to Christ's victory over the devil, symbolically speaking, God put Jesus in the chariot and chained the devil and his demon hordes to the back of the chariot. And they are **still there** if we understand what God's Word says.

Where are we in this picture? Because we are "in" Christ, according to Romans 8:1, we are in the chariot with Christ Jesus, enjoying the spoils of winning the war! That is the reason we don't have to beg God for what has already been accomplished. We aren't standing on the sidelines, hoping a small part of the victory will rub off on us by chance. **We are always triumphant in Christ!**

If that is true, why do some Christians have so much trouble with the devil? Why are some Christians suffering from the assaults of the devil through fear, sickness, depression, sin and want? Once again, they are believing the devil's version of what their position is in Christ more than what God tells them about it in His Word.

Deceptions And Delusions

We are expressly commanded to, *"Put on the whole armour of God, that ye may be able to stand against the wiles of the devil."* The wrestling match or battle or spiritual warfare that we are engaged in today revolves around this area of deception or illusions which the devil uses to trick us into believing his lies about the situation instead of God's Truth.

For that reason we can't believe the sense realm or this world's system where the devil has freedom to manipulate the circumstances to fit his lies. **Now the battle is to see through the devil's deception** and to reject his way of life in this world for the **Life** God has given us through Christ—the ability to be more than conquers over this world's system, the flesh and the devil. (Romans 8:37)

When the devil tries to put his symptoms of fear and sickness on us, we battle them with the Sword of the Spirit which is the Word of God. When the devil says he is going to kill us or our children, we say, "No you're not because God's Word says this and this. Now get out of here in the Name of Jesus!" **We keep the devil behind the chariot where he belongs!**

He will try to pull us out of the chariot with his tricks. In fact, some Christians are bound behind the chariot and the devil is running loose in their lives, stealing, killing and destroying, because they don't understand it is their right, as a child of God, to keep the devil in a constant state of bondage! The fact is that the devil is terrified of Christians who stay in the chariot, believing God more than anything else.

We still have difficult times in our Christian life. The devil rages at us, trying to intimidate us into leaving the chariot of faith in God, but Peter says the way to handle him is to resist the devil (roaring lion) steadfast in the faith. (I Peter 5:8,9) James follows with, *"Resist the devil, and he will flee from you." (James 4:7)*

Understand now, the **condition** which keeps us in the chariot with Christ is that we, *"Submit ourselves therefore to God."* We have got to live this life according to God's rules. We can't be involved with the works of the flesh and sin and expect to continue triumphing. Sin opens us up to the fiery darts of temptation, unbelief and deception. When we sin, our shield of faith falls down and our armor develops holes that cause us to become prey to the devil's tricks and we fall off the chariot, symbolically speaking.

We Still Wrestle

Some Christians foolishly believe that because Christ won the war, they don't have to do **anything** now. If that is true, Paul wasted a lot of space instructing us on how to conduct ourselves in the wrestling match he says is **still in progress**!

But there is a vast difference between a wrestling match when the winner is in doubt and one that you **know you will win** if you obey God's rules of wrestling. There is a confidence that comes when you know the outcome even though the circumstances may look terrible in the natural, worldly realm.

Paul says that when we have done everything we know we should do, we are to stand confidently with our feet planted in God's Word and our Sword ready for action, knowing that the enemy is defeated and that Jesus is with us in the chariot and the devil is chained to the back of the chariot, naked, humiliated, bound and defeated! (Ephesians 6:13)

We aren't brash or overconfident about it—we just know what the Truth really is and we let it manifest itself in our lives because God's Truth will stand forever. Now be strong in the Lord and use the mighty weapons God has given us where they will do the most good! That is God's Plan for us in these last days.

Chapter 3

QUESTION: "What is my problem when I have closed all the doors in my life to the devil, but the situation doesn't seem to get any better. It sometimes gets even worse than when I first began praying about it?"

We probably get more cries for help in this area of spiritual warfare than anywhere else. To begin with let's lay the situation out as it appears to stand.

You are a child of God. You believe and have acted on God's Word with faith in your heart.

You have closed all the doors of your life to the devil by repenting of any sin, such as unforgiveness, bitterness, envy, strife, etc. in your life so that he has no opening in your armor to shoot in his fiery darts of temptation, unbelief and deception to harass you.

You have resisted and bound the devil in the Name of Jesus according to James 4:7, Matthew 18:18 and 16:19 and have loosed or invited the Holy Spirit to accomplish what He wants to do in your life.

You have asked the Holy Spirit to reveal any other areas you may have overlooked in your life that could be holding back the answer to your prayers.

But, the sickness remains the same as ever, the unsaved loved one is as rebellious as before, the financial pressure is unabated or the marriage problems are worse.

Many believe this to be a sign that God is saying "No" to your request or that He is punishing you for some reason or that He is using this to teach you something or that it is not His Will for you to have it. But remember this, we are asking for something God **wants to give us** when we believe His promises and meet His conditions. *"Ask, and it shall be given you;...for **everyone** that asketh* *receiveth;...if ye then, being evil, know how to give good gifts unto your children how much more shall your Father which is in heaven give good things to them that ask Him?"* (Matthew 7:7,8,11)

God's Word is clear, *"...with his stripes we are healed."* (Isaiah 53:54) He is, *"...not willing than any should perish, but that all should come to repentance."* (II Peter 3:9) *"...God shall supply all your need according to his riches in glory by Christ Jesus."* (Philippians 4:19) God wants your marriage to succeed because He instituted this relationship for the human race and, *"What therefore God hath joined together, let not man put asunder."* (Matthew 19:6)

The basic truth you must hold on to in this situation is this: **God does not go back on His Word.** You can trust God to carry out what He has promised you in His Word. When you asked Him to forgive your sins He didn't have to think about it—He did it, if you met His conditions and (1) confessed with your mouth the Lord Jesus Christ, (2) believed in your heart that God raised Jesus from the dead, (3) asked God to forgive you of your sins, (4) and received Christ as your Savior. The same will be true in **this** situation if you meet the conditions God's Word demands.

Getting To The Root Of The Problem

Here is how we help people get to the root of the problem:
I. First, we point out that we are not to walk according to what we see, feel, smell, taste or hear with our physical senses, but by faith in the Words of God. "For though we live in the flesh, we are not carrying on our warfare according to the flesh..." (II Corinthians 10:3 Amplified Bible)

If we believe what we see with our natural eyes we will be deceived because the devil stacks the circumstances against us in the natural realm for the express purpose of discouraging us from continuing on with the battle.

A friend of ours prayed for her hard-drinking husband after she accepted the Lord as her Savior. The more she prayed, the worse he got and the more he drank. After a period of time he finally accepted the Lord. When she asked him why he had drunk more heavily the more she prayed for him, he told her he felt the Holy Spirit convicting him as soon as she started praying. He just didn't want to get saved so he drank more whiskey to drown out the voice of the Holy Spirit.

The very thing that **appeared discouraging in the natural** was actually an encouragement because it was part of God's answer to her prayers. The Holy Spirit did exactly what she asked when He convicted her husband of sin. Her husband's **reaction** in the natural was the devil's attempt to discourage her to stop praying.

If she would have said, "I can't understand why God isn't answering my prayers—why doesn't God stop my husband's drinking—he's worse now than when I started praying so I guess God hasn't heard me or doesn't want my husband saved or wants to teach me something from this," or all the other things the devil whispers in our ear when the pressure is on, she may not have ever seen her husband come to the Lord.

*"But let him ask in faith, **nothing wavering**. For he that wavereth is like a wave of the sea driven with the wind and tossed. For let not that man think that he will receive anything of the Lord. A double minded man is unstable in all his ways."* (James 1:6-8)

The fact that people say, "I did everything I was supposed to do and **nothing happened**," is a sign of wavering and unbelief. James says very clearly what it will get us from God—**nothing**. So it is important to maintain faith in God no matter how things may appear in the natural, physical realm.

What Do You Say About Your Problem?

II. We try to ascertain if the people have done in reality what they say they have done in the area of closing all doors in their life to the enemy. Many people are playing mind games with themselves these days. They say and think they have closed all the doors, but after conversing with them their words reveal all the fear, doubt, bitterness and hatred they have failed to recognize in their heart. For that reason the devil still has an open door in their life to continue harassing and robbing them of God's Promises.

Listen closely to yourself when you are experiencing a blockage in your prayer life. If faith isn't coming from your heart, that could be the problem. *"...out of the abundance of the heart the mouth speaketh."* (Matthew 12:34)

What Are The "Wiles" Of The Devil?

III. When we are certain the individual has no holes in his defense, we point him to Ephesians 6:13. "Wherefore take unto you the whole armour of God, that ye may be able to withstand in the evil day, and having done all, to stand." The Amplified Bible says, "Stand therefore—hold your ground." (V.14) Stand in faith, stand in confidence, don't fear, don't worry, don't waver, don't listen to the devil or doubters or to your physical senses. Stand by what the Word of God says!

Stand in the confidence that God's armor is sufficient to help you defeat the enemy whenever he seeks to establish his will over the will of God in your life by deceiving you.

The enemy just **seems** to be winning. That is part of the "wiles" verse eleven talks about. The armor is to protect and help you recognize and defuse the wiles, deceptions, tricks and illusions of the devil. An *illusion* is something which has all the appearance of reality but is nothing more than air when you try to touch it. What the devil does or says, looks and sounds for all the world like it is real—**but it isn't because it has no substance**.

He tries to trick you just as he tricked Eve in the Garden of Eden. God said, *"You are not to eat of the tree of the knowledge of good and evil. If you do you will surely die."* (Genesis 2:17)

The devil told Eve in so many words, "Just look at that beautiful fruit. Does it **look** like it would kill you? Noooo, God is just trying to keep you from reaching your full potential."

Eve believed the devil more than God and was drawn away from God's Word to her physical senses by the enemy, leaving her unprotected and vulnerable. She **looked**, she **desired** and she **reasoned**, "It really does look like it will improve me." The jaws of deception closed over her and she sinned.

The devil's tactics haven't changed all that much in 6000 years. He still comes to us with the same old, tired routine dressed up with a little brightly-colored wrapping paper. That is why God's advice must dominate any circumstances the devil fabricates to try to make us believe God's Word is not true. **We don't give the devil room to turn his illusions into reality in our lives. We believe God's Word instead!**

24

Just keep standing in faith, using the armor of God and the sword of the Spirit on the devil until **he** gets discouraged and leaves you alone.

Abraham was noted for his faith in God's Promises and he, *"...staggered not at the promise of God through unbelief; but was strong in faith, giving glory to God."*

The Amplified Bible says, *"No unbelief or distrust made him waver or doubtingly question concerning the promise of God,...fully satisfied and assured that **God was able and mighty to keep his word and to do what he had promised.**"* (Romans 4:20,21)

How Do We Receive What God Has Promised In His Word?

IV. The last area we emphasize is to receive what God has promised in His Word. "Ask, and it shall be given you; seek, and ye shall find; knock, and it shall be opened unto you; for everyone that asketh, receiveth; and he that seeketh, findeth; and to him that knocketh, it shall be opened." (Matthew 7:7,8) God cannot be more positive about answering your prayers than He is in those verses.

Now it is up to you to reach out and take what you are asking for by faith. You believe, talk, think and act like you have it, whether it has appeared in the physical realm or not. Remember, we are talking about something you **know** is God's Will for you to have according to His Word. You have closed all the doors to sin and the works of the flesh so the devil has no right to block the flow of God into your life.

Sometimes you will immediately see in the natural realm what you have asked God for, but **most of the time you won't**. That is why you need faith. Faith is a **spiritual sense** that helps you bridge the gap between the natural world of man and the supernatural world of God. Faith reaches into the realm of God and says, "I receive that promise from Your Word for my situation or problem or need down here. Thank you, Father."

Then you confidently go about your business knowing that you have it, even though it hasn't materialized yet in the physical world. You encourage yourself by reading what God says about it every day in His Word. You speak about it as an already accomplished fact, just

25

as the farmer speaks of a crop that hasn't sprouted above the ground yet as though it already has.

When the devil tries to discourage you by pointing out that things are getting worse, you use the Sword of the Word of God on him and drive him away.

A friend told me the testimony of a lady who had an ugly, disfiguring growth on her face. She asked the Lord to heal her face and sensed in her heart that He had answered her prayer. She began testifying of the fact that her face was healed.

This went on for about two years with the growth still very much in evidence on her face. Finally some of the people of the church asked why she was testifying about something that they could **see** hadn't happened.

She was devastated to think that her fellow Christians would doubt that she had been healed. So she told the Lord that night before she went to bed, "Lord, **you** know and I know that you have healed me. Now I ask you to show **them** too."

The next morning when she bent over to wash her face, the growth fell off into her hands!

It is a sad fact that instead of encouraging people who are standing by faith on the Word, some Christians actually ridicule them for it. They suggest every negative, doubt-filled, cop-out they can think of to discourage those who choose to believe the Word of God. Jesus talked about this in Luke 18:8 when He declared, *"However, when the Son of man comes will He find persistence in the faith on earth?"* (Amplified Bible)

What an indictment today that believers, who use words of faith, are looked upon by some Christians as though they are mentally unbalanced when they make a stand of faith based on God's Word.

"Pit Bull Prayers"

Many Christians pray what I call, "French poodle prayers." At the first sign of a spiritual battle they bark a couple of times at the devil and run for cover. Then they try to discourage anyone else from standing up to the devil because it didn't "work" for them.

The days in which we live call for "Pit bull prayers." I am told that when a pit bull bites down firmly on something, two muscles on either side of his jaw slip down and overlap the jaw muscles, making it physically impossible for him to open his jaws—they have to be pried apart.

When we clamp down on a Truth or Promise of God's Word we shouldn't let go either until it manifests itself in our life. Nobody or nothing should shake us loose because we are convinced by God's Word that it is ours. We stubbornly, determinedly hang on to the Word of God because we know it is not in God's character to lie to us.

That is the kind of Christian who is going to make it in these perilous, dangerous, deceptive, fearful, last days—people who know who they are in God, know what God has said in His Word, know what God does and doesn't do in their lives, know what the devil can and cannot do to them and who have an unshakable faith in the Word of God.

"While we look not at the things which are seen, but at things which are not seen: for the things which are seen are temporal; but the things which are not seen are eternal." (II Corinthians 4:18)

FEAR IS REALLY: **F** alse
E vidence
A ppearing
R eal

Going Through The Wall

The world of athletics gives us a good example of how we should approach spiritual warfare today. They call it "hitting the wall." It is a time when they think one more step will cause their heart to explode. They have pushed their body to the maximum. Their legs feel like lead. Their body tells them, "This is it. I can't go one more step." But the experienced athlete knows that his body can't be trusted to make a decision at this point because there is still another dimension of performance to attain if he pushes beyond the "wall phase."

He not only must **hit** the wall, but he must go **through** the wall if he expects to supersede his past performances. Some call it getting their "second wind." From one moment to the next, the athlete is able to step up his level of excellence as never before. He runs faster, jumps higher, throws the ball harder and surpasses records he thought he could never reach, much less break.

Oh yes, it isn't easy to go through the wall. If it was, everyone would do it. Only a select few, who train correctly and pay the price through sweating and aching muscles, reach the pinnacle as recognized champions.

Do you see the similarity to spiritual warfare?

How many Christians give up just before they reach a breakthrough in their life because they feel they can't go any further—its just too tough and it looks like it will never get any better.

That's not the time to quit, but to reach down inside for the Power God has made available for you to get your second wind and go on to victory. Break through the wall and enter a level of living in Christ you have never experienced before.

Yes, there is a price to pay. You won't be able to indulge yourself in the works of the flesh (Galatians 5:19) and sin. You will have to read and hear God's Word, pray, tithe, make your body a living sacrifice, follow the leading of the Holy Spirit—the rules are all there in your training manual—the Bible.

But the rewards of breaking through to victory are worth seeing your family and friends saved; laying your hands on the sick and seeing them recover; hearing God's Voice leading and directing your life; seeing God do miracles in your life, family, business, church and finances.

The Three Hebrew Children

The three Hebrew children provide a perfect example of how to conduct successful spiritual warfare under the most difficult of circumstances. (Daniel 3:1-30) They didn't just hit a wall of concrete, but of fire.

Nebuchadnezzar had a golden image constructed which was 90 feet high. He sent word throughout his kingdom that all the leaders were to gather on a certain day and worship the image. Whoever did not fall down and worship the image would be cast into a fiery furnace.

On the appointed day everyone obeyed the King except Shadrach, Meshach and Abednego. They were Jewish young men who had been captured in Jerusalem and brought to Babylon. Instead of making them ordinary slaves, they were given three years of special training and made members of the king's prestigious court.

King Nebuchadnezzar commanded them to be brought to his throne room as soon as he was informed by spies that they had not bowed down to the gold image. He was enraged that his orders had been disobeyed. The fact that he didn't kill them immediately shows that he liked them because he gave them a second chance.

The musicians were reassembled and he told the three Hebrews in so many words that he couldn't believe they could be so foolish as to risk everything over a simple command to bow down to his image.

This is where the similarity begins in the way Nebuchadnezzar handled the situation and the way the devil tries to intimidate us into disobeying God in our lives.

(1) He singled them out and made them appear foolish for not doing what **everyone** else did without hesitation. The "everyone else is doing it so why don't you" syndrome is still with us today. But Shadrach, Meshach and Abednego didn't even blink. There was no loose linkage in their will. **What God said about the matter was more important than how they appeared to the world.**

They told the King in so many words, "We believe our God will deliver us from your furnace, but if He doesn't, we still will not bow down just on the principle alone!"

That did it!

(2) The King ordered the furnace heated **seven times hotter than it had ever been heated before.** Possibly the King thought the three Hebrews would say, "Oh my, that makes a difference. If it is going to be **that** hot we change our mind."

I see the three Hebrews actually saying, "Big deal. If it kills people at **normal** heat, what difference will seven times hotter make it?"

The devil tries to pull this same trick on us. He always tells us how awful things will get if we continue believing God's Word and living as He says we should. "What's a little bowing down going to do? You can't testify to the King if you're dead. Give him a little slack. He's really been good to you guys. If you do this favor for him, maybe he will make you more important in the kingdom and you'll have more opportunity to testify about the true and living God."

Looking at the situation from the natural side, the devil's advice looked pretty good. No lightning bolt had stopped the King from having them bound with their own belts. Traditional sources tell us the flames were shooting 100 feet above the walls of the furnace. That is a worst case scenario if there ever was one. **But learn to never trust the advice of the devil.** He's on his way to the Lake of Fire so what does he know. Who wants a loser's advice anyhow?

Can you imagine how the three Hebrews must have felt as they went flying into that terrible flame? The heat was so great that the "most mighty men" who threw them in were killed by the flames leaping out of the furnace door.

After a few minutes the King looked into the furnace, expecting to see the boys reduced to ashes by the awesome fire. To his astonishment the three were walking around in the inferno as if they were in their own backyard. And there was someone else with them who had the appearance of the Son of God!

The moment the three Hebrews passed through the furnace door, they broke through the "wall" and entered a level of living that superseded anything they had ever experienced before. **The fire was powerless to hurt them!** That makes up for a lot of hard training, doesn't it?

The only thing the flames had power to do was burn their bonds off and free them to show the power of God to the King in a way they could never have done if they hadn't been thrown into the fire!

No one likes to face these kinds of fiery furnace experiences. But if we keep our eyes on Jesus and our feet planted by faith in God's Word, we will go through the wall of fire to victory and show God's Power to our friends, family and the world around us like we could never have done **outside** the furnace.

Don't ever give up in spiritual warfare. If there is life, there is hope for victory.

Nebuchadnezzar had to back down and acknowledge that there was no God like the God of Shadrach, Meshach and Abednego. So will the devil when you nail him with the Truth of God's Word.

So don't quit—go through the wall!

Chapter 4

QUESTION: Can I be certain that God will answer my prayer when I stand against the devil? I've heard of people who tried spiritual warfare and got clobbered by either God or the devil, I'm not real sure which it was. So I've not really gotten into this because I don't want any more problems than I have right now.

We are astounded at how many Christians think God is the major reason they do **not** receive what the Bible promises them as children of God. They have the concept that God treats them like the farmer who dangles a carrot just out of his donkey's reach to make him work. They must continually strain, sweat and work to grab the "promises" dangling in front of their spiritual noses and then forcibly wrest them away from God.

Jesus tells us that His Father is not that way at all. Remember that Jesus was with God the Father in the beginning and knows Him more profoundly than anyone on this earth, so we must pay particular attention to anything Jesus says about His Father if we truly want to know Him. He says, *"Ask and it shall be given you:...for everyone that asketh receiveth;...if ye then, being evil know how to give good gifts unto your children, how much more shall your Father which is in heaven give good things to them that ask him?"* (Matthew 7:7,8,11)

"If God be for us, who can be against us?" (Romans 8:31) When believers finally understand that God is actually **for** them and truly wants them to be conquerors instead of whipped beasts of burden, it revolutionizes their entire relationship with God.

They begin to see that God is actually encouraging them to step out and become the son or daughter He wants them to be; doing exploits, spreading the Gospel around the globe, healing the sick and maintaining dominion over the devil in the Name of Jesus.

The sad fact is that great numbers of believers think God is a limiting force in their life who seeks every opportunity to humiliate them, push them down, keep them sick and poor and punish them in some of the most brutal ways imaginable. Then, magically, God undergoes a transformation in the millennium and begins treating them as He should while they rule and reign with Him forever, defeating the devil, sickness, poverty, abortion and the New Age.

Our Sonship

The only problem with that scenario is our sonship with God does not begin in the millennium or in heaven or after we get our new bodies. John tells us, *"Now are we the sons of God..."* (I John 3:2) There will be no need to do anything with the devil at that time any-how—he will be in the pit and later on in the lake of fire. There will be no sickness then because sickness, poverty, abortion and the New Age will have all passed away.

God wants us to be conquerors over those things **now**. And to accomplish that fact we need all of God's help, encouragement, power and the other things He has promised us in His Word.

Paul informs us that God is ready and willing to provide all of this in our life **now**. *"Now unto him that is able to do exceeding, abundantly above all we ask or think, according to the power that worketh in us."* (Ephesians 3:20)

"Let us therefore come boldly unto the throne of grace, that we may obtain mercy, and find grace to help in time of need." (Hebrews 4:16) The "grace" that we find at the throne is "help" or "support," when, where and to the extent that it is needed. God backs us up every step of the way as we operate within the perimeters of His great Plan.

After Jesus ascended into heaven the disciples, *"...went forth, and preached every where, the Lord working with them, and confirming the word with signs following."* (Mark 16:20) *"...and, lo, I am with you alway, even unto the end of the world."* (Matthew 28:20)

Jesus has given us authority over the devil to accomplish what He said we are to do before He comes back to set up His Millennial Kingdom on this earth. *"Behold, I give unto you power (**authority**) to tread on serpents and scorpions, and over **all** (100%) of the power of the enemy: and **nothing** (0%) shall by any means hurt you."* (Luke 10:19) We are to treat the devil just as Jesus treated him when He was here on earth. That frees us from the debilitating fear that if we fight the devil he will get angry and do terrible things to us or our family or our church in retaliation. That fear is nothing more than satanic in-timidation to make us meekly lay our weapons down instead of aggressively disrupting his plans and kingdom.

Is The Devil A Lion?

But isn't the devil a roaring lion? No, Peter said, *"...the devil as a roaring lion, walketh about seeking whom he may devour:"* (I Peter 5:8) The devil imitates or mimics a roaring lion; tries to make us believe he is a lion; wishes he were a lion. **But he is no lion if we are a child of God, living according to God's Word!**

If he really were a lion, Peter would not have added, *"Whom resist steadfast in the faith."* Under normal circumstances it would be suicide to resist a hungry, angry, vicious lion. But Peter knew something about this "animal" that is fundamental to spiritual warfare. This noisemaker is a bully, a fraud and a fake and the best way to defeat him is to resist him by faith in God.(James 4:7)

How do we combat the urge to run when he roars? **By believing the truth of what God says instead of the deception of the devil.**

I am told that lions use an old, decrepit, toothless male, who nevertheless can still produce an earthshaking roar, to literally drive the victim into the jaws of the pack because of its fear of the harmless lion's roar. Do you see the point? If the hapless victim had only known who was making the noise, he could have been saved from the lions by **not believing the roar**!

We have been given authority to bind the devil in the Name of Jesus and loose or allow the Holy Spirit to do what He wants to do in the situation. *"Whatsoever ye shall bind on earth shall be bound in heaven: and whatsoever ye shall loose on earth shall be loosed in heaven."* (Matthew 16:19 & 18:18)

We are to spoil and sack his house and release the prisoners bound by sin and lead them into the Light of the Gospel. *"...how can one enter into a strong man's house, and spoil his goods, except he first bind the strong man? and then he will spoil his house."* (Matthew 12:29) We are to cast the devil out of people, places and things. *"And these signs shall follow them that believe; In my name shall they cast out devils; they shall speak with new tongues; they shall take up serpents; and if they drink any deadly thing, it shall not hurt them; they shall lay hands on the sick, and they shall recover."* (Mark 16:17,18)

Christians back off from spiritual warfare because they don't understand that they have the **right** to do it as a child of God and that God **wants** them to do it and in fact **needs** them to do it because of the way He has set up His Plan.

Our Relationship To God

Understand now that our **relationship** to God is more important than our **authority**, but the truth is that we can have both! Jesus places the emphasis correctly in Luke 10:20, *"Notwithstanding in this rejoice not, that the spirits are subject unto you; but rather rejoice, because your names are written in heaven."* .

When we live according to God's Word it isn't any big deal to bind the devil—it is our right as children of God to be free from the devil and his works. *"If the Son therefore shall make you free, ye shall be free indeed."* (John 8:36) Binding the devil is just plain, old, regular, believer's work. *"And these signs shall follow them that believe;" (Mark 16:17)* What is the first thing Jesus says believers will do? *"In my name shall they cast out devils."* Are you a believer? That is the condition that you must meet. When you believe, the devil doesn't have a chance. It's nothing to even get excited about. **The really exciting fact in our lives is that our sins have been forgiven and that we are members of the family of God!**

Too many Christians practice a variation of what the indigenous tribes have done for centuries in the jungle when they want the devil and his demons to treat them well. To appease the demons they leave food and gifts at designated areas. Unfortunately, the more they try to appease the demons the more they get into bondage because the demons know the people are defenseless to protect themselves.

Christians hope to appease the devil in the same way by not bugging him. They think that if they just tip-toe around him, everything will be alright and he won't bother them. But the principle is exactly the same and "not bugging the devil" won't work any better than leaving him food and gifts. The only way the devil will behave himself is when he is comes into contact with Someone who is stronger than he is as Matthew 12:29 teaches. The devil only respects the Power and Name of Jesus. So the sooner God's people learn how to use the Power and Name of Jesus in these last days the better.

We even have pastors and leaders tell us they don't want to have a seminar or teaching on spiritual warfare for fear that it will get the devil stirred up. They say, "Don't rock the boat. Things are going good now so why open up a 'can of worms.'" That is no more than symbolically setting food in front of a tree in the jungle. It is an indication of a lack of knowledge about what Jesus and Paul said about spiritual warfare and sends a message to the devil that they are living in fear and believing his deception.

The truth of the matter is that if we aren't making the devil mad by what we are doing for God we aren't doing much that will stand for eternity. God **wants** the devil to remain bound, cast out and his house spoiled in our world today. One of the big problems these days is that the devil is running around unhindered, doing things he has no right to do.

I John 3:21 & 22 gives insight into why some Christians have bad experiences when attempting spiritual warfare. *"Beloved, if our heart condemn us not, then have we confidence toward God. And whatsoever we ask, we receive of him, because we keep his commandments, and do those things that are pleasing in his sight."*

A Great Problem
In The Body Of Christ Today

One of the great problems in the body of Christ in the U.S. is that Christians think they can sin and get away with it. *"Be not deceived; God is not mocked: for whatsoever a man soweth, that shall he also reap."* (Galatians 6:7) If we are not living in obedience to God's Word, it opens us up to the harassment of the devil. That is one of the reasons some Christians get zapped by the devil when they attempt spiritual warfare. They play free and easy with the devil and then expect to suddenly switch and start binding and loosing. They have bitterness, unforgiveness and rebellion in their hearts, they covet, lie, steal, smoke, drink alcohol, swear, commit adultery and fornication and then wonder why they can't shut the devil down in their life. Sin must be repented of and gotten under the Blood of Jesus **first**. Then when our heart doesn't condemn us, we have confidence that God hears and answers our prayers.

Submission Brings Authority

Remember, before we can exercise authority over the devil we must be under authority to God!

"We know (absolutely) that anyone born of God does not (deliberately and knowingly) practice committing sin, but the One Who was begotten of God carefully watches over and protects him (Christ's divine presence within him preserves him against the evil), and the wicked one does not lay hold (get a grip) on him or touch (him)." (I John 5:18 Amplified Bible)

That is not to say that sin is **always** the reason why bad things happen, but it certainly is one of the reasons. Nor does it mean that only perfect Christians can do spiritual warfare. The Name of Jesus gives us our authority to resist the devil. What it does mean is that the less we sin and are involved in the works of the flesh, the less the devil can hassle us.

A friend of ours was getting off a bus in Portland, Oregon with her children when a drug addict threatened her with a knife and demanded her money. She yelled at the top of her voice, "Jesus, Jesus, Jesus" and the thief ran off.

The police picked him up later, but released him for lack of evidence. The next day the same man **robbed and killed** another victim under similar circumstances.

The way we react to the devil's roar can be the difference between life and death. James recommends, *"Resist the devil, and he will flee from you."* The Christian's song is not, "Whatever will be, will be." There is no good or bad luck for God's people. We maintain life by faith in what God's Word says.

Spiritual warfare is simply believing God more than the devil; then acting on God's promises to us as though they are fact, not theory. When God says that believers can cast out devils, we don't question or analyze whether it is true or not. We believe, act and trust that it is done because we know God does not lie. Then we continue speaking what God's Word says about it because the Word is more real than the devil's deception and lies.

Do We Suffer If We Teach Spiritual Warfare?

People ask us, "Don't you have all kinds of problems with the devil because you teach on spiritual warfare?" (As if the devil punishes us because we have the nerve to stand up to him.) No, that is false information the devil uses to scare some Christians out of acting in the authority and power of a child of God. The truth is that the more we exercise our God-given rights and power over the devil, the **less** he will be able to harass us. Just think about it for a moment. If you learn how to protect yourself and as a result learn how to more skillfully use the weapons of spiritual warfare against the devil, who do you suppose is going to suffer more? That's right, the devil, and that is why he wants to keep us ignorant of our rights as a child of God.

So stop listening to the roar of the toothless, old devil and start believing God when He says *"...we are more than conquerors through him that loved us."* (Romans 8:37) Don't allow the devil to cheat you out of your right to shut him down in your life as you live according to the Word of God.

Chapter 5

QUESTION: "How can I know God's Voice and know the difference between what the devil tells me and what God is saying to me?"

There are three classes of spirits in our world; God's, the demonic and the human spirit. Each one of them has a voice that speaks to us and it is imperative that we recognize the difference between each one of them, especially when we are involved in spiritual warfare.

Did you know that the devil can appear and sound very "God-like" on occasion? We are told he can transform himself into an angel of light if it is to his advantage. (II Corinthians 11:14)

I read about a minister who was forced to leave his church because of health problems. One morning he woke up to find what appeared to be the Lord in his bedroom. The creature's clothes were shining and he told the pastor that he was there to inform him that it was not God's will to heal him. The pastor took this as a word from the Lord and stopped believing for his healing.

But was that really the Lord Jesus Christ talking to him? Would Jesus say it is His will to heal people in His Word and then contradict Himself to this pastor? No, He wouldn't. Isaiah 53:5 says, *"And with his stripes we are healed."* That is something which Jesus has accomplished for every believer who will receive it by faith.

If the being with shining clothes had told the pastor that he wasn't saved, would he have believed that also? Not if he knew anything about what the Bible says about salvation. But he was tricked out of his healing because he was deceived by the devil's God-like appearance.

The Content

One rule for knowing whose voice is talking to us is to note the **content**. Whenever a voice or person tells us anything contrary to the Word of God we automatically recognize that it is not God's Voice. *"But though we, or an angel from heaven, preach any other gospel unto you than that which we have preached unto you, let him be accursed."* (Galatians 1:8)

The Location

The **location** in our being where we hear God's or the devil's voice can also help us zero in on which voice is talking to us.

Satan has access to our mind to tempt us, but he cannot speak to our spirit or heart. That is God's territory if we are one of His children. The sinner's spirit is dead spiritually, which is why he lives according to what his bodily desires and emotions tell him. *"And you hath he quickened, who were dead in trespasses and sin; Even when we were dead in sins, hath quickened us together with Christ,(by grace are ye saved;)"* (Ephesians 2:1,5)

God communicates to us through our spirit or heart because He is a Spirit. *"God is a spirit and they that worship him must worship him in spirit and in truth."* (John 4:24) *"For as many as are led by the Spirit of God, they are the sons of God. The Spirit itself beareth witness with our spirit, that we are the children of God."* (Romans 8:14,16) It is a safeguard for us to know that Satan cannot control our spirit area.

How many times have we heard of a mother who killed her children because "god" told her to do it. But God would not command her in His Word, *"Thou shalt not kill"* and then contradict Himself by telling her to kill her children. What she heard was the voice of the devil. Because she didn't know the difference between the two voices a terrible tragedy occurred.

We've also read newspaper accounts of people who said they heard a voice in their head telling them to kill someone or themselves. That points up the fact that our mind is the devil's playground unless we renew it by filling it with God's Word. (Romans 12:2) So we must carefully weigh what we see, feel and hear so that we **only** believe what God says about whatever situation we encounter, instead of what the devil tells us. We have a new spirit placed within us when we accept Christ as our Savior that acts as a spiritual receiver for the voice of God. *"Therefore if any man be in Christ, he is a new creature:"* (II Corinthians 5:17) As we learn to fine-tune that still, small voice in the depths of our being, we are able to walk confidently in the Power of the Holy Spirit. And remember, the Voice of the Holy Spirit will **always** speak in harmony with the Word of God.

More and more these days we hear of Christians who say, "It doesn't matter if the Bible supports it or not. This message is so vital that it has to be from God." No, we can be **sure** it isn't from God if His Word does not support it! What they heard was a doctrine of devils which Paul warns will increasingly take place in these perilous, last days. *"Now the spirit speaketh expressly, that in the latter times some shall depart from the faith, giving heed to seducing spirits, and doctrines of devils;"* (I Timothy 4:1)

Then, there is the matter of differentiating between the voice of our spirit and that of our carnal, fleshly nature and our emotions. Our human spirit, that "new creature" that Jesus gave us, desires to be led by the Holy Spirit, while the devil seeks to exploit by force our flesh and emotions through temptation, unbelief and fear. Only as we keep our flesh and emotions under the control of the Holy Spirit are we able to live according to God's Will.

Our Body And Emotions

Romans 12:1 commands us to make a living sacrifice of our flesh; not obey or listen to what it says in spiritual matters. The reason we must do that is because we never, ever receive good spiritual advice from our body. When was the last time your body said, "I feel like going to church tonight?" No, the very opposite is true. That is why we never ask our body if we should pray or praise the Lord because we already know what the answer will be. Neither do we rely on our emotions to judge whether we are saved or not because there are times we don't necessarily **feel** saved. **Our emotions and body play tricks on us**. So we filter out the static of our body and emotional voices in spiritual matters and concentrate on what God communicates to our human spirit by His Word and Holy Spirit.

That does not mean that we don't practice good mental and health habits. When we abuse our health by not eating or sleeping correctly our body will let us know something is wrong. We pay attention to that. To be spiritually guided doesn't mean we stop using sound thinking and good logic.

But just remember that the **real you** is a spirit. To live according to the way God wants you to live, your body and soul or emotions must come under subjection to your human spirit, which in turn is under the direction and guidance of the Holy Spirit.

A Test To Find Where Your Spirit Is Located

If you don't understand what it means to listen to God's voice in your spirit, try a little experiment. Romans 8:16 tells us, *"The Spirit itself beareth witness with our spirit, that we are the children of God:"* When you wake up in the morning, take a few minutes to turn your mind toward God and quietly praise Him before you get up. Then listen for a song or chorus, or even new phrases of praise that many times will begin to spontaneously bubble up from the middle of your stomach area, right around the bottom of your rib cage. That is about where your spirit is located and that is where the Holy Spirit will communicate with you. Daniel said, *"I Daniel was grieved in my spirit in the midst of my body,..."* (Daniel 7:15) Jesus also located where the Holy Spirit lives in us when He said, *"He that believeth on me, as the scripture hath said, out of his belly shall flow rivers of living water."* (John 7:38)

We need to become more aware of these impressions from the Holy Spirit. He lives in us and is trying to direct our lives so we can accomplish His Will and live correctly. God wants to bless us and lift us up into heavenly places with Him. Life, with all its problems, will have a different perspective when we start the day out listening to the inner voice of the Holy Spirit. It is a practice that will fine-tune us to recognize the voice of the Shepherd as He speaks to us the rest of the day.

Most of the time His voice will be soft and still; under some circumstances it can be louder.

Some Christians think God has spoken to them in their minds when in reality they have received it first in their spirit before it then moved up to their mind.

Others may be pleased to find that they have been hearing God's voice all the time but they just haven't recognized it as His.

When you have learned to correctly focus in and obey the Spirit-led part of your being, your body, emotions and even the devil himself will not be able to trick you into sinning, being fearful or unbelieving or anything else that is against the will of God for your life.

"...he that entereth in by the door is the shepherd of the sheep. To him the porter openeth; and the sheep hear his voice; and he calleth his own sheep by name, and leadeth them out. And when he putteth forth his own sheep, he goeth before them, and the sheep follow him: **for they know his voice,** *And a stranger will they not follow, but will flee from him: for they know not the voice of strangers."* (John 10:2-5)

You **can** hear and know God's Voice and know beyond a shadow of a doubt that He is leading and guiding you into all Truth!

Terror At Tenerife

The book about the terrible collision which took place between two 747 jets at Tenerife, Canary Islands in 1977 is described by Norman Williams in his book, *Terror at Tenerife.* He tells of the terrible experience of being trapped in a jet plane with no escape. He said flaming debris was flying all over the cabin, cutting the people in terrible ways.

He had always heard sinners make the statement that they would repent before they died if they just had the chance. But he witnessed people, whose flesh was melting away because of the intense heat, who were swearing vehemently with their last breath damning God for letting them die like that.

Norman told Carol personally that before the accident, he and his mother, who lived in his house, would spend time each morning reading the Bible together and praising God in English and in their prayer languages for a while before he went to work.

He said that when it looked like he would burn up with the rest of the people, without even thinking, his prayer language began flowing out of his spirit through his mouth. It just rolled out. In just a matter of seconds he looked up, saw a hole in the roof of the jet, got up on the top of the seat, pulled himself through the roof, jumped onto the wing and then over the edge to the ground and away from the fire ball that had been an airplane.

Looking back on the incident, he knows an angel helped him because he is a large man and the roof was so high he could never have done what he did even with an adrenalin surge.

That illustrates that what we put into our spirit comes out under pressure. The computer people call it, "Garbage In - Garbage Out." Those who had programmed themselves to swear when things weren't going right, went into eternity doing that very thing in the flaming jet. But Norman had programmed God's Word and the working of the Holy Spirit into his spirit and that is what saved his life.

It pays to program your spirit correctly ahead of time—before the crisis occurs!

"How can you speak good things when you are evil (wicked)? For out of the fullness (the overflow, the superabundance) of the heart the mouth speaks. The good man from his inner good treasure flings forth good things, and the evil man out of his inner evil storehouse flings forth evil things. But I tell you, on the day of judgment men will have to give account for every idle (inoperative, nonworking) word they speak. For by your words you will be justified and acquitted, and by your words you will be condemned and sentenced." (Matthew 12:34-37 Amplified Bible)

Chapter 6

QUESTION: "Can I really trust God the Father? I've been taught that He does bad things to us when He is angry or to teach us a lesson or to test us. I'm always afraid God will do something terrible to me. But I'm also not sure when the devil is involved in my life because he does bad things too."

It is absolutely necessary that we have total confidence in God the Father if we are to conduct healthy, successful, biblical, spiritual warfare. If our shield of faith in God and His Word is taken away from us, we are left exposed to the devil's deception. That produces disastrous results in our life and is one of the reasons Christians have trouble living the victorious life that is their right as a child of God.

When we understand the truth about our heavenly Father we are better able to judge when He is doing something in our life and when it is really the devil who is responsible. This is important because if we become confused about what God does in our life and what the devil does, it keeps us from acting decisively spiritually.

Who Is Doing What To Us?

A very simple way to judge **who** is doing **what** to us is to apply this test to whatever is going on: is this something "Godly" that is happening in my life or is it "devilish?" Is this giving me faith and strengthening my spiritual vitality or is it robbing me of those things? We must remember that God does Godly things and the devil does devilish things. It is as impossible for God to do something devilish as it is for the devil to do something Godly.

We can distinguish between what is actually Godly and what is devilish by looking at the character of God and the character of the devil. Character tells us what people are really like. We know and

43

recognize each other by our characteristics and the same is true of God and the devil.

If we have a friend who never repays a loan, we know what will happen when he asks us for financial help. His character helps us anticipate what the results will be and we can save ourselves a lot of grief by telling him, "I'm sorry but I can't loan you the money."

The same is true in our dealings with God and the devil. If God is doing something in my life, I want to cooperate with Him. But if it is the devil, I want to stop him from doing whatever he is doing as soon as possible, which is my right as God's child.

Who Is God?

First, let's consider the various sides of God's character. By studying **who** God is, we can get a clear picture of how He deals with us in a given situation. That is not putting God in a box nor are we saying it is all God will ever be. One of the wonderful features of Heaven is that God will continue revealing Himself to us throughout the ages of eternity. God is so great that we will never know all there is to know about Him. But the features of God's character that we will consider now are those God has revealed about Himself to this point in His Word.

GOD IS A SPIRIT. We are not dealing with some kind of super human being. God is in a category all by Himself. If we want to communicate with God we must do it on His terms, *"God is a Spirit: and they that worship him must worship him in spirit and in truth."* (John 4:24) That is why it is so important to recognize **where** we hear God's Voice in our being so the devil can't trick us by sounding God-like. When we know in our spirit that this is really God we are communicating with, we can be absolutely sure that we are hearing and walking in Truth.

GOD IS HOLY. He has never been touched in any way by sin nor will He be involved with sin. So if what you are experiencing has anything to do with sin you know God is **not** the author of it. *"Let no man say when he is tempted, I am tempted of God: for God cannot be tempted with evil, neither tempteth he any man:"* (James 1:13) This is also a tipoff on how to get along with our heavenly Father. If God doesn't like sin, the less we are involved with sin the better our relationship!

GOD IS ETERNAL. He was not born and He will not die. He has always existed and always will exist. Time, therefore, may not have the same impact on God as it does on us. We are pressured by time, but God isn't. That may be one of the reasons we have trouble with God's timing in some of our situations. The fact is, though, that God's timing is always perfect.(Ps. 90:2;102:25-27)

GOD IS INFINITE. His Power is without limits except when He limits Himself. For instance, God has the power to force every person in the world to accept Christ as their Savior in an instant. But God wants us to accept Christ because WE want to do it, not because we are forced into it. So He has limited Himself to allow us to choose, by our own free will, what we will do with Jesus. (Ps. 103:19)

GOD IS OMNIPRESENT. He is everywhere in the Universe at the same time. *"Whither shall I go from thy spirit? or whither shall I flee from thy presence? If I ascend up into heaven, thou art there: if I make my bed in hell, behold, thou art there. If I take the wings of the morning, and dwell in the uttermost parts of the sea; even there shall thy hand lead me, and thy right hand shall hold me."* (Psalms 139:7-10)

GOD IS OMNISCIENT. He has all knowledge. He knows everything there is to know about everything in the entire Universe. (Ps. 147:5)

GOD IS OMNIPOTENT. He has all power. Therefore there is not anything God cannot do if He has promised it to us in His Word. (Col. 1:16,17)

GOD IS TRUTH. He never, ever lies. We can count on His Truthfulness in His dealings with us. On the other hand we can be absolutely sure that wherever a lie is involved, we are dealing with the devil, not God.(John 14:6)

GOD IS JUST. He is 100% fair in His dealings with us. *"For there is no respect of persons with God."* We always receive justice from Him. He doesn't play favorites. (Romans 2:11)

GOD IS GOOD. He is totally good. *"Every good gift and every perfect gift is from above, and cometh down from the Father of lights, with whom is no variableness, neither shadow of turning."* (James 1:17) A good God does good things, not evil. (Mark 10:18)

GOD IS UNCHANGEABLE. *"...with whom is no variable-ness, neither shadow of turning."* (James 1:17) He is *"...the same yesterday, and to day, and for ever."* (Hebrews 13:8) That is why it is necessary to understand God's character. When we do, we can be sure that He won't act out of character because He's had a bad day—He will always be the same as He has always been. If you or I were God and someone came to us with some insignificant request on a day when we weren't feeling good, we would cut them off in mid-sentence with, "Oh get out of my face, I'm having problems in Europe. Can't you see I'm busy?" If we come to Him according to His Word He is always ready to listen to us and do what He has promised. (Malachi 3:6)

GOD IS LIFE. He isn't just alive, He **is** life. All life flows from God. If God ceased to exist, the Universe would stop existing in an instant. Whatever God touches, turns to life because He is the, *"...way, the truth, and the life."* (John 14:6)

GOD IS SOVEREIGN. He is the absolute supreme ruler of the Universe. Many feel this is where God occasionally does bad things to people because He can do whatever He wants. But understand that God's Sovereignty is in complete harmony with His other attributes, such as Love, Justice and Mercy. His attributes never get out of balance with each other.

As humans, we have days when we do things that are "out-of-character" because we are under pressure or tired; things we would never do when we are our normal selves. But God **never** does anything that is "out of sync" with the rest of His characteristics. He is the most perfectly balanced personality in the Universe! (Daniel 4:35)

GOD IS LOVE. God is not just loving, He is the very personification of love. Think of the most loving person you know and he or she will not even begin to compare with our Loving Heavenly Father. One of the most difficult areas the Pharisees had a problem accepting in the teachings of Jesus was about His Father. How is it possible for a loving God to do the terrible things people have attributed to Him? (I John 4:8)

This does not mean that God can be manipulated or that He is soft, as happens when humans are blinded by their love for unreliable people. It is impossible to "pull-the-wool" over God's eyes because He has all knowledge and sees exactly what is in our heart.

GOD IS FAITHFUL. He is absolutely trustworthy. Many Christians do not get too close to God the Father for the reasons stated in the original question at the beginning of this chapter. But we must understand that God does not take, **He gives**. The only thing He ever takes from us is sin and we **want** that taken away. God the Father is the greatest Giver in the Universe. We can have complete trust in God and His Promises. He will **never** take unfair advantage of us in any facet of our life. He longs for us to just relax like a baby in His Arms, unafraid, trusting, secure in the fact that He will take care of our every need as He has promised. *"Behold the fowls of the air: for they sow not, neither do they reap, nor gather into barns; yet your heavenly Father feedeth them. Are ye not much better than they? Therefore take no thought saying, What shall we eat? or, What shall we drink? or, Wherewithal shall we be clothed? ...for your heavenly Father knoweth that ye have need of all these things. But seek ye first the kingdom of God, and his righteousness; and all these things shall be added unto you."* (Matthew 6:26,31-33)

We should not carry this to the extreme that we don't do our part and work for a living. The scripture also says, *"...that if any would not work, neither should he eat."* (II Thessalonians 3:10)

GOD IS MERCIFUL. His Mercy is beyond human comprehension. *"But God, who is rich in mercy, for his great love wherewith he loved us,..."* (Ephesians 2:4)

GOD IS PROVIDENT. He did not create us only to go off and forget us. He watches over and cares for His Creation. The Salvation of mankind is the number one priority in God's Mind. This scripture applies not only to this characteristic, but to His Mercy. *"The Lord is not slack concerning his promise, as some men count slackness; but is longsuffering to usward, not willing that any should perish, but that all should come to repentance."* (II Peter 3:9)

There is no such thing as luck in the Christian life. We do not have luck, we have God. We have bad luck when, because of ignorance, being deceived or willfully sinning, we allow the devil to have his will in our life.

The Bible also says that God gets angry and jealous, but this is a **righteous** anger and jealousy because God does not sin. It is not the same kind of sinful anger and jealousy that we usually experience. However, Paul acknowledges that there is a righteous anger that is not sinful. *"Be ye angry, and sin not:"*

I usually feel a righteous anger when dealing with the demon-possessed that feels wonderful. It is an overwhelming feeling of power over the demons that includes a holy anger because the demons have taken advantage of the individual involved. At times I have had to restrain myself from slapping the person because I was so incensed with the demons within him. Only when I remembered that I shouldn't punish the person for what the demons were doing was I able to control my desires. I believe that is the kind of anger Jesus felt when He cleansed the temple. (John 2:12-16)

In answer to those who feel God does terrible, vicious, cruel things to people, we must understand that God would never be found guilty of doing things He commands **us** not to do. What kind of an example would that be? Would He tell us not to kill, lie, steal and cheat and then do it Himself? You can be sure He wouldn't! **God is not a child abuser!** He doesn't abuse His children under any circumstances.

Who Is The Devil?

We are going to see, as we review the devil's character, that many times people have attributed to God the actions of the devil. Can you see what a terrible, insensitive act that is: to blame God for things He is not guilty of doing? That is why we must be careful to know **who** is doing **what** in our lives so that we can cooperate with God and resist the devil instead of resisting God and cooperating with the devil.

Let's look at the devil now. I warn you in advance, it isn't a pretty picture. Some feel that we shouldn't talk about the devil because it gives him glory. But we must examine the enemy so that we know what to expect from him and as a result, be able to shut him down when he begins his activity in our life. "General Matthew B. Ridgeway in his autobiography *Soldier* wrote, 'There are two kinds of information that no commanders can do without—information pertaining to the enemy which we call combat intelligence and information on the terrain. Both are vital.'

"Accurate and up-to-date intelligence on the enemy is crucial in making tactical decisions in war. A thorough knowledge of the strength of your opposition, the enemies probable line of attack and the enemies tactics, all help determine the course a nation's land, sea and air divisions will take." (Christ for the Nations, pg.10, author, Kay Arthur, 6/93) Ignorance is not bliss in spiritual warfare, it is deadly!

The devil is a liar, cunning, a tempter, deceitful, totally evil, a thief, an adversary, wicked, cowardly, a murderer (he does the killing),without principles, rebellious, fierce, cruel, a sower of discord, a destroyer and proud. Whenever we encounter these areas of behavior, we can be sure we are dealing with the devil in one form or another. **God is never involved in any way with these character traits!**

Study the two lists. God and the devil never exchange characteristics. The devil will try to convince you that God is involved with evil, but don't believe it. The devil uses the same tactics children use when their parents catch them in wrong-doing. They point their finger at their brother or sister and say, "He did it!" The devil has been doing this for centuries. Only when you know who your Friend is and what you can expect Him to do, in accordance with His characteristics that are according to His Word, will you be able to shout back at the devil, "That wasn't God's action, devil, that was **you**. Now get out of here in the Name of Jesus. I will not tolerate that in my life anymore. Jesus has given me freedom and I receive that freedom now into my life. Thank you Jesus for your Love and Mercy, etc."

When we understand that God isn't doing bad things to us or it isn't something we have to put up with because everyone in our family has it or it isn't bad luck, we can begin living life as God wants us to live. I spoke with a pastor who said, "When I realized it was actually a demonic spirit working on me and that I had the Power through Jesus to stop it, it changed my life. What a wonderful feeling to know I don't have to put up with the devil's tricks anymore!"

Some people believe the devil is a negative equivalent of God, with the same attributes as God—the opposite pole from God so to speak. The truth is that Satan is only a **fallen** angel. He isn't even as powerful as a good angel. Where did we ever get the idea that when Lucifer fell from his position of power because of sin, he got **stronger**? Does sin make **you** stronger? No! Sin makes whatever it touches **weaker**. Satan is only a shadow of what he once was. On top of that, Jesus defeated the devil so thoroughly that just the mention of His

Name sends shivers of terror through the kingdom of Satan. *"Thou believest that there is one God; thou doest well: the devils also believe, and tremble."* (James 2:19)

To illustrate how far Lucifer has fallen, it requires only **one** good angel to cast Satan into the pit at the end of the Great Tribulation. *"I saw an angel come down from heaven, having the key of the bottomless pit and a great chain in his hand. And he laid hold on the dragon, that old serpent, which is the Devil, and Satan, and bound him a thousand years."* (Revelation 20:1) Notice that this is just one, plain, ordinary angel and it only takes one of his hands to grab Satan by the scruff of his scrawny neck and throw him into the pit. The other hand is holding the key to the bottomless pit and a great chain!

What Are The Works Of The Flesh?

It is a different proposition if we get into the works of the flesh (Galatians 5:19-21) and sin. That is the devil's area of expertise because he invented Sin. Speaking of the devil Jesus said, *"He was a murderer from the beginning, and abode not in the truth, because there is no truth in him. When he speaketh a lie, he speaketh of his own: for he is a liar, and the father of it."* (John 8:44) He is a master at tricking us once we are away from the protection of God's Word. The devil knows how to push the buttons of our flesh to present temptation in its most appealing light.

But when we keep the devil within the boundaries of what God's Word says about the situation, he is helpless and we are more than conquerors over him through Jesus Christ our Lord! (Romans 8:37)

God's ultimate purpose in our life is more than keeping us from going to Hell. His greatest desire is that we have a loving, Father-child relationship with Him that is so deep and open that we will have absolute, total confidence in Him as our Heavenly Father. As the years go by and throughout the endless ages of eternity our relationship will grow and deepen as He reveals Himself to us and we respond with our love, worship and fidelity to Him.

The more we truly **know** God, the more we will give Him the honor and obedience He deserves and the less we will sin or disobey Him. Once we understand that He wants to lavish His Love on us and help us become what He knows we can be, so that we can experience

Life in the fullest sense of the word, it is easy to give our life fully to Him. He is the greatest Friend we have in the entire Universe and we can never thank Him enough for what He has done for us.

The blatant lie of the devil is that it isn't intelligent or even fun to live for God—that it is more satisfying to sin. To expose that nonsense, all we need to do is ask the devil what sin ever did for him. Sin knocked the devil out of heaven, caused him to lose every good thing he ever had and will separate him from God, in Hell, for eternity.

God wants us to miss the tragedy of sin, so He warns us in His Word, *"The wages of sin is death."* (Romans 6:23) "Don't do it!" He pleads. "It will kill you!" Can you hear the concern in God's voice as He tries to guide us away from the evil deceptions of the devil so that we can experience the abundant life that is available to us if we will just trust and obey Him?

The Israelites are a prime example. As long as they obeyed God's rules for living, their quality of life was outstanding because that's what God's Life is. When they followed the devil, they were abused, beaten-up, carried into slavery and killed. God didn't want that for them—they chose it when they chose to believe the devil's deception and sinned.

Two Reasons People Don't Trust God

One of the problems some Christians have in all of this is that they really don't trust God for a variety of reasons. The two major ones are: (1) their earthly fathers abused them and this has carried over into their relationship with their Heavenly Father or (2) they have been taught that occasionally God does such bad, evil, terrible things to His children that it would get an earthly father jailed if he did it to his children in our evil society today. How anyone could ever think that a Just, Holy, Loving God would ever be guilty of crimes our society considers so evil that the perpetrators are locked away from the rest of the citizens, is beyond me.

We must understand beyond a shadow of a doubt that God doesn't do devilish things to His children nor does He ask the devil to do it for Him. God does everything possible to **protect** His children from the devil, **provided** they don't chose to follow the devil by sinning. In that case, God has no other alternative but to allow His children to not only choose what they want, but to also receive what that choice brings—harassment by the devil and eventually—death, if they continue their rebellion against God and His Word without repenting.

We read about this in I John 5:18, *"We know (absolutely) that anyone born of God does not (deliberately and knowingly) practice sin, but the One Who was begotten of God carefully watches over and protects him—Christ's divine presence within him preserves him against evil—and the wicked one does not lay hold (get a grip) on him or touch (him)."* (Amplified Bible)

John adds that we know the Son of God came to this world to give us, *"...understanding and insight...to know better and more clearly Him Who is true;...the true God and Life eternal."* (verse 20)

Pay particular attention to what Jesus said about God the Father because mankind had gotten a mistaken idea of who God is and what He actually does as opposed to what the devil does. Jesus said that if we want to know what God the Father is really like we should just look at Him (Jesus). *"He that hath seen me hath seen the Father."* (John 14:9)

We know that Jesus did only good things for the human race while He was here on earth. *"How God anointed Jesus of Nazareth with the Holy Ghost and with power: who went about **doing good**, and healing **all** that were oppressed of the devil, for God was with him."* (Acts 10:38)

And that is what God the Father does also. We can trust Him to do what is right in our life. God wants to keep the devil from even touching us and will do so as long as we choose God's way of living and have faith in His ability to protect us.

Now, let's apply this close relationship with God to our everyday life and spiritual warfare today. If we truly believe that God loves us, protects us from the devil and doesn't let us down in the clutch, then we can be sure that the Promises of His Word will come to pass in our life when we place our life in His Hands.

It is absolutely necessary to know this down in your **heart** when the battle is raging around you and the bullets or "fiery darts" of unbelief, temptation and deception are flying all around you. The enemy tells you all kinds of things are going to happen to you and your family if you don't cave in to what he wants you to do.

But you know God is there to protect and deliver you! All you have to do is make your stand of faith according to your rights as a child of God and then **stick to that no matter how the circumstances appear in the natural.** From that moment on you refuse to believe anything that is not supported by what God says about the situation in His Word.

"But, but, but..." There are no "buts" about it. The enemy **can not** wipe you out. He absolutely can't win because our Father says the devil was whipped—totally humiliated by Jesus according to Colossians 2:15—and now we are applying that victory to our personal life by faith in God's Promises. (Colossians 2:15 Amplified Bible, I John 3:8) We believe the **devil** is defeated, **not us. We** are the conquerors through Jesus over the devil and we don't let up the pressure on the enemy until that victory is visible in the natural realm.

When All Looks Lost — Do This!

When it looks like everything is going wrong and it looks impossible, we **know** our Father has not abandoned us. **We never quit** because of natural circumstances as long as we are walking in Truth. We **trust** our Heavenly Father to do exactly what He has promised in His Word.

That takes all the fear out of our lives. *"...perfect love casteth out fear:"* (I John 4:18) When we are totally convinced God really loves us, we know He will do everything possible to protect and provide for us just as He has promised.

Trust your Heavenly Father. He loves you and has provided for your every need. He doesn't give you bad things—only that which is good for you. The truth is, **the closer you live to God, the better and sweeter life is!**

For those of you who have been angry at or fearful of God because of terrible, evil things that have taken place in your life, it will be of benefit for you to ask God the Father to forgive you of those feelings. He understands that you thought these things about Him because of a lack of information, but it will still help you begin a new, healthy relationship with Him to humbly ask for His forgiveness.

Just talk to Him as you would to the most loving person you have ever known. Say, "Heavenly Father, I ask you to forgive me for being fearful of you and for harboring anger in my heart toward you for the bad things that have happened in my life. I can see now, according to Your Word, that You love me more than I can ever understand and that it is Your Will to protect me from the devil. I'm so sorry for ever blaming you for what the devil was actually doing to me.

"Thank you for your forgiveness for my sins. Help me to draw ever closer to you and to trust you with every part of my life. I give myself completely to You because You will not take advantage of me, but will help me to become all that You know I am capable of being. I love you with all of my heart, Father. Amen."

"I rebuke you devil for deceiving me about my Heavenly Father and from this point on I'll resist you because now I know when you are doing your dirty work in my life. I have repented of fear and anger in my life so you cannot use those open doors to harass me anymore. I am free from your bondage forever because the Word of God says, 'If the Son therefore shall make you free, ye shall be free indeed.'" (John 8:36)

"Thank you, Lord Jesus, for your freedom. I open my heart to Your Holy Spirit to lead me into all Truth so that I can be used of You to accomplish Your Will in my life. Amen."

Chapter 7

QUESTION: "Why is there such an extreme in the Body of Christ today over spiritual warfare? It seems like Christians are either so frightened of it that they don't do anything or else they become some kind of 'wacko' that is 'off the wall.' Why isn't there some kind of balance?"

An important aspect of spiritual warfare is that we must live and work within the framework of the legal authority God has established for His Church. God does not operate "helter-skelter" in any aspect of His Character, His Word or His Kingdom. He wants us to obey and operate within those Laws because He knows that only then will we experience Life in abundance. (John 10:10)

His Laws do not cause bondage, but give liberty to live life as it should be lived. If we disobey God's Laws, we pay for the results of that disobedience, up to and including physical death at the hand of the devil and eternal separation from God if we don't repent of the disobedience and get into right relationship with God once again. (Romans 6:23)

The Two Extreme Problems

The two problem extremes that Christians face in doing spiritual warfare is that they either do not know about the legal authority that is available to God's children over the forces of evil or they try to operate above and beyond the authority that God's Word provides.

A traffic policeman who fails to exert his legal authority by not clearly demonstrating to the motorists what they should be doing in certain traffic situations may end up getting run over by those same automobiles. He has the uniform, the rights, the badge and the name, but because he is fearful of standing up to the traffic, he actually places his life in jeopardy.

Let us also suppose that there is a policeman who does not thoroughly understand the law he is supposed to enforce due to a lack of study, understanding or faulty teaching. Because of that lack of knowledge, this officer makes things up as he goes along. When another policeman who knows the law, points out that the proper proceedure has not been followed he the answers, "Its OK, I tried it this way in a situation the other day and it worked just fine."

We can see what a disaster this hypothetical policeman would make of the Law.

Situational Spiritual Warfare

In like manner some Christians are doing "situational" or "experiential" spiritual warfare that is not only incorrect but actually dangerous. **The end does not justify the means**. When spiritual laws are circumvented for whatever reason, someone suffers the consequences down the line somewhere. ("experiential"—"Any doctrine or theory that maintains that personal experience is the only or principal basis of knowledge." The Random House Dictionary of the English Language)

Experiences must **always** conform to God's Word no matter how great or mighty they may be. We have heard people say, "It doesn't matter that it isn't according to God's Word. It was so powerful that it has to be from God." **Not so!** If it doesn't measure up to what God says, it must be completely disregarded before it leads to error. Nor should we try to make experiences fit into what God's Word says. We are to study what God says about it and then **do it that way to begin with.**

That is why we continually stress the need to stay as close to what God's Word says about spiritual warfare as we possibly can. What does **God** call a spirit? How did **Jesus** deal with demons?

"But I asked the demon his name and he said it was such and such." someone says, "So that has to be correct because the person had real freedom after we cast it out." Once again, the end does not justify the means. How can we possibly place any confidence whatsoever in what a demon tells us? They are pathological liars so how will we **ever** know when they are actually telling us the truth?

The only time Jesus asked a demon its name, the demon lied to Him, telling Him how **many** there were, "legion," which signified a number that varied anywhere from 4200 to 6000. (Vines Expository Dictionary of Old and New Testament Words, page 329) This would be the equivalent of asking someone what their name is and having them answer, "5000." The obvious conclusion is that if the demon didn't tell Jesus its correct name we certainly can't believe **anything** demons say to us. We never see Jesus doing that again, but yet "asking demons their names" is standard procedure for many today. Mark 16:17 instructs us that demons go in the Name of Jesus because we **believe** the Word of God, not because we ask them what their names are in order to be able to cast them out more effectively.

Wouldn't it be more correct to ask the Holy Spirit what the demon's name is or find out what God calls a demon spirit in His Word, if it was necessary to know their names before we could cast them out?

Further, the less conversation we carry on with demons the better. We have heard of people supposedly leading demons in the sinners prayer after spending lengthy sessions conversing with them. That's how crazy it can get!

The problem is that such steps taken away from God's Word have taken spiritual warfare to extremes that are ridiculous and have given a bad name to something that is vital for successful Christian living in these last days.

Another problem in this area of authority is that if we expect to exercise authority, we must be under the authority of those who have been placed over us in God's chain-of-command.

Why did Jesus get so excited about the Roman centurion who came beseeching Jesus to heal his servant who was some distance away, sick of the palsy? Because he understood how authority in the Kingdom of God operates. He told Jesus to just speak the word and his servant would be healed. He added that the reason he could be so confident in Jesus' Power to heal his servant was because he, too, was under authority to his superiors in the Roman army. When he told his soldiers what to do they had to obey, just like the sickness had to obey when Jesus commanded it to leave his servant. (Matthew 8:5-10)

Christians who are living in sin or allowing the works of the flesh to dominate them are not going to have success in spiritual warfare because not only are they **not** under authority to God, but they are actually fraternizing with the enemy!

Many Christians in the "do-your-own-thing" atmosphere we find today will not come under authority to anyone. In that condition they can bind and loose all they want, but it won't work. James 4:7 says first, *"Submit yourself to God."* Then, *"Resist the devil and he will flee from you."*

We have got to stop the nonsense that is going on today in the Church of Jesus Christ and get back to basic obedience to God's Word.

Unfortunately, there are times when the authority structure breaks down because those over us have not obeyed God and His Word. In that case we are released from having to follow their orders and directions up to a certain point. For instance, in the fourth chapter of Acts we see Annas the High priest and other Jewish leaders who were very upset with the doctrine of Peter and John. They commanded them in v. 8 not to speak or teach again in the Name of Jesus.

The disciples knew God's Holy Spirit had moved upon them to say what they had said, so they obeyed God rather than the carnal Jewish leaders.

We have seen abuses today in cases where carnal leaders have lost their direction and as a result have exploited those under their care, telling them to do or not to do certain things and leading them away from God's perfect will for their life or ministry.

Act According To The Word And The Holy Spirit

But make absolutely sure you are acting according to God's Word and the voice of the Holy Spirit before you disobey those God has placed over you in His authority structure! If you are wrong, **you will be the one in rebellion against God.**

The positive side of operating **correctly** within God's authority structure is tremendous! We are more than conquerors over sin, the flesh, the devil and this world's system.

"Then he called his twelve disciples together, and gave them power and authority over ALL devils, and to cure diseases." (Luke 9:1)

"And these signs shall follow them that believe; in my name shall they cast out devils; they shall speak with new tongues; they shall take up serpents; and if they drink any deadly thing, it shall not hurt them; they shall lay hands on the sick and they shall recover." (Mark 16:17,18)

Jesus has transferred His Power of Attorney—His Name—to us, which gives us the legal right, authority and power to do whatever needs to be done on this earth which relates to His Kingdom, that is according to His Word and which is under the direction of His Holy Spirit.

The world looks at God's people with disgust. We appear so helpless in this vicious, devilish world, singing our hymns and going to church. But under the mild-mannered appearance of "Clark Kent" is a child of God who possesses **power** that makes Superman look anorectic!

We have been placed in this world to dominate it spiritually until Jesus returns to rule as King of Kings and Lord of Lords. (Luke 19:13) But until that time we must be responsible in using the Power of the Holy Spirit to reach this world with the Gospel of Jesus Christ by carefully following God's instructions in His Word.

Don't let this world's lying, corrupt, insane system intimidate you into giving up and thinking you can't make an impact for God. *"The effectual fervent prayer of a **righteous** man availeth much."* (James 5:16)

When you speak in the Name of Jesus, the demons tremble and must obey. They have no other alternative but to obey because when you speak in the Name of Jesus, according to God's Word, it is just as if Jesus is giving them the command personally! If the demons try to talk back, just tell them to, "Shut up in the Name of Jesus. You have no choice in the matter." This is, of course, if the person you are dealing with wants to be free. God honors the will of man and we must also. (Whether the person wants to be delivered or not should be ascertained before you begin dealing with them.)

"For though we walk in the flesh, we are not carrying on our warfare according to the flesh and using mere human weapons. For the weapons of our warfare are not physical [weapons of flesh and blood], but they are mighty before God for the overthrow and destruction of strongholds." (II Cor. 10:3 Amplified Bible)

In the spirit realm we are mighty because we live and operate in the Power of the One who created the heavens and the earth! As we walk by faith in God's Word, the physical manifestations will follow just as God says they will.

Live in accordance with God's instructions—respect those in authority over you—have faith in God and His Word—resist the devil and he will flee from you. These are some of the key elements in successful spiritual warfare and Christian living.

Chapter 8

Question: "I'm a pastor and a lady in my church has been creating a problem by trying to cast demons out of everyone she can get her hands on in the church. She also advocates that the people should throw-up the demons into paper bags and other things which I have a problem with. When I talked to this lady she gave me your book on the Strongman with the comment, 'I don't agree with everything the Robesons teach on demon possession, but their book is very good in helping identify evil spirits.'"

This pastor's phone call focuses on a couple of areas that need clarifying: (1) whether or not Christians can be demon possessed, and (2) whether or not unpleasant manifestations have to take place when demons come out of people who actually are demon possessed.

We are always thankful whenever our book is helpful to God's people in dealing with any facet of spiritual warfare. It would be wishful thinking on our part to believe that everyone would agree completely with what we have written or taught about spiritual warfare because there is such a wide variety of thought on most subjects within the Body of Christ. No one has complete knowledge about any particular subject so we are certainly open to further information that conforms to God's Word.

We have been accused by people of teaching that Christians can be demon possessed even though we have clearly indicated in our book, seminars and newsletter that this is **not** our belief. On the other side of the coin, we have been criticized by people who believe Christians **can** be demon possessed because, once again, we have clearly stated our belief that we don't. (Some use the terms, "demonization," "having a demon," or "the demon having the Christian," the meaning of which can vary from one person to another. When these terms were explained to us, they usually boiled down to the fact, after working through the conflicting terminology, that demons needed to be cast out of people in order for them to have freedom.)

Although we cannot agree with those who believe **true** Christians can be demon possessed, we still appreciate them for the fact that they are at least willing to be engaged in spiritual warfare. **We have many dear friends who believe true Christians can be demon possessed, so as we address this subject, please understand that it is not our purpose to discredit them in any way as individuals.** But we feel it is important to carefully follow God's Word in these treacherous times. If that causes us to disagree with people we love and appreciate, we are sorry. **It is not our desire to be divisive. But error is dangerous, no matter how it is arrived at, and as such, must be corrected.**

When John pointed out to Jesus that a man was casting out demons who wasn't one of the disciples, (*"he followeth not with us"*), Jesus told John, *"Forbid him not: for he that is not against us is for us."* (Luke 9:49,50) Notice that it wasn't a matter of error in the casting out of demons, but the fact that he was an outsider that was the problem.

We hear people, trying to walk the middle line, who say, "It doesn't really matter whether the demons are inside or outside of Christians—just so they get rid of them." That sounds reasonable, as most compromises do, but if a teaching cannot be supported by God's Word it certainly does matter whether they are inside or outside. In fact, it would be devastating to our faith in God if our protection and freedom was so weak that demons could enter into us whenever they pleased and do whatever they wanted. What kind of freedom would that be? Jesus tells us in Luke 10:19, *"Behold, I give unto you power to tread on serpents and scorpions, and over **all** the power of the enemy: and **nothing** shall by any means hurt you."* Does that sound like Jesus is talking about demon possessed Christians? **How can something we have all power over, turn around and possess us?**

The Pharisees accused Jesus of casting out demons in the power of Beelzebub, the prince of devils, thereby implying that Jesus was demon possessed. This illustrates how far afield people can get in saying who is demon possessed. (Matthew 12:24)

It is interesting to note that Jesus never cast demons out of His disciples, although many today would feel justified in doing so because of the disciple's actions. Peter had many problems that people, who believe like that, would tell us could only be resolved by casting demons out of him.

How Did Jesus Do Spiritual Warfare?

But Jesus didn't, and this gets to the heart of how spiritual warfare should be conducted today. How did Jesus do it? How did **He** handle it? If we follow Jesus' example, we will have the same results He did, as we all desire. *"He that believeth on me, the works that I do shall he do also; and greater works than these shall he do; because I go unto my Father."* (John 14:12)

In this case, He told Peter that the devil desired to have the opportunity to "sift" him like wheat. Then He prayed that Peter's faith in Jesus would not fail and that after he came through the temptation, he would have knowledge he could use to help others weather the temptations of the devil. (Luke 22:31,32) Many spiritual warfare teachers these days would consider that to be far too soft an approach in dealing with the devil.

Judas is a different story. The Bible actually says the devil entered into him—one of Jesus' own disciples. (Luke 22:3, John 13:27) Doesn't that prove that Christians can be demon possessed? **This is where we feel the major error is committed**. We believe Judas is a prime illustration of how someone who appears to have it together spiritually, can actually have severed his/her relationship with Christ and be involved with the demonic to the point of possession. The difference between Peter and Judas is that Jesus prayed for Peter, but He did not pray for Judas. He only told him to be quick about what he had decided to do. (John 13:27) Judas had crossed a line in the spirit realm that Peter hadn't crossed, which opened Judas to demon possession.

Jesus didn't teach his disciples or anyone else for that matter, how to cast demons out of true believers. In fact, there is no account in the Bible of a true believer being demon possessed. Isn't that strange in the light of the all the demons supposedly being cast out of Christian believers today?

This is not to say that Christians can't be attacked from without by demons in their mind, will, emotions and body. They can be troubled, pressed, buffeted, harassed, depressed, obsessed, oppressed, in bondage and bruised and **still not be possessed of the devil.** It is not God's will for them to continue in the above states. He wants them to overcome the attacks of the devil with His Word and be the more than conquerors that He says His children are to be in Romans 8:37.

Nor are we saying that deliverances do not take place in Christian's lives, **we are just saying they aren't deliverances from demon possession.** To be delivered from a spirit of fear does not necessarily mean the spirit was inside the individual. In the case of a Christian, it means he has fought off the attack of the spirit of fear by taking authority over the spirit in the Name of Jesus and believing what God has to say about the fearful situation the devil has used to weaken his/her faith. James 4:7 shows that when we, *"...resist the devil, ...he will flee from..."* us. When the Christian realizes he has power over fear in the Name of Jesus, a "deliverance" from fear takes place—**fear is no longer able to harass him as it did in the past.**

Those people who are actually in the final state of possession, or are indwelt, have long since severed their relationship with God by an act of their will. (either choosing to stop serving Jesus or neglecting to maintain their spiritual walk with Christ) They may still hang on to a form of godliness, but it is only an empty shell, camouflaging their true spiritual condition. They are "possessed" by a spirit of fear that has totally dominated them and taken up residence in their spirit.

Jesus teaches further in Matthew 12:43-45 that it isn't just a matter of casting demons out of people. **It is also important to keep them from coming back in.** *"When the unclean spirit is gone out of a man, he walketh through dry places, seeking rest, and finding none. Then he saith, I will return to my house from whence I came out; and when he is come, he findeth it empty, swept and garnished. Then goeth he, and taketh with himself seven other spirits more wicked than himself, and the last state of that man is worse than the first."*

Jesus makes it plain in this particular case that the individual involved is not a Christian because there is nothing within the "house" to keep the demon from re-entering it again. There is no Word, no armour of God, no Holy Spirit, no defense of any kind. That would not be possible in the case of a Christian because true Christians have the Holy Spirit living within them and since when are demons any match for the Holy Spirit and the Sword of the Spirit, which is the Word of God? The **last** place a demon wants to be is where the Holy Spirit dwells!

The Definitive Word Concerning Christians & Demon Possession

I Corinthians 6:19,20 gives us the definitive word concerning all of this, *"What? know you not that your body is the temple of the Holy Spirit which is in you, which ye have of God, and ye are not your own? For ye are bought with a price: therefore glorify God in your body, and in your spirit, **which are God's**."* This contradicts those who feel that demons can possess a Christian's body or mind without possessing his spirit. God says He dwells within our **total being**. We aren't some kind of condominium with demons living in one or two rooms and God in the other. That kind of fragmentation of the individual is a heathenistic concept which should have no part in Christian teaching. Although we have three parts, we are still **one** person. And, *"Greater is he (Holy Spirit) that is in you, than he (devil) that is in the world."* (I John 4:4)

Then, the above scripture says we are not our own, or we don't belong to ourselves anymore, but to God. Does that mean that God would allow demons to possess something which He possesses? That is impossible. The very word, "possession," means "one owner." **We are either "owned" by God or "owned" by the devil!** We can't have it both ways.

"There is therefore now no condemnation to them which are in Christ Jesus, who walk not after the flesh, but after the Spirit." (Romans 8:1) Look carefully at that scripture. Does that mean that Christians who are **in** Christ can have demons **in** them, thereby inferring that demons are **in** Christ? Certainly that is not the case, but it points out the danger and inconsistencies of a teaching that is not supported by Scripture.

Jesus does not violate man's free will. He is pictured in Revelation 3:20 as standing at the door, knocking, waiting for the door to be opened so He can come in. If God, who is All-Powerful, cannot violate man's will, demons must also honor man's will if the individual knows what the Word says and chooses to follow it. The demons will try to force people to open the door, but the principle still remains that we are the ones who decide when the door is to be opened or remain shut.

Experience VS. God's Word

Invariably these teachers will use experiences they have witnessed to substantiate their theory instead of the **weight of scripture** in God's Word. As a result, what they really attempt to do is cast the **works of the flesh** out of people, which is not only impossible to do, but is extremely frustrating for the people they are trying to do it to. The people never arrive at the state they desire because there are always more demons to be cast out of them. The truth is that we all have to contend with our flesh until Jesus gives us a new body. **It is impossible to cast the flesh out**—as much as we would all like to do so. Usually there is total silence about the works of the flesh by people who believe Christians can be demon possessed.

One evangelist tells his listeners, "We'll cast 50 demons out of you tonight and tomorrow we'll cast 50 more out." This not only creates a dependency in the people for the evangelist, which is not healthy, but there is never any lasting "victory" because they are forever having to have demons cast out. On the other hand, when Christians obey God's Word and discipline the flesh, there is victory. We may fail at times, but there is a sense of progress when we repent and God's Spirit gives us the power to extinguish the devil's fiery darts on our shield of faith the next time.

Also, people who are continually having demons cast out of themselves have a great tendency to become so demon conscious that they nearly forget about Jesus. They spend more time talking to, rebuking and thinking about the devil than they do about Jesus. They are continually chasing demons. It becomes a demonic wild-goose chase that only leads to confusion. They see demons everywhere instead of Jesus and the Power of the Holy Spirit. Jesus is the author and finisher of our faith and that is where our eyes, attention and faith must be centered. (Hebrews 12:2)

Paul instructs true Christians to present their bodies or fleshly desires as a living sacrifice to God. (Romans 12:1) He adds, *"...those who belong to Christ Jesus, the Messiah, have crucified the flesh* (the godless human nature) *with its passions and appetites and desires."* (Galatians 5:24 Amplified Bible)

The inference here is that those who are living according to the **flesh do not belong to Christ** and therefore need to repent of their sins and get in right relationship with God so they can use the Power of the Holy Spirit to keep their fleshly, carnal desires from ruling their life. **That is probably the primary reason so-called "Christians" manifest in a demonic manner when they are confronted by the power of God!** Paul says it is an understood fact that, *"...you are living the life of the Spirit, if the [Holy] Spirit of God [really] dwells within you [directs and controls you]. But if anyone does not possess the [Holy] Spirit of Christ, he is none of His [He does not belong to Christ, is not truly a child of God]."* (Romans 8:9 Amplified Bible)

The Requirements

Living for Christ requires a life of discipline which many of the Christian community refuse to embrace—opting instead for the lazy, irresponsible, noncommittal, last-day mentality that will (1) not only cause them to be hassled by the devil because they leave vast, open doors in their life that gives the devil a right to harass them unmercifully, but (2) there is some doubt that they will be ready to meet Jesus when He returns for His Church.

"Not everyone who says to me, Lord, Lord will enter the kingdom of heaven, but he that doeth the will of my Father which is in heaven." (Matthew 7:21)

"...strait is the gate, and narrow the way, which leadeth unto life, and few there be that find it." (Matthew 7:14)

This is serious business. Jesus is looking for a people who are faithful to obey His commandments. When teachers tell people they will be OK if they have demons cast out of them, they are not addressing the real problem, which is usually some kind of spiritual breakdown in their life; sin, unbelief, fear, unforgiveness, envy, strife, immorality, ignorance of God's Word, generational weaknesses/doors that need to be acknowledged and shut, and the deception of the devil. Until these people repent, close the doors to the devil's temptations and the flesh's desires and **live a holy life**, they will not only continue to be harassed, but will also be in danger of losing their salvation.

That is what we are trying to accomplish with our Strongman teaching as we point out what God's Word says about those open door areas that must be dealt with by **repentance** and then **discipline** through the Power of the Holy Spirit. **The doors must be closed tightly by a decision of our will.** We must take the vote away from our flesh in spiritual matters and obey what God's Spirit and Word dictate to us.

Jesus has defeated the devil and has given us His Holy Spirit to help us maintain that defeat over the flesh, the world and the devil on a daily basis. When the lure of temptation comes, we recognize it for what it is and apply the Word of God, just as Jesus did when He told the devil, "It is written..." (Matthew 4:1-10)

It is not our desire to cause Christians to doubt their salvation or get into fear over this matter because doubt and fear are of the devil. **But Christians need a good dose of holiness in their lives today.** *"Follow peace with all men, and holiness, without which no man shall see the Lord:"* (Hebrews 12:14) This is not the "holiness" of "dress codes" from pasts years which were possibly installed in good faith, but degenerated into a pharisaic nightmare of rules and regulations that produced more bondage than freedom.

There just seems to be a blindness to sin in the Body of Christ these days. Not only with what we might call surface sin (although sin is sin in God's eyes), but blatant, in your face, gross sin. These people can sit under Holy Spirit preaching and teaching and not put two and two together in their life. They come up afterward and ask, "How come I'm having all these problems in my life?" When the Holy Spirit pinpoints areas of sin in their life, as we talk with them, they say, "Do you suppose there's a connection between that and my problems?" Then they usually want **us** to do something to resolve their problems when it is **they** who must repent, discipline and obey.

Possibly this is where this "casting demons out of Christians" came from. Instead of telling these people they need to get right with God and repent of their sin, they are told that this is the devil's fault and when he is cast out, the problem will be resolved. How cunning of the devil to use the very issue of demon possession to deceive Christians into living sub par lives because they fail to do those basic things required of them to maintain the life in Christ a Christian must live. After all, if the demons are to blame for my "weaknesses", then all I have to do is have someone cast them out, instead of disciplining my flesh as the Bible clearly teaches. (Romans 12:1,2)

In the final analysis, each individual is responsible for the choices he/she makes. Many Christians have adapted the "no fault divorce and no fault auto accidents" to Christianity. Everything that happens is the demon's fault.

The "Loose-Liver" Plague

As a result there is a plague of loose-living "Christians" these days who are indistinguishable from sinners. They come to church, raise their hands during the worship service, looking like true believers, calling themselves Christians, and then go out and do the most ungodly things imaginable.   Here is what God has to say about it: *"Now the doings (practices) of the flesh are clear (obvious): they are immorality, impurity, indecency, idolatry, sorcery, enmity, strife, jealousy, anger (ill temper), selfishness, divisions (dissensions), party spirit (factions, sects with peculiar opinions, heresies), envy, drunkenness, carousing and the like. I warn you beforehand, just as I did previously, that those who do such things shall not inherit the kingdom of God."* (Galatians 5:19 Amplified Bible)

These are things your flesh wants to do. The devil knows this, so he floats temptations by your eyes and ears that appeal to those areas of your flesh which he knows you are especially vulnerable to. Hebrews 12:1 refers to this as, *"...that sin which so readily (deftly and cleverly) clings to and entangles us,"* (Amplified Bible) He has a pretty good idea of what he can deceive you with by what your family has succumbed to over the generations and by observing your actions and decisions over a period of time. **At this point it is your choice as to what you will do.** Nobody, not God, the devil or any other person can force you to do something contrary to what you **will** to do because God has given you a free will.

Let's say that a Christian in this position chooses to sin, gives in to his flesh and commits the sinful act. Does that mean a demon has come into him? No, he gave in to his flesh. However, the longer he continues giving in to his flesh in this area, without repenting, the more he is in danger of walking away from the Grace of God and losing his Salvation. The length of this process can vary from one person to another because everyone is distinct and there are many variables to be considered. (An example is Peter and Judas in the scenario mentioned earlier) While in this state, he will be harassed by the devil because sin causes open doors, which gives the devil the right to do things to him he couldn't do if the door were closed. A Christian who refuses to repent eventually will lose out with God and cross the line. **Now**, the devil's power to lead the individual deeper and deeper into sin becomes increasingly powerful, until the final stage of possession results, which is a possibility with any sinner. Even Paul had to be careful that this process would not happen in his life so that after preaching to others, he would not become a castaway himself. (I Corinthians 9:27)

Paul addressed this to the Galatian church and told them that unless they repented of their sins and disciplined their flesh by the power of the Holy Spirit, they would miss Heaven and go to Hell. We seldom hear this taught or preached these days for fear the people will be unhappy and leave the church. The truth is that they have already left the church—in spirit—the only thing that remains, symbolically speaking, is their body.

One evangelist uses a Pentecostal pastor as an example in his book to "prove" that Christians can be demon possessed. When the evangelist began praying for this pastor of 40 years experience, he manifested demonically. Understandably this would be a shock and the natural assumption would be that this "Christian" was indeed demon possessed.

But listen to what this pastor's problem was—**He hated his mother!** Although we live in a time when many people are realizing they have grown up in dysfunctional families and as a result have deep areas of hurt toward family members, it is no small matter to hate your mother for whatever reason.

What does the Bible say about someone who hates? *"Whosoever hateth his brother is a murderer: and ye know that no murderer hath eternal life abiding in him."* (I John 3:15, 4:20 & Revelation 22:15) Somewhere along the line the pastor's hatred of his mother carried him outside the boundaries of eternal life and, as a result, opened him to demon possession.

Not only **doesn't** the Bible support the fact that the pastor was in right standing with God at this particular time, but **it illustrates the fact that we cannot use experiences to form our doctrines.** The weight of scripture in the Bible is very clear concerning the fact that true Christians cannot be demon possessed. Therefore something was definitely wrong with this experience that seemed to be in conflict with the weight of scripture which God has given us for just such an occasion as this. **If our experiences do not match up with what God's Word says, then the experiences must be discarded—not God's Word.** The ground around experiences is shifting sand because no two experiences are ever exactly the same. That is why we must absolutely demand that God's Word be our ultimate standard of what we believe in these deceitful times. *"Heaven and earth shall pass away, but my words shall not pass away."* (Matthew 24:35)

The Case Of Ananias And Sapphira

The case of Ananias and Sapphira is similar to that of the pastor above. (Acts 5:1-10) Through the Gifts of the Spirit, Peter exposed the heart of their problem—**lying to the Holy Spirit!** The scripture text does **not** say that they were possessed of the devil. Peter says in verse three that Satan had filled their heart or had **tempted** them to do the deed. Then in verse four he lays the blame where it belongs, *"...why hast **thou** (Ananias and Sapphira) conceived this thing in thine heart."* They became convinced, because of the temptation and deception of the devil, that they could get away with this con game and **of their own will** they committed the act. They were not forced to sin anymore than any of us—they just received the wages of sin, albeit, more quickly than usual.

This instance shows the cop-out of blaming demon possession for actions the Christian is responsible for choosing him/herself, for what it is. True, the devil tries to tempt and deceive us, but we have God's Word, the Armour of God and the Holy Spirit to counteract the devil's tricks and keep us on the road of Truth **if that is what we truly desire.**

Another occasion people use to justify that Christians can be demon possessed is when Peter rebuked Jesus after He told the disciples He would have to suffer, die and rise from the dead. Jesus turned to Peter and said, *"Get thee behind me, Satan: for thou savourest not the things that be of God, but the things that be of men."* (Mark 8:31-33) They feel this means that Peter was demon possessed because Jesus addressed Satan instead of Peter. But Peter had simply fallen for the same trick the devil had tried to use on Jesus when he tempted Him after 40 days in the wilderness. He tried to convince Jesus to accomplish mankind's salvation the easy, carnal, blood-less, cross-less way. Jesus recognized it for what it was, labeled the source correctly and dealt directly with the devil.

Peter probably realized the error soon after the words left his mouth, as happens to you and me at times, and was sorry he had ever opened his mouth. Otherwise you can be sure Jesus would have said more to Peter than He actually did.

There are those who think such slips of the tongue are because the demons are talking from within the Christian. But Jesus says that what we speak is what we **will** to speak, which in turn is determined by what is already in our heart. *"...for out of the abundance of the heart the mouth speaketh. A good man out of the good treasure of the heart bringeth forth good things: and an evil man of the evil treasure bringeth forth evil things."* (Matthew 12:34)

"Therefore, my dear ones...work out (cultivate, carry out to the goal, and fully complete) your own salvation with reverence and awe and trembling (self-distrust, with serious caution, tenderness of conscience, watchfulness against temptation, timidly shrinking from whatever might offend God and discredit the name of Christ)" (Philippians 2:12 Amplified Bible) This scripture reveals that we must carefully guard our Salvation and relationship with Christ or it will slip through our fingers and be lost eternally.

It's Crunch-Time In World History

This is crunch-time in world history. We cannot make up doctrines as we go along because of experiences. *"Henceforth be no more children, tossed to and fro, and carried about with every wind of doctrine."* (Ephesians 4:14)

As we live according to God's Word, get sin out of our life, stop believing the devil's lies and deception and receive by faith what the Word of God has made available for us, He lifts us out of our weakness and places us on the Solid Rock and gives us the Power to be more than conquerors through Jesus Christ our Lord!

A sword is for cutting and our Sword of the Spirit cuts spiritually—it hurts demons. They don't like it—they will do anything to get away from the Truth of God's Word.

Must Deliverance Have Sickening Manifestations?

Now, let us see what God's Word has to say about vomiting up demons. (please excuse the use of this unpleasant terminology, but it is necessary to be specific so that no one is able to say, "That isn't what they really meant.") Once again, there is no reference in the Bible that supports such teaching—not one scripture. In fact, one of the reasons some have avoided having to deal with demon spirits is because this aspect of it caused such disgust and even fear in people that it created more problems than it cured. Just because the devil and his demons are foul, loathsome creatures does not mean we have to be subjected to their filthy displays. **Demons will put on as ridiculous an exhibition or sideshow as they are allowed to do.**

When we know in advance that we are going to be casting demons out, we bind them ahead of time and tell them just exactly what they are going to do and **how** they are going to do it. Even if it is a spur-of-the-moment situation we can still lay down the rules to them.

Understand that we are not saying there will be no manifestations whatsoever such as crying out, falling down or even shaking. These all took place in Jesus' ministry in Mark 1:26, Luke 4:35, Mark 9:26 and Acts 8:7. What we would like to show is that these actions are momentary—not a long drawn-out process that goes on and on. Secondly, that the manifestations were not sickening, repulsive kinds of things such as vomiting, etc. When the crying out took place in Jesus' ministry it was a brief, short action and then it was over.

The question we get from the people who believe they must have these manifestations is this: "If they don't throw-up or cough or yawn or breath them out, then how will you ever know they have really come out?"

The answer: "Since when does faith in God's Word need physical manifestations to prove what God's Word has promised will come to pass? Don't we walk by faith and not by sight?" (II Corinthians 5:7) Jesus teaches that, *"...these signs shall follow them that believe; In my name shall they cast out devils;"*

Isn't this promise Jesus made good enough for us to believe that the results will take place, just as He says they will, without having to have some gross, physical manifestation of the devil to prove it?

If the individual, who is demon possessed, **wants** to be delivered and if you believe what God says about it, then the demons have no alternative but to come out. We have **all** Power over them in the Name of Jesus, so what do you think the demons are going to do, argue with Jesus? They never did when He was here on earth and if they do now, just use the Sword of the Spirit, which is the Word of God, on them and they will **have to go**.

A sword is for cutting and our Sword of the Spirit cuts spiritually—it hurts demons—they don't like it—they will do anything to get away from the Truth of God's Word.

Two Things That Will Stop A Deliverance

Only two things will stop a deliverance from happening: (1) the will of the person who needs deliverance. So it is very important to make sure they **really** want to be free. As violently possessed as the man from the country of the Gadarenes was in Mark 5, he still desired to be free and was completely delivered, or (2) if there is unbelief present among those dealing with the demon possessed person. While Jesus was being transfigured on the mountain, as recorded in Matthew 17:1-20, his disciples were trying to cast the demon out of the boy down in the valley. When Jesus came back, He saw the situation and cast the dumb and deaf demon out. The disciples questioned Jesus later about it, *"Why could not we cast him out? And Jesus said unto them, Because of your unbelief:..."* (verses 19 and 20) There is a possibility that the disciples had been involved with the scribes in a heated, or contentious, discussion. Such things will always affect the anointing of the Holy Spirit and thereby limit the quality of your faith. (verse 14) Don't allow fear, unbelief or strife in your heart while dealing with the devil because those are tricks he uses to keep you from accomplishing God's Will in the situation. The truth is that the demons are afraid of you when you walk in the Power and Authority of God's Word as the child of the most High God.

The one instance when foaming at the mouth is even mentioned in a case of demon possession did not take place at the time of the deliverance, but had been an ongoing condition in the boy's life for who knows how long. (Matthew 9:20)

A sidelight in this case is shown in verse 25, which we feel is important in conducting deliverances. Before casting the spirit out,

Jesus took time to ask the boy's father pertinent questions about the child. Sometimes this information is revealed by the Holy Spirit through the Gifts of the Spirit, but, especially when dealing with children, it may be necessary to deal with the parents, because sometimes the parent's spiritual condition has contributed to the problems of their children. (such as parents who have been in the drug and witchcraft scene) In this case, Jesus had to deal with the father's faith, *"...help thou mine unbelief."* (verse 24)

In the next verse it says, *"When Jesus saw that the people came running together, he rebuked the foul spirit, saying unto him, Thou dumb and deaf spirit, I charge thee, come out of him, and enter no more into him."* Look at two significant actions here: (1) Jesus didn't allow this confrontation to turn into a circus. As soon as He saw the curiosity-seekers coming to see the show, He immediately terminated the encounter by dispatching the spirit. That, alone, would end many deliverance ministries today because the excitement and action of the casting out of demons is the high point of the night for their audiences. That's what the people come to see. The real question, though, is: who is exalted more, Jesus or the demons? When it is possible, we always limit the number of people who are present to those who are mature in the Lord. (2) Jesus revealed the name of this particular foul spirit—dumb and deaf spirit.

There was no need to ask this demon his name so that Jesus could cast him out more easily. And God's Word has given us the names of 16 major spirits or strongmen so that we need not spend unnecessary time making conversation with lying demons. That is what we have presented in our "Strongman's His Name, What's His Game" book to pinpoint the areas of demonic activity the devil uses to accomplish his program in people's lives today.

The "Demon's Nest Theory" Dismantled

One last reference to ugly things which some people say must take place when casting out demons is that the person must not only throw up the demon, but also the demon's so-called "nest."

Obediah, verse 4, uses the word "nest" to describe, through the law of double reference, the residing place of Satan "among the stars." But to say this has any reference to demons having a nest in people is not dividing the Word correctly. Stars are just not people.

The contex has to do with the Horites when Edom expelled them from the area around Petra. The Horites were dwellers in caves in those mountains. God tells Satan that he can try to hide as high up in the caves as he wants, even in the stars, but he will still be brought down because he cannot hide from God.

Another reference in Habakkuk 2:9 might seem to refer to demons and nests. But the Amplified Bible clarifies the meaning. *"Woe to him who obtains wicked gain for his house [who thinks by so doing] to set his nest on high, that he may be preserved from calamity and delivered from the power of evil!"* The Babylonians thought that by having vast riches they could miss calamity—evil befalling them. But God informed them that they would be plundered inspite of their riches.

Jesus tells us to cast out demons, not nests. Demons are spirits who have no physical bodies therefore have no need of a physical nest. Once again, it is a trick of the devil to make the casting-out-of-demons so repulsive that a certain amount of Christians will become disgusted and stop doing it. We have friends in the ministry who told us personally that they got tired of people vomiting all over everything and now only instruct the people do other, less sickening things to "let the demons out."

When demons **enter** people they don't have all these sickening, ridiculous things taking place so why do they have to occur when they leave? When people teach that the demons must be "breathed" out, it would only make sense that they are also "breathed" IN. But the truth is that demons are not limited to entering or leaving only through orifices in our body. They are spirits that aren't limited by physical substances or materials—walls, bodies, steel, concrete, anything. They can enter or leave through any part of the human body that suits them in cases of possession.

It always amazes us that these kinds of things didn't occur in Jesus' ministry when He cast demons out of people. So where do these ideas come from? "Just because it happens is not sufficient reason to build doctrines.

Chapter 9

QUESTION: "How do we know when to deal with an individual in spiritual warfare and when to cut them loose? What is a good test to know the difference between someone who really needs help and someone who is only wasting our time?"

We are hearing real horror stories about troubled people who are monopolizing, through lies and trickery, the time and lives of Christians who are trying to help them get their lives straightened out. These apparent victims tantalize the Christian by saying they want help, but in reality they are being used of the devil to cause havoc, destroy relationships and rob the Christian of time they could spend in more productive ministry.

The question that usually reveals where people are is simply, "Do you truly want help?" By this we mean, "Are you willing to do what is necessary to change your life from what it is to what God's Word says it must be?"

A simple example of this would be to ask a thief if he is willing to stop stealing and begin working at a legitimate job. Or will he continue playing games with himself and you—doing just enough to take the pressure off for a short time before sliding back into his old habit pattern again.

We are not downgrading the ability of the Holy Spirit to lead us because we must depend on His discernment to know what the truth is in any situation. But God also expects us to use good, common sense in all parts of our life.

Jesus never helped anyone, while He ministered on earth, who didn't **want** help and who didn't have faith to accept that help from Jesus and who didn't do what he/she needed to do so that Jesus could help them.

Do You Want To Be Healed?

How many times did Jesus ask people, "Do you **want** to be

healed?" Why did He ask such a seemingly unnecessary question? Because it was important that they want to be healed before He could actually heal them. Jesus never forces us to do anything we don't want to do, even if it involves something so important as the healing of our bodies.

The rich young ruler is a case in point. (Luke 18:18-25) He asked Jesus for help and then refused to do the one thing Jesus told him he would have to do to inherit eternal life. Did Jesus run after him, trying to counsel him and help him see the mistake he had made? No, and we never hear anything more about the rich young ruler again because he had made his choice.

We must understand that the human will is supreme in the spirit world. God will not violate it in any way. He gives us absolute freedom to choose whatever we want to choose. The devil, on the other hand, will try to force us, through deception and fear, to do something we may not have really wanted to do to begin with. But if we reject his deception through an act of our will, he must back off until he feels he has a chance to deceive us again in the future.

The Pivotal Point Of Deliverance

The will of the individual we are trying to help is the pivotal point in how far we can go in trying to assist him/her in receiving God's answer to their situation.

It would be unwise to think we could **make** someone get saved who doesn't want to accept Christ. When an individual demonstrates that he isn't ready yet, we stop dealing with him until he is ready. We can pray that he will see his error by binding the evil powers in the Name of Jesus that are causing him to continue on in sin and loose, or come into agreement with God's Will for the situation, which is that he be saved, so the Holy Spirit will continue speaking to his heart. But that's as far as we can go until the person is ready to accept Christ.

The same is true in receiving healing in our body. Jesus didn't heal one person while He was on earth that (1) didn't **want** to be healed, (2) didn't have **faith** in His ability to heal him/her and (3) didn't have faith to **receive** the healing that He extended to him/her. There were probably many godly, sick people in Jesus' day who did not get healed because they did not meet all of the above basic requirements to be healed.

Jesus didn't go around haphazardly healing everyone who was

sick. So why do people believe Jesus would do something today that He didn't do while He was on earth? Yet an entire doctrine has evolved in religious circles that tries to explain why God doesn't heal certain people who **outwardly** seem to qualify for healing, yet are not healed.

The truth is that healing has already been bought and paid for by the sacrifice of Jesus, so the question isn't **if** God is going to heal, but **will we receive it by faith?** Instead of blaming God when people aren't healed, we should be looking for the breakdown somewhere in the person's will that is keeping them from making contact with the Source of their healing. That is the only way we can thwart God's Will in our life and keep Him from accomplishing what His Word says will **absolutely happen** if we ask for it, believe He can do it and receive it.

"Ask and it shall be given unto you...for everyone that asketh receiveth...If ye then, being evil, know how to give good gifts unto your children, how much more shall your Father which is in heaven give good things to them that ask him?" (Matthew 7:7-11)

Now, let's apply this to the problem of knowing just how far we should go with people before we know it is time to back off until they are ready to receive God's answer to their problem which is deliverance. Understand that there are cases when the devil actually uses satanic plants to exhaust and discourage the Christians who are involved in spiritual warfare so that they will get burned out and not be as ready and willing to help people who really want help in the future.

Deliverance is no different from anything else God has provided for us. When people become involved in practices, lifestyles and problems that require God's help to get them free, the same basic requirements still must be met by the individual needing help or **deliverance will not take place.**

What If Nothing Happens?

You will know something is wrong, somewhere, when what God has promised will take place, **doesn't take place**.

When the individual meets the requirements to be delivered, the deliverance takes place as quickly as Salvation happens. How long did it take Jesus to cast demons out? "But that was Jesus," you say. No, He says we can do it just like He did it if we follow His Word and the individual really wants to be free and **follows through with his decision.** (John 14:12-14)

Any breakdown in getting people delivered, just as in Salvation and Healing, always revolves around the person's will, provided **we** are following God's Word in dealing with them. We must instruct

79

them to do what is according to God's Word and advise them to do **healthy, Biblical things** so they can escape the unhealthy, unbiblical practices they have been involved with.

If you are truly hearing from God and what God's Word promises will happen, has not happened, **then something is wrong.** Somehow, somewhere the devil still has an open door which the individual has allowed to stay open, either through ignorance, choice or deception of the devil.

However, when the open door is located and the person chooses to close it once and for all, the struggle will be over in deliverance or anything else God has promised.

Then we must get them full of the Holy Spirit and build them up in the Word so they can recognize the devil's deception and not fall for his tricks when he comes back to check things out later, **as he always will,** whether it is deliverance, salvation or healing.

God's Word says, *"...these signs **shall** follow them that believe; in my name shall they cast out devils."* (Mark 16:17) If you believe and the devils don't come out, then the individual has a problem and, as a result, is not able to cooperate with you and the Holy Spirit or the demons are leaving and coming right back through the door the individual hasn't closed yet **or** the individual is playing games with you to get attention, rob your time or exhaust and discourage you. Something is definitely wrong, **not with God,** but with the individual's will.

When you point out the open door and you are absolutely certain the person understands what must be done and the person does not change, then tell them, "When you are willing to do what you know must be done, let me know. Until then I will not waste my time with this nonsense!"

Don't let the person wheedle you into continuing unless there is **ample proof** that they are now ready to get all the doors closed, **stick with that decision,** and **walk it out for an extended period of time**.

Jesus gave the disciples some advice in this regard when He sent the twelve out. *"Heal the sick, cleanse the lepers, raise the dead, cast out devils:...**and whosoever shall not receive you, nor hear your words**, when ye depart out of that house or city, **shake off the dust of your feet**...Behold, I send you forth as sheep in the midst of wolves: be ye therefore wise as serpents, and harmless as doves."* (Matthew 10:8,14,16)

These days God's people must distinguish between reality and the deception of the devil. The time is too short to play games with demons. We must show mercy and help deserving people, but don't be afraid to cut off people the devil is using to disrupt your life and who have no desire to stop following the devil.

Chapter 10

It seems that whenever there is any kind of horrendous occurrence in nature these days, some Christians begin telling the whole world that this was an action of God, as if they are members of some kind of terrorist group taking credit for the latest bombing.

Homes are inundated by floodwaters, leveled by earthquakes and hurricanes, people are killed by the hundreds, misery and tragedy spread across the scene like a malignant nightmare and these Christians seem to relish telling sinners, "This is something God did."

Can they honestly believe this kind of destructive, malevolent disaster is actually going to **draw** sinners to God? Aren't sinners trying to get away from that kind of evil taskmaster?

The usual kind of "decisions" that are made under these circumstances are "fox hole" decisions and many times they only last until the danger has passed, although there are always exceptions for which we are thankful.

The point is that **driving** people to Christ through fear does not give good results because fear is a tool of the devil. The Holy Spirit **draws** people to Christ. *"And I, if I be lifted up from the earth, will draw all men unto me."* (John 12:32) God doesn't need the devil's help to send a message to mankind. He speaks to them by His Word, through His Holy Spirit.

The Real Destroyer

Jesus instructs in John 10:10 that killing, stealing and destroying are actions of the devil, not God. God is, *"...not willing that **any** should perish, but that **all** should come to repentance."* (II Peter 3:9) It would be counterproductive for God to cause people to perish as a result of His judgment when He wants **all** of them to be saved. Would God act against His own Will? Never!

What mankind is experiencing in these natural disasters is a combination of, (1) the wages of sin which is death, (2) mankind's abuse of the ecology (the great flood of 1993 was exacerbated because reportedly the engineers had messed with the Mississippi's channel) and (3) the results of the curse of sin on the earth. The earth has been fractured because of man's sin, thus creating the possibilities for earthquakes. (Each time an earthquake occurs it should be a reminder of how destructive **sin** is, not how ferocious God is.)

The shocking truth is that after all of these terrible things have taken place on earth during man's lifetime, he **still** must face God's judgment **after** death. *"...it is appointed unto men once to die, but after this the judgment:"* (Hebrews 9:27) **God is saving people now, not judging them. The devil is the killer!**

God Is Not A Child Abuser!

Some would say, "But people really wake up to the fact that life is short when these terrible things happen, so God must be sending them."

It is true that **after the fact** God uses what has happened to point out what His Word says about life and death, but that doesn't mean He **sends** or **causes** them to happen.

For instance, let's say you instruct your child not to play in the street so a car won't hit him. Your child ignores you and continues playing in the street.

To teach your child a lesson, you wouldn't ask your neighbor to get into his car and deliberately hit your child, would you? No, you love your child and that is why you told him not to play in the street— to **keep** him from getting hit by a car. Besides, there is a law against child abuse.

But, if your child is hit by a car and ends up in the hospital, you would surely have his entire attention when you tell him, "This is what I've been warning you about. This is the reason why you shouldn't play in the street."

You didn't cause or plan for your child to be hit, but you used the situation to impress the fact upon him that you love him and for that reason he must obey what you say from now on.

God does not abuse His creation. He is not a child abuser. And our message to sinners should express that truth. Instead of telling people that God **causes** these terrible disasters, we should tell them, "If you will believe and live according to God's Word He will **protect** you from these things the **devil** causes. It is the devil's plan to kill you, destroy your possessions, wipe out your job, hurt your children and make you live in fear and bondage. But God wants to give you freedom from the results of sin and protection from the devil's actions in your life if you will just obey Him and have faith in His Word. The Good News is that the reason He does all of this is because He really loves you!"

In our ministry in Latin America we preached that simple message night after night in the open-air crusades. We found that sinners already know their lives are a disaster. They don't want to be threatened by a God of vengeance. They want to find Someone who really loves them and will help them get away from the devastation in their life.

After two and 1/2 years of preaching that message every night in our open-air crusades in Managua, Nicaragua, not one member of our denomination's churches, who was living a righteous life, was killed when the earthquake destroyed Managua in 1973! On the contrary, miracles took place that saved their lives.

People in one of the new crusade churches were warned by the Holy Spirit 30 days in advance that an earthquake was coming. So they prayed, fasted and bound the devil in the Name of Jesus and that suburb of Managua suffered very little damage, although the full force of the earthquake was felt!

We've got to get this simple fact straight in our thinking: God gives life in abundance and the devil is the one who tries to take life from us. When we accept Christ, stay out of sin and the works of the flesh, believe and act on God's Word, **He will deliver us** out of the clutches of the devil and make us members of the family of God with full privileges.

Luke 10:19 tells us that Jesus gives us 100% power over the devil IF we will believe and use it by faith. When the devil tries to rob, kill and destroy in our life, we recognize it for what it is and command the devil to **stop it in the Name of Jesus** and then allow the Holy Spirit to have His complete Will in the situation. (Matthew 16:19 & 18:18)

When we recognize **who** is doing **what** to us, it blocks out uncertainty, fear and doubt so that we can be the, *"...more than conquerors..."* that God says we are in Romans 8:37. Not only that, but we won't blame God for the actions that Sin and the devil are responsible for causing.

Chapter 11

QUESTION: "I have such a difficult time dealing with the invisible part of spiritual warfare. How can I get beyond the problem of not being able to physically see what is going on in the spirit realm?"

I agree that there are times when it would seem more satisfying if we could feel a real sword in our hand and see it make contact with the demons when we swing it. We could be sure it was actually working if we could see the demons tremble when we speak the Name of Jesus or see them running away from us when we resist them in the Name of Jesus. This certainly would satisfy our physical nature, but the reason the human race is in the shape it's in **is** because Adam and Eve followed their physical senses and sinned in the Garden of Eden. That made mankind's physical senses suspect because through them Adam and Eve fell and sin entered human nature and brought eternal death.

So Jesus took the conflict out of the physical realm and into the spiritual when He defeated Satan at the cross. He allowed His body, which included His five physical senses, to be nailed to a cross and allowed death to take place, thereby becoming the sacrificial Lamb which paid for our Salvation and freed us from the results of Sin.

This was all too good to be true as far as the devil was concerned. He thought he had actually killed God's Son. What a victory! He had won the war and kicked God forever out of mankind's affairs on this earth.

But three days after Satan had taken the best shot he will ever get at God, he found that he had forgotten one very important detail about God. **He is life!** Death could only hang on to Jesus as long as God said he could hang on.

That fateful Sunday morning almost 2000 years ago, God backhanded death and the devil like a giant swatting a fly and Jesus rose Victor over death, hell and the grave!

Now, when the devil tries to tell you he is going to defeat you, that you aren't going to make it, that he is going to do this and that to you or your family, you just point back to the Resurrection and say, "You've got it all wrong devil. **You** are the one who is defeated and I apply the victory Jesus won over you to this situation I am dealing with today."

Because Jesus changed the arena from the physical, where mankind was defeated, to the spiritual, where Jesus defeated the devil, we now have a different set of rules to play by. Now we don't have to be a strong, physical hulk of a man to be victorious over the devil. **All we have to do is believe that Jesus won the war!**

We Believe God's Version Of What Happened

Little children, grandmothers, 98 pound weaklings, **anyone** who believes in their heart that God raised Jesus from the dead and confesses with their mouth the Lord Jesus, shall be saved. (Romans 10:9) Saved from what? Saved from sin, the devil, death, sickness, fear— anything that had to do with mankind's bondage to the devil and his kingdom.

We live by faith in God now instead of our physical senses. In the spirit realm or arena **we** are now the conquerors because of what Jesus has done for us—**provided we truly believe God's version of what happened at the cross.** We believe, or have total confidence in God and His Word more than the defeated, lying, snake of a devil who tries to drag us back into a physical type of warfare in which we depend on our physical strength, senses or feelings to live our life.

When God says it doesn't pay to sin, we **believe** Him instead of the devil who tells us it won't hurt us or that we can get away with it if we want.

When God says our body was healed when Jesus took the stripes on His back, we **believe** him instead of the devil who says we will never recover, or all our family puts up with that kind of sickness so we will have to also, or what makes us think we are so good that God would heal us?

When God says He will protect us, we **believe** Him instead of the devil who tells us God sometimes lets bad things happen to us to teach us a lesson. We know our Father doesn't resort to devilish tactics to teach His children, so we hang on to the truth of God's Word by faith.

We believe that God provides for our every need. We believe that His Holy Spirit is bringing our family and friends to Salvation. We believe that there is absolutely nothing to fear because 365 times in the Bible in one form or another we are told, "**fear not**."

I'm Going To Kill You!

A young man's friend dared him to rob five convenience stores in the same day, one after the other. So he took his .357 magnum revolver and proceeded to rob four of them in 45 minutes.

While his buddy waited for him in the car, he approached the fifth store to wrap it all up. But this one was different. He said that for some reason he couldn't understand he could hardly walk through the door this time. Understand now, this man was full of hate and the devil; mean, vicious, animalistic, ready to kill at the slightest provocation.

He finally shoved the door open and saw a young girl bent over the counter. He walked up behind her and put his gun to her head and said, "This is a robbery!"

She turned around, looked him in the eye and said, *"Silver and gold have I none but such as I have, I give you in the Name of Jesus. God loves you."*

He banged his gun down on the counter and said, "You don't understand, this is a holdup!"

The young girl calmly took the key to the cash register, locked it and threw the key away.

He screamed at her, "I'm going to kill you."

She turned and went over to her purse. He thought she was going to give him her personal money. Instead she pulled out a gospel tract with a yellow smiley face on it that said, "Smile, Jesus loves you."

He put his gun back to her head and snarled, "I'm going to blow your head off."

She answered, "Sudden death—sudden glory!"

He fell back away from her, stumbled out of the store, got into the car and slumped down in the seat. His friend said, "What took you so long, man, where's the money?"

He answered, "There's a guy in there with 22 inch biceps. It was all I could do to get my gun back and get out of the store!"

That confrontation with a child of God, who believed God more than the circumstances she could see in the physical realm, caused the young man to accept Christ as his Savior.

Many Christians today really don't believe that God keeps His Word. They live in constant fear and dread of the unknown. As far as they are concerned the Bible was written for everyone else except them. They have a spiritual inferiority complex. The devil has completely convinced them that they are the exception to God's Promises in spite of the fact that God's Word plainly states that He is not a *"...respecter of persons:"* (Acts 10:34)

How Do We Escape This Brainwashing Of The Devil?

Jehosaphat received instructions from God on how to war against the Moabites, Edomites and Ammonites that is just as powerful in today's world of spiritual warfare as it was back there in the physical. (II Chronicles 20)

(1) Jehosaphat, *"...set himself to seek the Lord, and proclaimed a fast throughout all Judah."* (verse 3) He wanted to make sure he and the nation were where they should be in their relationship with God. If we want to receive the benefits of God's family we have to obey the rules of His family. We must deal with sin and repent of it. We must close any open doors of disobedience to God in our life so the devil has no opening or loophole to legally harass us. *"The effectual fervent prayer of the righteous man availeth much."* (James 5:16)

(2) Jehosaphat **prayed a prayer of faith**. It was only 224 words, but it was powerful. Look at some of the key phrases, *"...in thine hand is there not power and might so that none is able to withstand thee."* (verse 6), *"...thou wilt hear and help."* (verse 9), *"...we have no might against this' great company that cometh against us; neither know we what to do: but our eyes are upon thee."* (verse 12, author's emphasis)

Many of our problems in the faith realm involve the matter of God's timing. In our push-button, microwave society we usually think God has refused our request if it doesn't happen 30 minutes after we ask for it.

Faith involves patience, determination, endurance, even stubbornness to the degree that God's Promises are stated in His Word. **The Christian life isn't a 100-yard-dash, but a marathon**. Paul's testimony was, *"I have fought a good fight, I have finished the course,*

I have kept the faith." (II Timothy 4:7)

(3) The very first thing God said when He responded to Jehosaphat's prayer was, *"**Be not afraid nor dismayed by reason of this great multitude;**"* (verse 15) In other words, physical circumstances have nothing to do with the problem.

We cannot allow physical circumstances to dictate how we are going to live for Christ. We cannot live by how the situation looks or feels. The spirit of fear must be brutally eradicated from our lives if we are ever going to be victorious.

(4) God told them this wasn't their battle, but His. **Then He instructed them on the exact way they were to conduct themselves.**

"...set yourselves, stand still, and see the salvation of the Lord." (verse 17) Ephesians echoes this advice, *"...and having done all, to stand."* (Ephesians 6:13) One of the hardest things to do in the physical is just to stand when every fiber of our being is screaming, "Do something!" But if we have total confidence in God, we will know that He keeps His Word. It is not how strong we feel physically, but how much faith we have in God's strength that brings victory in our life.

(5) **They sang and praised God before they saw any kind of physical evidence to substantiate what God had said would happen.** (verses 21,22) That takes confidence in God. We get that kind of faith by hearing God's Word. (Romans 10:17) It was only **after** they stepped out in faith that they actually began seeing the answer to their prayer come into physical manifestation.

What happened? The enemy was thrown into confusion and destroyed each other. **How sad that because many today are not following God's instructions in spiritual warfare, it is the Christians who are confused and destroying each other and the devil is running loose in our world!**

(6) Verse 25 illustrates why it pays to follow God's way in dealing with the enemy—**victory brings rewards.** It took God's people three days to haul off the riches of the defeated enemy. The devil has to pay when he loses. He has to give up his victims; he has to restore what the cankerworm has eaten; he has to give back our children and relatives; he has to return the money he has robbed from us and he has to give our health back. *"And when Jehoshaphat and his people came to take away the spoil of them, they found among them in abundance both riches with the dead bodies, and precious jewels, which they stripped off for themselves, more than they could carry away: and*

they were three days in gathering of the spoil, it was so much."

Don't give up! Keep the devil in the realm of God's Promises—the spiritual realm. Believe **that** more than anything else and then act on that Word in the crisis time or whenever you are tempted not to believe God. That's the way God's family is supposed to live. It doesn't matter what the problem or circumstance may be, you are a conqueror through Jesus Christ our Lord! (Romans 8:37)

End Of The Party!

We arrived in Modesto, CA for a seminar in a pastor friend's church on Saturday evening. We were very tired and looked forward to a good night's rest in the beautiful motel room the pastor had graciously reserved for us.

When we checked in, we noticed the room next to us was jammed full of balloons. But we were so tired the significance didn't register on our minds. The motel was a huge complex with a large indoor swimming pool and all the games and activities that children could enjoy.

We went to bed early so we would be refreshed for the next day. About midnight we were awakened by the sounds of a large group of people yelling and playing in the swimming pool right outside our window. I waited for someone to call the motel manager to complain about the noise, but apparently everyone else was waiting for someone else to do so also.

Then, to our utter dismay, the party moved from the pool to the room full of balloons next to us! We tried to sleep with pillows over our head, but the noise was incredible.

At 2:00 a.m. I suddenly thought, "Why are we putting up with this? We are being robbed of valuable sleep and these people have no right to carry on like this in a motel full of people."

So Carol and I agreed together in prayer that the party would break up. We bound the devil for disturbing our sleep and released the Holy Spirit to accomplish His Will in the situation. The moment we started praying, the noise stopped. As we prayed I watched the outline of the people quietly leave the room and walk by our window as they headed home. When we finished praying there was utter calm and we were able to sleep in peace the rest of the night!

As I fell asleep I thought, "Why didn't I do that sooner?"

Chapter 12

QUESTION: "Why do you use Matthew 18:18 as a spiritual warfare scripture when many believe it has to do with church discipline?"

15. More over if thy brother shall trespass against thee, go and tell him his fault between thee and him alone; if he shall hear thee, thou hast gained thy brother.

16. But if he will not hear thee, then take with thee one or two more, that in the mouth of two or three witness every word may be established.

17. And if he shall neglect to hear them, tell it unto the church: but if he neglect to hear the church, let him be unto thee as an heathen man and a publican.

18. Verily I say unto you, Whatsoever ye shall bind on earth shall be bound in heaven: and whatsoever ye shall loose on earth shall be loosed in heaven.

19. Again I say unto you, That if two of you shall agree on earth as touching any thing that they shall ask, it shall be done for them of my Father which is in heaven.

20. *For where two or three are gathered together in my name, there am I in the midst of them.*

The reason there seems to be a conflict over this passage is a basic misunderstanding of spiritual warfare. Those who feel these scriptures refer only to church discipline believe it is wrong to use Matthew 18:18 for spiritual warfare purposes. But what is wrong with approaching the church discipline from a spiritual warfare standpoint? Why can't the two compliment each other?

Let's look at the situation here. Why is there a **need** for church discipline? **Who** causes brother to trespass against brother? The **devil** of course. What do people who teach spiritual warfare say should be done in dealing with this kind of church discipline problem? **Bind the devil in the Name of Jesus!** When the devil is bound, people are able to see what they are involved in and follow the leading of the Holy Spirit more closely.

When the **root cause** of church discipline is dealt with in a spiritual way, instead of an ecclesiastical way, we are able to cut through the carnal infighting that has characterized church problems for centuries! (1) We bind the devil, whose deception has caused people to act as they have acted, (2) Show the people involved what God has to say about their conduct and (3) ask the Holy Spirit to accomplish His Will in each life represented in the situation. When church discipline is conducted in that manner, the passage is beautifully compatible with both church discipline **and** spiritual warfare!

The Greek Translation Supports This Action

There is also solid evidence in the Greek translation of the Bible to substantiate that Matthew 18:18 belongs in the arena of spiritual warfare not only for church discipline, but across the board in dealing with the deception of the devil.

No one doubts that Jesus was talking about spiritual warfare in Matthew 12:29 when He said, *"...how can one enter the strong man's house, and spoil his goods, except he first **bind** the strong man? and then he will spoil his house."* The word, "bind" in Matthew 12:29 is the **same Greek word** Jesus used in Matthew 16:19 and Matthew 18:18 when He says, *"Whatsoever ye shall **bind** on earth shall be bound in heaven;"* (word #1210 in Strong's Concordance of the Bible, "deh'-o")

Further, the Greek language structure that is used to describe **what** we are to bind in the three scriptures above does not refer to the binding of **persons,** but of **things** who have no gender form—they are **neuter**. (*"...they neither marry, nor are given in marriage; but are as the angels which are in heaven." Mark 12:25)* That would have to be the case in the binding of Satan and demonic spirits because spirits are not masculine or feminine—**they are neuter. THEY ARE THE THINGS WE ARE TO BIND—NOT PEOPLE!**

Secondly, the word, "whatsoever" in the Greek is "ho" which is the **neuter** singular in 16:19 and, "hosa" which is the **neuter** plural in 18:18. So the reading of Matthew 16:19 and 18:18 would be, *"Whatsoever* (not masculine or feminine in gender) *ye shall bind* (not masculine or feminine in gender) *on earth shall be bound in Heaven."* (page 1288, The Hebrew-Greek Key Study Bible, Spiros Zodhiates, Th.D)

Even in English, when referring to people we say, **"who**soever" and in referring to **things**, as the case is here, we say **"what**soever."

Therefore it is perfectly clear that Jesus was speaking about prayer and spiritual warfare in Matthew 16:19, 18:18 and 12:29, which makes it imperative that we obey what He says about binding the devil. When we bind the enemy in the Name of Jesus, we are acting according to the authority Jesus gave us in Luke 10:19 which gives us "all" (100%) power over the devil. We do our part by commanding the **devil** to take his hands off of people, places and situations. Then, all of Heaven stands behind us because we are coming into harmony with what is the perfect Will of God. It is always God's Will that the enemy be bound when he is trying to rob, steal and destroy, as the case is in church discipline or any other conflict caused by the actions of the devil.

The second promise concerning, *"...whatsoever ye shall loose on earth shall be loosed in heaven,"* naturally follows the binding of the devil. We know that the "loosing" cannot refer to the devil because we certainly would not want to "loose" something that we have just bound. So "loose" has to do with the loosing of something positive into the situation.

The only other party left to loose in spiritual warfare activity is God. Of course we know God isn't tied-up so that He needs to be loosed, but on the other hand there is a point in dealing with humanity when God must wait for us to choose which way we will go, whether it be God's way or the devil's way. The Holy Spirit is a gentleman and will not force His way into our lives. Only as we invite Him to do what He wills in the situation is He able to accomplish in our lives what He knows should be done.

Many fine Christians are binding the devil correctly, but do not receive all God has for them in their life because they refuse to allow the Holy Spirit to heal the hurts in their life or they are afraid to receive the Power to be the overcomer God wants them to be or they neglect to give up the sin that has opened up their life to an attack of the devil in the first place, thereby making their life a revolving door of continually having to bind the devil because the door remains open for him to attack.

So, the other side of the coin is to loose or release or allow the Holy Spirit to do in our life whatever He feels is necessary so that God's Will is accomplished. We are not demanding or telling God how to handle the details—we just have the faith to believe He will do it the best way possible. As we cooperate with God's Holy Spirit, He is able to make us into the person He knows we can become in Christ. The rough edges are smoothed off, the Holy Spirit helps us to forgive ourselves and finally, the hurts and misunderstandings we carry because of the abuses we may have suffered in our background, are revealed and explained so that we can forgive those who caused them and thus release ourselves from bondage to them and get on with accomplishing God's Will in our life.

The Greek word used here for "loose" is "luo." The primary meaning is, "to loosen (literally or figuratively) (word #3089 Strong's Concordance of the Bible)," which is what we are doing figuratively when we "loosen" or allow, permit and cooperate with what the Holy Spirit chooses to do in the situation.

Many times we are like the children of Israel in the desert. We have been delivered from the enemy (Egypt-the devil), but we still have so many hang-ups, hurts and fears that we cannot enter the abundant life God wants us to experience and enjoy. By opening ourselves, we release or allow the Holy Spirit to lead us out of the desert experiences and into the Promised land of freedom, peace and joy.

QUESTION: "Shouldn't we be more respectful of the devil when we speak to him. After all the archangel, Michael, was careful when he spoke to the devil, saying, 'The Lord rebuke thee.'" (Jude 9)

This incident occurred in the Old Testament before Jesus had accomplished the complete defeat of the devil and his kingdom. Also, Jesus did not die and rise from the dead for the angels and give them the authority of His Name as He has done for us. Although the angels occupy a higher position than the human race at this time, we will eventually judge the angels in the future. (I Corinthians 6:3)

Another scripture people use, attempting to prove that we must be careful of the power of the devil, concerns the seven sons of Sceva. (Acts 19:13-16) Apparently a vagabond group of Jews had come up with a method of casting out demons. They would tell the demons to come out of the possessed people by saying, "We adjure you by Jesus whom Paul preacheth." It is apparent that these wandering Jews were not believers in Jesus and had no idea of what they were doing. They were similar to some people today who are well-meaning in their efforts, but do not follow what God's Word says about dealing with the devil.

The seven sons of Sceva decided to try this method out and, to say the least, they had disastrous results. *"And the evil spirit answered and said, Jesus I know and Paul I know; but who are ye? And the man in whom the evil spirit was leaped on them, and overcame them, and prevailed against them, so that they fled out of that house naked and wounded."* (verses 15,16)

This incident does not prove that we are to be afraid of the devil—it shows that we must know how to deal with the devil **correctly**, according to how the Word of God teaches us. First of all, unsaved people have no power over the devil, no matter what they say or do, until they become a child of God. Even Christians who are not in obedience to God and His Word are in danger of having these kinds of results because they can't play "footsie" with the devil and then, all of a sudden, get spiritual and start ordering him around. *"And beloved, if our consciences (our hearts) do not accuse us [if they do not make us feel guilty and condemn us], we have confidence (complete assurance and boldness) before God. And we receive from Him whatever we ask, because we [watchfully] obey His orders [observe His suggestions and injunctions, follow His plan for us] and [habitually] practice what is pleasing to Him."* (I John 3:20,21 Amplified Bible)

Because we are children of God, habitually practicing what is pleasing to Him, we have the right to use His Name, with all the Power and Authority it carries over the devil. *"These signs shall follow them that believe; In my name shall they cast out devils;"* (Mark 16:17) When we realize that the victory Jesus has given us over the devil is total, absolute and irreversible, there is nothing to fear from the devil. As long as we keep our dealings with the devil within the realm of the Word of God, the devil is "dog-meat"—he doesn't have a chance—he has no alternative but to obey what we command him to do, in the Name of Jesus, according to God's Word.

But if we get into sin and the works of the flesh (Galatians 5:19-21), we get into the devil's area of expertise, where he is able to do things to us that he can't do if we stay within the protection of God's Word. This area is where bad things can happen to Christians who stray into his clutches out of ignorance or because they choose some aspect of the devil's deception.

Sin and the works of the flesh are the **only** areas where the devil demonstrates any kind of intelligence. For instance, I Corinthians 2:8 tells us that if the devil and his minions had known what the crucifixion of Jesus would accomplish, they would never have been a part of the crucifixion. Even after God totally stripped and humiliated the devil at that time, (Colossians 2:15) the devil continues to fight Him, as if there is some question as to what the final outcome will be. Sin strips whoever it touches of the ability to think correctly. *"For God hath not given us the spirit of fear; but of power, and of love and of a SOUND MIND."* (II Timothy 1:7)

There really needs to be a de-glorification of the devil so that God's people will not be afraid to stand in authority over the devil and accomplish what God wants accomplished in these last days!

QUESTION: "Is prayer important in spiritual warfare?"

Yes, throughout scripture we see a pattern of God's men and women asking God for strategies to defeat the enemy. God always answered and gave them insight to win the battles. A good example of this would be in 2 Kings 6:8-17, when Elisha was able to inform Israel of all the plans of the King of Syria. When his servant trembled with fear at what he saw, Elisha prayed and asked God to open his eyes to see into the spiritual realm.

Prayer preceeds our seeing into the spirit realm and knowing things from God's perspective. Never underestimate the power of prayer in spiritual warfare.

"Call to Me, and I will answer you, and show you great and mighty things, which you do not know." (Jeremiah 33:3) **Call**, qará (kah-rah); (Strong's Concordance #7121): To call out to someone; cry out; to address someone; to shout, or speak out, to proclaim. "Qará" often describes calling out loudly in an attempt to get someone's attention, or for calling upon the Lord or upon His name.

God is telling us to take the time to call out to Him and He will answer us by giving us insight into "great and mighty things" that we would not know in any other way. God wants to give us revelation knowledge of the enemy's strategies when we are under attack and give us the route to a sure victory.

Prayer and the Word of God are like the two wings of a bird. Without either one or the other, the bird would fly in circles. With both intact, the bird flies directly to his destination.

"'...but we will give ourselves continually to prayer and to the ministry of the word.'" (Acts 6;4)

The boldness needed in spiritual warfare comes as a result of a developed prayer life. *"And when they had prayed, the place was shaken where they were assembled together; and they were all filled with the Holy Ghost, and they spake the word of God with boldness."* (Acts 4:31)

Chapter 13

QUESTION: "Does 'pleading the Blood of Jesus' give us protection from the devil?"

Yes, it certainly does. We spend a great part of our teaching on the "binding and loosing" aspect of spiritual warfare, but that does not mean we think that is the only way to keep the devil in his place and have the victory in our life which God's Word promises. The Word of God, the Name of Jesus, the Power of the Holy Spirit within us and the Armour of God that includes the Sword of the Spirit are all part of the weaponry that God has given us to accomplish His Will in our lives and on this earth.

If we have neglected to teach concerning the Power of the Blood of Jesus please forgive us. We were gone from the U.S. for the better part of 20 years and as a result there are many things we assumed Christians already knew in God's Word, when we wrote Strongman I, that we have since realized they do not fully understand as they should. That is one of the reasons for this book—to add to and amplify the information in Strongman I that we see needs emphasizing in greater detail.

Revelation 12:9-11 shows how effectively the Blood of Jesus stops the devil from doing what He would like to do in our lives. *"And the great dragon was cast out, that old serpent, called the Devil, and Satan, which deceiveth the whole world: he was cast out into the earth, and his angels were cast out with him. And I heard a loud voice saying in heaven, Now is come salvation, and strength, and the kingdom of our God, and the power of his Christ: for the accuser of our brethren is cast down, which accused them before our God day and night.* **And they overcame him** *(the accuser—the devil)* **by the blood of the Lamb and by the word of their testimony;"**

The scene is like a court room. God the Father is the Judge, Jesus Christ is our Lawyer and Satan is the prosecutor. Satan accuses you of this sin and that sin as he rails on and on about what a terrible person you are.

God asks our Lawyer and Defender, Jesus, if that is true and Jesus answers, "No, it is not." God then inquires if there is a witness in the case.

Jesus responds, "Yes, there is. My Blood which I shed on Calvary is the witness—the Blood of the Lamb! This child of mine has received cleansing from all sin by confessing with his mouth that I am his Lord and believing in his heart that You raised Me from the dead." (Romans 10:9)

So God the Father throws the case out of court and Satan loses again. Why? Because of what the Blood of the Lamb has done for you and your testimony or confession of faith in the blood-sacrifice which Jesus offered for your sins. You have overcome Satan by the Blood of the Lamb and the word of your testimony!

It is an open and shut case as long as we continue believing God's Word and living according to His Rules. The devil can't touch us as I John 5:18 clearly states, *"We know [absolutely] that any one born of God does not [deliberately and knowingly] practice committing sin, but* **but the One Who was begotten of God carefully watches over him and protects him**—**Christ's divine presence within him preserves him against the evil**—*and the wicked one does not lay hold (get a grip) on him or touch [him]."* Amplified Bible

Back in the Old Testament we have a foreshadow of this when the Israelites were delivered from Egypt. The last plague was to be the death of the first born child in each home, and even the beasts, if the blood of a lamb without blemish was not sprinkled on the doorposts of the homes. (Exodus 12) Because of the sin of Pharaoh and the Egyptians as well as the Israelites, God was going to withdraw His Hand of protection and allow Satan to destroy only the first born of every family and the beasts that did not follow His instructions for survival. The Bible clearly states that, *"... the wages of sin is death;"* (Romans 6:23) This was judgment time for sin and death was the wage people would receive if they did not obey God.

That is why it is called the Passover. Because the Israelites **believed** God and obeyed His instructions, the destroyer—Satan—was **compelled** to pass over their house! And that is exactly what happens now when we are washed in the Blood of Jesus, provided we will **believe it** and **testify of our faith in it**. Satan is overcome and cannot do what he would like to do in our life.

If the blood of a lamb could protect the Israelites and even their animals, how much more can the blood of Jesus protect us, our families and our property today?

That is why Satan does everything he can to downplay the Blood.

98

Does 'Pleasing The Blood Of Jesus' Protect Us?

In the modernistic hymnbooks all references to the Blood of Jesus have been deleted. They call it "slaughter-house religion." But we must not allow Satan to trick us out of such a powerful part of our inheritance. We can plead the Blood of Jesus over our family, our property, our health, our finances, over everything God has given us because the Blood is a witness of what Jesus accomplished for us on Calvary. Because of the Blood we are free from the power of sin, sickness, bondage, depression and death!

So plead the Blood everyday. Say, for example, "I plead the Blood of Jesus over every member of my family." And name them. Then, "I bind you devil in the Name of Jesus. I rebuke your spirit of fear that would try to cause my faith to be weak. I loose God's power, love and sound mind into my life according to II Timothy 1:7. I allow Your Holy Spirit to have Your Will in my life. Thank you for the Armour you have given me. Thank you for your Word that gives me faith, wisdom and strength."

By that time you will sense the Power of God starting to surge through your body so you can bind the spirit of infirmity and loose the Resurrection Life of God into every cell of your body.

When you get done using all the spiritual weapons God has placed at your disposal you should be ready for whatever happens that day.

Missionary-evangelist Bernhard Johnson relates about the time he was challenged by the 15 leading witchdoctors that dominated the area around a city near Rio de Janeiro, Brazil where he was holding one of his huge evangelistic crusades.

The first night 35,000 attended and the attendance grew more each night. This surprised Bernhard somewhat because the Sunday night crowd is usually the largest. What he didn't know, and the people did know, was that the witchdoctors had gotten together and cast their spells, curses and mumbo jumbo to destroy Bernhard and the crusade. They spread the word around the city that Bernhard would be dead by Wednesday night!

By Thursday night the crowd had grown from 35,000 to 55,000 and although Bernhard was supposed to be dead, he was healthy and preaching up a storm. He knew nothing of the witchdoctors who were in the stadium each night, lighting their candles in front of images of Satan and praying to Satan while he was preaching. Friday night he was still preaching unaffected by the efforts of the witchdoctors.

"After the service Friday night, a crowd of about 10,000 waited for the witchdoctors at the stadium's gate. They surrounded them and declared, 'You have held us in bondage for years. You dominated our families and our businesses. We have to pay you to keep our stores open. And now the 15 of you can't handle this one man. You said he'd be sick by Monday, in the hospital by Tuesday, and dead by Wednesday. But look at him! He's stronger than ever. If you don't do something to him by Sunday, we're running you out of town'"

The next day the 15 witchdoctors had a meeting and drew straws to see who would stab Bernhard on the platform and make a sacrifice to Satan out of him in front of everybody.

The crowd grew to 65,000 on Sunday night. This was the great showdown—Mt. Carmel revisited, so-to-speak. That night Bernhard preached on the Power of the Blood of Jesus. He preached under such a heavy anointing that he could physically feel oil being poured on his head and roll down under his shirt to his shoes.

All of a sudden, 20 minutes into his sermon, everyone heard the sound of screams and wailing like a pack of wolves had invaded the stadium. A pastor ran up and told Bernhard that 1 of the 15 witchdoctors was headed to the platform to carry out the planned sacrifice to Satan.

Bernhard prayed, "'Lord, what am I to do?' Immediately the Holy Spirit said, 'Is not your life clean? Aren't you covered by the Blood? You're preaching about the Blood. Take command of the situation.'"

He thanked the Lord, grabbed the microphone and commanded silence. When the crowd became quiet, he told the people that he had just learned about the witchdoctors and what they were trying to do. Then he spoke to the 15 witchdoctors and gave them two choices: They could either run out of the stadium as fast as their legs would carry them before he came up after them in the stands, or, they could run down to the front of the platform and fall on their knees.

Eight of the 15 ran out of the stadium and the other seven came to the platform, dropped to their knees, accepted Christ as their Savior and were delivered from demon possession. Today four out of the seven former witchdoctors are elders in the Assemblies of God churches in the city of Duque de Caxias, Brazil! (Evangelists Fellowship Newsletter, Winter issue, 1992, Vol. 20, No. 1. Taken from the abridged keynote address at the 1991 Evangelists Seminar.)

We have nothing to fear, *"...because greater is he that is in you, than he that is in the world."* (I John 4:4) If your life is clean before the Holy Spirit, then you are covered by the Blood of Jesus. SO TAKE COMMAND OF THE SITUATION IN YOUR LIFE. Stop letting the devil do things to you he has no right to do.

What a wonderful thing it is to serve our Great and Mighty God!

Chapter 14

QUESTION: "What is it about the Vietnam war that makes it so different as far as the veterans and their behavior is concerned?"

We will take most of our information from the material of Point Man International Ministries which provides individual and group counseling, literature and seminars to help Viet Nam veterans. Point Man is comprised of Viet Nam Combat and Era Veterans from all branches of the Armed Forces and has dedicated themselves to the comfort and aid of their brothers in arms. They can be contacted by writing to: P.O. Box 339, Sheridan, MI 48884.

Like many people who were not directly involved in the Viet Nam war Carol and I did not realize that curses had been placed on the soldiers by the Buddhist monks or that the soldiers had been encouraged to take part in demonic religious activities by the Vietnamese friendly soldiers. (the ARVN)

Other aspects that attributed to the problems that Viet Nam veterans experience now was the fact that it was a non-conventional war. All of Viet Nam seemed hostile, the enemy was all around. American troops were often forced to kill women and children combatants. The enemy struck by ambush and booby trap and was rarely seen.

Viet Nam was a political, no-win war that was not fully supported by the people back home. It was America's first teen-age war, the average combatant was 18.7 years old. Students all across the U.S. were actively protesting the war. Many veterans were degraded, egged and spat upon when returning home.

With the advent of jet travel, many combatants found themselves standing in a major U.S. airport less than 24 hours after a fire fight or rocket attack. They were expected to put on civvies and "get a job," as though they had just returned from a vacation or a semester at college.

As a result, here are some of the shocking statistics about Viet Nam veterans:

—Since the war officially ended in 1975 approximately 150,000 have committed suicide which is 86% higher than their peer group!

—Their suicide rate is 33% above the national average!

—70% of fatal, one-car accidents have been Viet Nam veterans!

—There are 100,000 in prison today, and over 200,000 on parole!

—In Washington State alone there are over 4000 living in wilderness isolation, reminiscent of combat conditions in Viet Nam!

—80-90% of Viet Nam veterans have been divorced which is double the national average!

—In a recent survey of runaway "street kids" in Seattle, WA, 87 out of 100 were children of Viet Nam veterans!

—Viet Nam was America's longest war!

In late 1989 Point Man Ministries headquarters received a verbal report that an ex-Buddhist monk had shared some vital information with an American pastor regarding demonic curses being cast upon American troops during the Viet Nam war.

According to this ex-Buddhist monk an entire sect of Vietnamese Buddhist monks spent years heaping specific curses on all Americans who came to fight in their country. These specific curses were:

1. That the American soldiers would become wandering men for the rest of their lives.

2. That they would never find peace.

3. That they would be angry men and women for the rest of their lives.

Of course those are the major problems the veterans struggle with to this day.

The demon god, Cao Dai has been pinpointed as the major demon power over that area of Asia. The interpretation for its name is "the eye of God" or "from the high places." The Strongman over the Cao Dai spirit would be the spirit of divination.

A small pamphlet inviting the American troops to attend the Tet celebration, which is the Vietnamese New Year's Day, illustrates how they were unwittingly exposed to this demonic activity. Here is some information the pamphlet gave concerning this heathen festival.

"TET is a religious feast in which people express their prayers and worship for their saints, gods and ancestors.

"Because of the Vietnamese belief in Astrology, in which the life of each individual is governed by the stars that change every year, TET brings hope for everybody that the change will work for the better.

"They have another custom which is divination. They often divine in the theater. The people who come to divine need not watch all the play. They can watch only a part of it and from that part determine if their fortune is going to be good or bad during the coming year."

A point of interest is that the ceramic nick-knacks made in the Orient have holes in the bottom of them so the spirits can come and go as they please.

Prostitution was another area that contributed to the spiritual problems of the soldiers. The Bible clearly states that two become one flesh in the sex act. Bonding and transferences occur during the sex act and many things are passed between two people so engaged.

Only a small percentage of soldiers did not frequent the prostitutes while in the country. Many pimps and their contingent of girls would actually follow some American units out on patrol to make paid-for-sex available at every rest period. It was very enterprising, but it had a devastating effect on the young troops.

In the sex act, that usually involved drugs and alcohol, there were also exchanged the feelings of anger, hatred, revenge, rape, repressed murder, despair, and homesickness. No doubt many of the problems veterans have today with family relationships can be traced to this ungodly bonding in a very pagan and demonic environment. And of course the drug use opened up huge doors to demonic possession.

Information About Post Traumatic Stress Or P.T.S.

These factors in themselves are enough to cause deep spiritual problems in the lives of the young soldiers, but another problem area surfaced as a result of the traumatic experiences that took place in the fighting—Post Traumatic Stress or P.T.S.

P.T.S. isn't just limited to war experiences, but of course combat circumstances are a prime area for the problem to begin. It is caused by a crisis that is outside the range of normal human experience, and is something beyond more common experiences such as simple bereavement, chronic illnesses, business losses, or marital conflict.

An event causing P.T.S. may be experienced alone (such as rape) or in the company of groups of people (military combat, airplane crashes, natural disasters). The syndrome is evidently more severe and longer lasting when the event is caused by human means and designs,(bombings, shootings, etc.)

Many P.T.S. victims suffer with denial that the event affected them in any way. **Helping the P.T.S. sufferer relate to the experience (s) by "talking it out" is the first step in the healing process**. Of course Christians have the Promises of the Word of God to rely on for the strength and wisdom they need to overcome this attack by the spirit of fear.

Here are a few major P.T.S. symptoms to help identify the problem and give a few clues in working through the problems with a P.T.S. victim.

*Intrusive thoughts and flashbacks *Anger *Isolation *Emotional constriction *Depression *Substance abuse *Survivor guilt *Hyper-alertness *Suicidal feelings and thoughts *Alienation *Negative self-image *Problems with intimate relationships *Emotional distance from children, wife and others *Denial of any social problems, or even denial of active service during the war.

The wives and children of the Viet Nam veterans also suffer terrible stress and wounds, both physical and emotional, in living with their husband or father. So special care must be taken in dealing with them because the trauma of living with a P.S.T. victim causes the family to become P.S.T. victims also. In fact, over 80 million Americans, nearly 30% of our population, have a direct, personal link to a Viet Nam era veteran such as parents, wives, children, etc. That is a major reason why we felt we should devote this much attention to it in our book. Anything that affects 30% of the people is something which must be exposed and remedied.

The Good News is that God has given us spiritual tools to deal with P.T.S. The above symptoms help us identify which Strongmen are involved in this continuing demonic attack on people who have become vulnerable to the devil's lies through the trauma they have experienced. We would advise you to get a copy of our Strongman's His Name I book that has the listing of the 16 major Strongmen that are listed in God's Word by name. Then begin taking the authority over the devil that God has given us through the death and resurrection of Jesus Christ and loosing or allowing the Holy Spirit to have His will in the situation, which is to save, heal and deliver the victim from the clutches of the devil!

One of the important aspects of getting free from P.T.S is to forgive the ones who caused the trauma. Here is a revealing look at what one anonymous veteran had to say about it.

"We MUST forgive. Unforgiveness is the root cause of most infirmities and personal problems. The Scriptures insist that we forgive if we are to be forgiven and have our prayers answered. The damaging effect of unforgiveness is its deposit of the gall of bitterness in our innermost being. Most infirmities are the result of the leavening of bitterness working its effects on our bodies.

"God revealed the relationship between bitterness and infirmities at the waters of Marah (Exodus 15). As He sweetened the bitter waters He revealed a new attribute of His Nature—**I am the Lord that healeth thee**.

"True forgiveness cannot be initiated by emotions or feelings. It is set in motion by an intellectual decision. We must never 'feel like' forgiving. We must exercise our will and decide to forgive.

"Not long ago I was speaking at a national conference for Vietnam veterans, and I touched on the importance of forgiving such notable figures as Jane Fonda, Richard Nixon, Lyndon Johnson, etc. The reactions were mixed, especially when I mentioned truly forgiving Jane Fonda (the Viet Nam veteran's arch-enemy) for her activities during the war. **One particular veteran**, who had been paralyzed and wheelchair-bound for twenty years, **forgave her and got out of his chair and walked**! As far as I know he is still walking, and most of all he is praising the Lord for setting him free of his unforgiveness!"

Please Note
This tree diagram is an illustration of what you can find in our previous book, *Strongman's His Name...What's His Game?* We recommend that you read <u>that</u> book also because it has the foundational, basic instruction that we build upon in this book, *Strongman's His Name II*. The diagram here is just <u>one</u> of the <u>16</u> strongmen mentioned by name in the Bible. You can get a copy of the first Strongman book in most Christian bookstores.

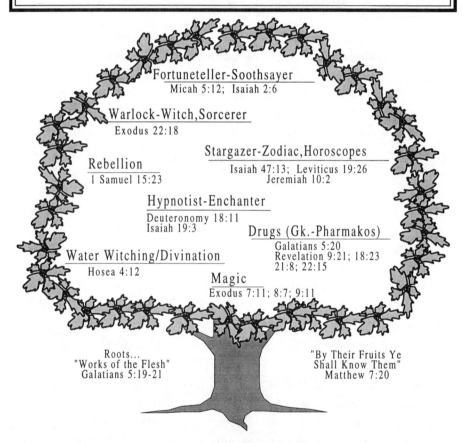

Fortuneteller-Soothsayer
Micah 5:12; Isaiah 2:6

Warlock-Witch,Sorcerer
Exodus 22:18

Rebellion
1 Samuel 15:23

Stargazer-Zodiac,Horoscopes
Isaiah 47:13; Leviticus 19:26
Jeremiah 10:2

Hypnotist-Enchanter
Deuteronomy 18:11
Isaiah 19:3

Drugs (Gk.-Pharmakos)
Galatians 5:20
Revelation 9:21; 18:23
21:8; 22:15

Water Witching/Divination
Hosea 4:12

Magic
Exodus 7:11; 8:7; 9:11

Roots...
"Works of the Flesh"
Galatians 5:19-21

"By Their Fruits Ye
Shall Know Them"
Matthew 7:20

According to Matthew 18:18...

Bind: Spirit of Divination
Loose: Holy Spirit and Gifts
1 Corinthians 12:9-12

Spirit of Divination 15

Take a look at this list and see if this is what you want your child to be involved with:

DEVILS	BLACK MAGIC
DRAGONS	DRUIDS
MYSTERIOUS FORCES	WITCHCRAFT
MYTHICAL GODS	WITCHES
EVIL WIZARDS	SORCERY
WARRIORS	POTIONS
MAGIC POWER	DEMONS
BLACK PRINCES	CURSES
MINIONS OF HELL	NECROMANCY
MAGIC SCROLLS	HOLY WATER
EVIL MONSTERS	BUDDHA
MAGIC ITEMS	MONSTERS
BAALZEBUB	MAGICAL SPELLS
ECTOPLASM	MAGICAL SWORDS
CURSE OF DEATH	MAGICAL BOOKS
EVIL SPIRITS	MYTHICAL BEASTS
BABYLON	

The items in this list were taken off the backs of the boxes in which the Nintendo Games are packaged. Check it out for yourself the next time you are in a store that sells these games. (idea from Shirley Smith-Lake Hamilton Bible Camp magazine)

This whole area of children's games, toys, television cartoons and activities has been inundated by the occult to steal your children away from you and from God. Don't let them get away with it.

(1) Supervise what your children are doing.

(2) Bind the spirit of divination, that wants to ruin and destroy physically, mentally and spiritually, in the Name of Jesus.

(3) Plead the Blood of Jesus over them.

(4) Come into agreement with the Holy Spirit that they will be saved and live for Jesus the rest of their lives.

(5) Lead them in the prayer to accept Jesus as their Savior.

(6) Teach them to look out for these kinds of deceptions so they won't be tricked by the devil.

The scriptures you can stand on are, *"...Believe on the Lord Jesus Christ, and thou shalt be saved, and thy house."* (Acts 16:31)

"The Lord is...not willing that any should perish, but that all should come to repentance." (II Peter 3:9)

QUESTION: "Is it wrong for Christians to be involved in the Martial Arts, such as karate and kung fu? What about acupuncture?"

Yes, it is.

Once again we see the deception of the devil sneaking into our churches these days. We have seen classes for Karate and Kung Fu being taught little boys on family night **in churches** where we were holding our seminar! They defend their actions by saying only the physical part is taught for self-defense. But who is to say what those 10-year-old boys will do later on? They learned the principles in church so what makes them think they will always stop short of the ocultic part, especially if they are attracted to this demonic deception? Anyhow, I thought we believed we should have faith in the protecting Power of God, not the arm of flesh?

"The original religious philosophy of kung fu dates back as far as 2696 B.C. where it was rooted in the occultic forms of divination known as the I-Ching and the 'Book of Changes.' Lao Tzu, the Chinese sage born in 604 B.C., added further demonic embellishments. His teachings were set forth in a 5,280 word manuscript called 'Tao te ching,' often called simply 'the tao,' or 'the way. He taught that salvation could not be found in prayer but rather in the observance of nature, the natural way.

"The next development in the history of kung fu took place when a monk named Bodhidharma brought Buddhism to China in the sixth century A.D...Known as 'I-chin-Sutura,' it combined kung fu with the philosophical principles of Zen to develop a highly sophisticated form of weaponless defense. As the martial arts spread beyond the monastery to the fields of war, some of the religious flavor was lost. But the essential undergirding of pagan principles has never been completely overshadowed, even to this day."(Speaks Out, March-April, 1978, page 2)

"The Zen undercurrent of the martial arts is more apparent when one explores the source of its strength and the intent of its 'salvation.' The term 'ki' is recurrent in the explanation of both acupuncture and yoga. It is seen as a universal source of energy that pervades and sustains the material world. The 'Handbook on Martial Arts' by William Logan and Herman Petras states, 'Some call ki God; others call it Buddha.'

"...in The History of Kung Fu author Earl Mederiros says, 'This then, is the real purpose of kung fu. It is not the breaking of bricks or the crushing of bones, but rather the purpose of kung fu is a spiritual discipline through which one may establish a pattern for life. In this way, man discovers within himself an inner serenity. It brings us a step closer to truth and the real meaning of life." (Speaks Out, May-June, 1978, pages 2,4)

Statements like these should be a chilling reminder that this is a tool of the devil to entrap people into a system that leads only to eternal destruction. The big question is why are certain elements of Christianity trying to tippy-toe along the line between Good and Evil? As with "Christian" Rock and Roll, we are told that it is an evangelism tool that attracts sinners who wouldn't normally listen if we just preached the Gospel of Jesus Christ. But nothing that has its roots planted deeply in the demonic **deserves** to be used in winning souls—it is counterproductive because what are we **winning** them too? Will the devil just sit by meekly and allow Christians to use **his** tactics to win souls to Jesus? No, he will lay low until the hook of deception is well planted in the "jaw" of the church before using it to cause the destruction and death that sin always causes.

Just as the devil is using New Agers and satanists to infiltrate our churches, he is also using Rock and Roll and the Martial Arts to accomplish the same purpose—chaos in the Body of Christ! On a secondary plane, "Christian" Rock and Roll, "Christian" Martial Arts, "Christian" acupuncturists, "Christian" Yoga and all the rest are nothing more than tentacles (either knowingly or ignorantly) of the Luciferian Initiation of the New Age to separate out from the Body of Christ those who are open to deception in those particular areas, creating a wide-open door in their lives to the overpowering deception of the last day! **Don't be tricked by the enemies tactics, run to God's Word for the direction we need in these last days!**

"To keep Satan from getting the advantage over us; for we are not ignorant of his wiles and intentions." (II Corinthians 2:11 Amplified Bible)

If the Holy Spirit has convicted you in any of these areas it is necessary to repent of that sin, bind the spirit of divination that has tried to trick you in that area of your life, in the Name of Jesus and tell it you will no longer be a part of those activities. Then ask God's Holy Spirit to fill you with His Power so that you won't fall for the devil's tricks again. Get into God's Word and allow the Holy Spirit to have His Perfect Will in your life. Keep that door shut and live the victorious life God has for you today!

QUESTION: "Can a Christian be tricked into interacting with demons?"

Yes, they can.

We were holding a seminar and after the first session that Carol had taught, which covered the activities of the spirit of divination and familiar spirit, a member of the church approached Carol and said, "This may sound strange, but for some time now I've been talking every day with, I guess you would call it, a spirit that only I can see. It's a friendly sort of thing and it hasn't said or done anything bad to me. Do you think it is from the devil?"

Carol told him in no uncertain terms that there was no doubt that it was a familiar spirit because God's angels don't mess around making small-talk with people. They get right to the point, deliver whatever message they were sent to deliver or do what they were sent to do and then leave.

As they talked she was somewhat shocked to find that he was on the church board, one of the leaders of the church. Out of ignorance,

110

this man, who was a fine person as far as people go, had been conversing with a demon and didn't know it.

Carol told him he needed to bind that evil spirit at once and never talk to it again because it was an open invitation to the devil to participate in such an activity. When she asked if he would do that he readily agreed, and right there in the vestibule of the church he bound the familiar spirit in the Name of Jesus and asked the Lord to forgive him for doing it and promised Him that he would allow His Holy Spirit to lead him into Truth so it would not happen again.

We returned the next year to that same church for another seminar and the man told Carol, "Do you remember me from last year?" When Carol told him that she did, he said, "Well, since we prayed a year ago, that spirit has never appeared to me again. Thank you for showing me what was really going on."

It is amazing how much of this stuff is going on these days, even in Pentecostal churches where people should know better. But the problem is that Christian's are suffering from a lack of knowledge. That is why God has called us back from the mission field to the U.S.—to expose the enemy for what he is and teach people how to live a life of victory.

Christian people in the churches tell us of demonic aberrations that take place in their homes with familiar and lying spirits torturing and taunting them, throwing up things they have done in the past that are under the Blood of Jesus—seeking to discourage and frighten them.

But when they go to Jesus and ask for His help, He never fails. So if you are having these kinds of activities in your life or home or church, just do as Carol showed the man to do, ask the Lord to forgive you of being involved in such activity, bind the spirit in the Name of Jesus and then allow the Holy Spirit to speak to your heart or spirit and listen only to his Voice. Get into the Word and find out what God has to say about these things so you won't fall for these tricks anymore.

QUESTION: "Can a person be a Christian and still play with Ouija boards and read their horoscopes?"

Christians who dabble in the occult are walking in the flesh according to Galatians 5:19-21 and are in danger of not going to heaven as a result of such practices. When people become involved and fascinated with familiar spirits and spirits of divination, little by little they turn their back on God and His Word and look to divination for their daily guidance. The end result is spiritual confusion and finally bondage to Satan.

"Now the works of the flesh are manifest, which are these;-
*...Idolatry, **witchcraft**, hatred...and such like: of the which I tell you*
before, as I have also told you in time past, that they which do such
things shall not inherit the kingdom of God."

QUESTION: "Do computers have a spirit of divination?"

No, but they can be used as a method to prognosticate (predict) by means of knowledge programmed into them. There are many good things a computer can be used for and it would be wise to only run programs that are totally free of the occult.

QUESTION: "How do we know that Satan cannot read our minds?"

The Bible is clear that **only** God has all knowledge or omniscience. The fact that He is the only one that possesses the attribute of omniscience immediately eliminates man, angels, or Satan (who is a fallen angel) from possessing all-knowledge or being able to know the thoughts and intents of our minds and hearts.

God's knowledge is perfect, He does not have to reason, find things out by observation, or learn gradually. His knowledge of the past, present and future is instantaneous and continuous.

Angelic intelligence exceeds that of men in this life, but is still limited. Angels cannot directly discern our thoughts and their knowledge of the mysteries of God's Saving grace is limited to observation only.

Read the passages in Isaiah 14 and Ezekiel 28 to see that Satan has wisdom and knowledge, but that he is just a created being (an angel) and as such has only limited wisdom. In fact, on the day of judgement people will look at him and say, *"Is this the man that made the earth tremble, that did shake kingdoms..."* (Isaiah 14:16) He does not possess God's supernatural wisdom that knows the thoughts of man. Satan and his demons can only observe and listen in order to gain advantage over mankind. His thinking has the same earthly processes as mankind's has...he is not divine! See Matthew 16:23.

By the way, whatever gave people the idea that Satan got stronger or more spiritual after he sinned? Sin always makes whatever it touches weaker. Therefore we can be assured that Satan is weaker, dumber, and uglier now than when he was created. Mankind also became weaker when sin entered the human race.

Satan can only use tricks and deception to make us think he is as intelligent and powerful as God. Only in the arena of sin and the works of the flesh does Satan have any power. So if we keep the devil in the arena of the Spirit, he can't touch us. *"We know that whosoever is born of God sinneth not: but he that is begotten of God keepeth himself, and that wicked one toucheth him not."* (I John 5:18) Satan has never been equal to God and never will be equal. He is the great deceiver!

"Then hear thou in heaven thy dwelling place, and forgive, and do, and give to every man according to his ways, whose heart thou knowest; (for thou, even thou only, knowest the hearts of all the children of men:)" (I Kings 8:39)

Psalm 139 relates the intimate knowledge God has of you. There are many scriptures that uphold the fact that only God knows the heart, mind and thoughts of man.

Other scriptures to read on this subject: Deuteronomy 29:29; I Chronicles 28:9; Daniel 2:20-23; Amos 4:13; Psalm 147:4,5; Psalm 94:11; Proverbs 15:3; Ecclesiastes 12:14; Isaiah 29:15-16 and 40:28; Jeremiah 17:9,10; Ezekiel 11:5; Luke 16:15; Acts 15:18; Romans 8:27; Romans 11:33-36; I Corinthians 2:10-12; I Corinthians 3:19,20; Hebrews 4:12,13; I John 3:20; Revelation 2:23.

QUESTION: "What are some of the scriptures forbidding water witching? Some people think this is a gift from God."

"Staff" or "mak•kale'" in Hebrew means: A rod for striking, guiding or divining. (Strong's Concordance #4731)

"My people ask counsel at their stocks, and their staff declareth unto them: for the spirit of whoredoms hath caused them to err, and

they have gone a whoring from under their God." (Hosea 4:12)

"Saying to a stock, Thou art my father; and to a stone, Thou hast brought me forth: for they have turned their back unto me, and not their face: but in the time of their trouble they will say, Arise and save us." (Jeremiah 2:27)

"And it came to pass through the lightness of her whoredom, that she defiled the land, and committed adultery with stones and with stocks." (Jeremiah 3:9)

"But they are altogether brutish and foolish: the stock is a doctrine of vanities." Jeremiah 10:8

The gifts of the Spirit include a Word of Knowledge which led Moses to water during 40 years on the desert. Divination by rods is Satan's counterfeit of God's gift. Why should we settle for second best when we have access to the authentic?

A willingness to follow after divination for quick answers and power results in long-term problems in other areas because we open a door that allows Satan to harass us and our family to the 3rd and 4th generation. *"Thou shalt have no other gods before me. Thou shalt not make unto thee any graven image, or any likeness of any thing that is in heaven above, or that is in the earth beneath, or that is in the water under the earth: thou shalt not bow down thyself to them, nor serve them: for I the Lord thy God am a jealous God, visiting the iniquity of the fathers upon the children unto the third and fourth generation of them that hate me;"* (Exodus 20:1-4 Also see: Exodus 34:7, Numbers 14:18, Leviticus 26:36 and Jeremiah 32:18.)

QUESTION: "Is all magic wrong? What about children's magic shows, circus tricks, etc.?"

The Bible says magic (all magic) is an abomination to God. How are children going to discern between the different types of magic? They will assume that all magic is O.K. especially if they see it in church or Sunday School.

When Bible teachers use chemical stories or other methods of teaching, it is best to call them "chemical stories," or whatever else they really are and not confuse the children. Children love chemistry and think it is fascinating. It may even encourage some of them to become chemists.

A person who practices magic is referred to in scripture as a sorcerer. Rev. 21:8 says they will have their place in the lake of fire. *"But the fearful, and unbelieving, and the abominable, and murderers, and whoremongers, and sorcerers, and idolaters, and all liars, shall have their part in the lake which burneth with fire and brimstone: which is the second death."*

QUESTION: "Is bio-feed-back the same as bio-rhythms?"

It follows the same basic pattern of trying to read our bodily functions by prognostication. It just uses a different method. We are more secure trusting in the Lord for our day to day health rather than charts or body feedback through meditation, etc.

Question: "Why don't you include the Jezebel, Ahab and Leviathan spirits in your list of strongmen in your book?"

We have purposely chosen to list only those evil spirits that are specifically mentioned by name in the Bible. We feel that if we base our knowledge on what God's Word calls a spirit we will always be on a firm foundation. Jezebel and Ahab were certainly evil people, but there is no evidence that there is such a thing as a Jezebel, Ahab or Leviathan spirit in the Bible.

I like to ask people what they called these spirits before Jezebel and Ahab were born? Did the demonic spirits come into existence only after the birth of Jezebel and Ahab or when they were teenagers or possibly after they became King and Queen? Of course that shows the error because demons are spirits and have been around much longer than Jezebel and Ahab.

Someone took it upon themselves to decide that since Jezebel and Ahab were so evil, they deserved to have a demonic spirit named after them. But is that how we are to arrive at truth? Wouldn't it be more accurate to label the demonic activity that surrounded Jezebel and Ahab according to Bible terms of what a demonic spirit is named? For instance, I read an article that spoke of a number of different demonic manifestations as being a Jezebel and Ahab spirit which could have been more correctly labeled a lying spirit, a spirit of jealousy, a spirit of divination and a familiar spirit. That seemed to be what ener-

115

gized the activity of Jezebel and Ahab so there is a good possibility it would also apply to people engaged in the same activities today.

Some say it doesn't really matter what we call them, but in the spirit realm it is always more effective to be accurate both in our prayer to God and in dealing with the devil. Just as there is a difference between using a shotgun, which has a wide pattern and a rifle, which goes directly to the mark, so it makes a difference how we address the devil in stopping his activity in our life.

One of the most damaging and, unfortunately, true accusations made against some people in spiritual warfare is that they base their teachings on experiences they have had or observed or even heard from demons themselves, instead of what the Bible says about it. As a result, there are all kinds of weird, wacky things going on under the name of spiritual warfare that are not only unscriptural, but actually dangerous. Total chaos results when people make up demonic names to fit the situation or, worse yet, ask the demons what their names are so they can cast them out.

We certainly appreciate the fact that these people desire to be used by the Holy Spirit to keep the devil from harassing people, but they will never accomplish that goal if they do not follow God's Word. We should especially pay attention to how Jesus dealt with the devil when He was physically ministering here on this earth

It is incredibly naive to believe that any demon will actually tell the truth about **anything**, much less its name, if it knows we will have more power to cast it out when we know what its name is. Jesus said the devil is the father of all lies. (John 8:44) When someone lies on a regular basis, we can't believe anything the liar says because who knows when he is lying or not? Yet a whole segment of people converse with demons before supposedly casting them out, and accept whatever the demons tell them as truth. They spend hours asking the demons their names and other information and even propagate what the demons tell them as sound doctrine to be followed in dealing with demons because, after all, they got it from the horse's mouth. (See the question, "Is conversing with demons dangerous even when doing spiritual warfare? Chapter 16)"

The truth is that we are supposed to receive our information and truth from the Holy Spirit, not from demonic spirits. *"But the Comforter, which is the Holy Ghost, whom the Father will send in*

my name, he shall teach you all things, and bring all things to your remembrance, whatsoever I have said unto you." (John 14:26) Why anyone can stand to communicate with filthy, lying demons is beyond me. Personally, we command the demons to shut up in the Name of Jesus because that's what Jesus did. Secondly, it is more important to talk with the **individual** who is possessed to see if he really wants to be free, and if so, to tell him what he must do to be set free and to stay free from the demons. If someone is truly going to be delivered from demon possession they must **desire** to be free or else they will become a revolving door—the demons coming right back in because, for whatever reason, the person still enjoys some part of being possessed and invites them back in.

The only biblical text that even remotely suggests that we should ask a demon its name is the case of the demoniac from the country of the Gadarenes. *"And he asked him, 'What is thy name?' And he answered, saying, 'My name is Legion: for we are many.'"* (Mark 5:9)

Notice that when Jesus asked the "spirit," singular, its name, the demon did not tell Jesus what He asked for. "Legion" is a number, (anywhere from 4200-6000-Vine's Expository Dictionary of Old and New Testament Words, page 329) not a name. This is an example of why it is non-productive to ask demons their name. If they didn't tell Jesus the truth, why do people suppose it will be any different in their case?

Jesus didn't say, *"Come out of him, you spirit of Legion"* because everyone in those days knew that "legion" is a number, not a name. There is no other indication in the Bible that even remotely suggests that there is a "legion spirit." Why Jesus asked this question is not known, but we never see Him asking it again in the recorded scriptures. The equivalent of this account today would be if someone asked you your name and you answered,"175, because that's how much I weigh."

Yet people try to cast out the spirit of "blue jeans" and "nail polish" and other names they have either made up to fit the situation or else demons have "revealed" to them. Wouldn't it be better to address the demons according to what God's Word calls a spirit? Isn't it safer to be sure we are using a name that really exists? God has already given us the names of 16 Strongmen and their symptoms or manifestations or fruit. That should be all we need.

QUESTION: "Can Christians have curses put on them?"

"...so the curse without cause shall not alight." (Proverbs 26:2 Amplified Bible)

"Christ hath redeemed us from the curse of the law, being made a curse for us: for it is written, Cursed is every one that hangeth on a tree." (Galatians 3:13)

The **condition** that must be met before the promises of God come into effect is that the Christian must be faithfully living an over-coming life of victory over sin, the flesh, the world and the devil. **That is always the condition that MUST be met if we expect to receive anything God has promised His children.** God will not rubber stamp our sin by healing us so we can sin better. He will not bless us financially so we can have more money to waste on the lusts of the flesh.

We must meet God's conditions **first** before we see even the beginning of the Promise. It is that step of faith that separates us from the rest of the world. We believe God and His Word enough to "step out of the boat," "stretch forth thy hand," "give and it shall be given unto you." When we make the step of faith, God meets us there at that point before our foot even touches the ground, because He is looking for the faith in our heart so He can do what He has promised. *"Then said the Lord unto me, Thou has well seen: for I will hasten my word to perform it."* (Jeremiah 1:12)

The book of Numbers, chapters 22-24, narrates the saga of Balaam the prophet who was hired by Balak to put a curse on Israel. Try as he might, Balaam could not curse God's chosen people. He told Balak, "I'm sorry. I've tried everything, but all I get is the bless-ing of God for the Israelites that is irreversible." In the spirit realm God had made a pronouncement concerning His people and no one could change it. "Behold, I have received commandment to bless: and he hath blessed; and I cannot reverse it." (Numbers 23:20)

If those God blessed under the old covenant were curse-free, how much more are we free of any curse if we walk in obedience to God. We have the Holy Spirit within us, the Armor of God, the Shield of faith and the Sword of the Spirit. The angels are all around us to protect and deliver us from danger. *"The Angel of the Lord encamps around those who fear him—who revere and worship Him with awe;*

and each of them He delivers." (Psalms 34:7 Amplified Bible)

Looking at it from the other side, when Israel turned from God and sinned, then all the curses of Deuteronomy 28 came upon them just as they will come upon anyone who disobeys God and falls into the clutches of the devil. If we are bothered by curses of any kind, we should check where we are leaving an open door that gives the devil the opportunity to beat on us, because **that is the only way a curse can have an effect on a true Christian.** The open door may be ignorance of the Word, fear, sin, pride, whatever, but it leaves us vulnerable to the shots of the devil. *"Leave no [such] room or foothold for the devil—give no opportunity to him."* (Ephesians 4:27 Amplified Bible)

We are promised in God's Word that the devil can't even touch us if he has no opportunity or foothold. *"We know [absolutely] that any one born of God does not [deliberately and knowingly] practice committing sin, but the One Who was begotten of God carefully watches over and protects him—Christ's divine presence within him preserves him against the evil—and the wicked one does not lay hold (get a grip) on him or touch [him]."* (I John 5:18 Amplified Bible)

Some people call generational weaknesses a curse. But it is a curse to us as true Christians only if we choose to fall back into the sin our family has been especially vulnerable to through the generations. Because the devil has had great success with our ancestors, he feels we will also follow their example. There is usually a time in all of our lives when we have a show-down with the devil over something that has come down our generational line. Those from alcoholic families will feel the heat of temptation in that area in an exceptional way because the devil can't believe we are really going to be able to resist it. When we **do,** we set a precedent that can be built upon so that it ceases to continue down our family line, **at least in our branch of it!**

Paul refers to something like this when he recommends to us, *"...let us strip off and throw aside every encumbrance (unnecessary weight) and that sin which so readily (deftly and cleverly) clings to and entangles us..."* (Hebrews 12:1 Amplified Bible) That is our area of vulnerability or weakness which may or may not be generational in nature. Whatever it is, we have to be especially careful to "ride herd on it" or keep it in check by the Power of the Holy Spirit and by living according to how God's Word tells us to live.

I remember one night when I came to the first Crusade lot in Managua, Nicaragua and found some kind of foul-smelling substance under the platform. The people said it was someone's attempt to put a curse on us and the crusade. We just bound the devil in the Name of Jesus, turned over to the Holy Spirit what needed to be done and had our service. Nothing happened because we knew Who the greater Power is and we had more faith in Him than in some stinking curse. We had services there every night for 18 months straight, in the middle of the red-light district, where 85% of the crime originated in Managua—a place that the people called, "A section of Hell," and the devil could not touch us! Not only that but thousands upon thousands of people were changed by the preaching of the Word and the Power of the Holy Spirit!

How can someone with a lesser power, curse or harm some- one with the GREATEST POWER living within them? It just doesn't make spiritual sense. *"No weapon that is formed against thee shall prosper; and every tongue that shall rise against thee in judg- ment thou shalt condemn. This is the heritage of the servants of the Lord, and their righteousness is of me, saith the Lord."* (Isaiah 54:17)

Do not fall into the trap of believing some doctrine the devil would like to promote instead of what God is saying. There are al- ways those who would rather have a demon cast out of them or a curse broken, or some other copout, instead of doing what God de- mands, which is to get sin out of their life, discipline their flesh by the Power of God, live a consistent life of faith in God's Word and follow what the Holy Spirit would like for them to do.

If we will do that, God says the devil can not touch us and I believe God!

Familiar Spirit 16

QUESTION: "What is hypnosis and what does it really do?"

Let me share with you what a wide variety of experts on this subject have to say.

Hypnosis is a passive mind state that an individual is placed into by a process called *induction*. Induction usually involves deceiving the patient to believe things that are not really true, such as, telling him his arm is too heavy to move or he no longer feels certain stimuli.

"Hypnosis can be described as an altered state of intense and sensitive interpersonal relatedness between hypnotist and patient, characterized by the patient's nonrational submission and relative abandonment of executive control to a more or less regressed, dissociated state." (Simeon Edmonds. *Hypnotism and Psychic Phenomena*, North Hollywood: Wilshire Book Co., 1977, p.139)

According to hypnotherapist Peter Francuch, "It is very important to utilize every reaction of the client to deepen his trance." (*Principles of Spiritual Hypnosis*, Santa Barbara: Spiritual Advisory Press, 1981, p.99)

"The relationship of a hypnotizable patient to the hypnotist does not differ in any essential way from the relationship of a lunatic to the superintendent of an asylum." (Pierre Janet, *Psychological Healing: A Historical and Clinical Study*, trans. by Eden and Cedar Paul, Vol. II New York: Macmillan, 1925, p.340)

"The hypnotherapist uses techniques such as repetition, deception, stimulation of the imagination, and emotionally overtoned suggestions to effectively influence the will and condition the behavior of the subject." (William Kroger and William Fezler. *Hypnosis and Behavior Modification: Imagery Conditioning*. Philadelphia: J.B. Lippincott Co., 1976, pp.25-26)

Professor Ernest Hilgard says, "With critical abilities reduced, imagination readily becomes hallucination." (Ernest Hilgard, *"Divided Consciousness in Hypnosis: The Implications of the Hidden Ob-*

server." Hypnosis: Developments in Research and New Perspectives. Erika Fromm and Ronald Shor, eds. New York: Aldine Publishing Co., 1979, p.49)

"Humanitarian fervor aside, it's the therapist's job to take power over the patient, push ahead with solving the problem, then convince the patient he or she is better, even if it means being devious." (John S. Gillis, "The Therapist as Manipulator," *Psychology Today,* December 1974, p.91.)

"Successful therapy can almost be reduced to a formula." The major part of the formula is convincing the "client that the therapy is definitely working apart from any objective evidence of a change." (ibid p.92) In short, psychotherapy will use flattery, distortion, lies and all forms of "false feedback" to convince people that they now have what they came to the psychotherapist to receive.

The whole structure of hypnosis and psychotherapy using hypnosis is built on deceptions and lies. We should be seeking Truth, not opening doors to the enemy by walking into areas of obvious deception. We should take our problems to the Lord and leave them with Him.

QUESTION: "Are there different degrees of hypnotic trances?"

Much research has been done to measure the different stages or degrees of hypnosis. They all seem to confirm the same basic fact that the power source behind hypnosis is none other than that of a familiar spirit guide that the Eastern religious mystics use.

Professor of psychology Charles Tart used a man named William to do indepth studies about hypnosis. They devised a number system to describe the different levels William went through in his trances. The first level brought a feeling of relaxation and departing from his physical body which William describes as, "just a thing, something I've left behind." He then progresses through different stages until, "...there is no longer a self to be peaceful or not peaceful beyond this point."

In the primary stages William is aware of himself, but then he becomes "centered in his head." Later he feels he has "potential to be anything or anyone." At the more profound levels there is "an awareness of some sort of chant or humming sound that is identified with

the feeling that more and more experience is potentially available."
Tart notes, "The chant William reported may be related to the Hindu
concept of the sacred syllable Om, supposedly a basic sound of the
universe that a man can 'hear' as mind becomes more universally
attuned." He then concludes, "William moved into stages similar to
Eastern descriptions of consciousness of the void." (Charles Tart,
"Measuring Hypnotic Depth." *Hypnosis: Developments in Research
and New Perspectives.* Ericka Fromm and Ronald Shor, eds. New
York: Aldine Publishing Company, 1979, p. 590-596.)

A former professional hypnotist says, **"Once you've been hypnotized, your mind will never be your own again."** ("Hypnosis in
Court," KNX, Los Angeles, Newsradio editorial reply, April 7,1982.)
This statement is definitely true for the unbeliever, but not for the
born-again child of God who has repented of it, is transforming his
mind daily with the Word of God and knows that he now possesses
the mind of Christ that Paul mentioned in 1 Corinthians 2:16.

**QUESTION: "Can hypnosis really take people back to the womb
or beyond to earlier lives they say they have lived?"**

No, but familiar spirits will gladly fill in any of the gaps that
people want to know if they will subject themselves to mind control
or hypnosis. These methods open a person up for evil spirits to take
control and give false information. The Bible reminds us, *"It is appointed unto men once to die."* (Hebrews 9:27) Reincarnation is
nothing but a doctrine of devils. (1 Timothy 4:1)

Social psychologist Carol Tavris concludes: "Memory is, in a
word, lousy. It is a traitor at worst, a mischief-maker at best. It gives
us vivid recollections of events that could never have happened, and
it obscures critical details of events that did." (Carol Tavris, "The
Freedom to Change." *Prime Time,* October 1980. p.28)

QUESTION: "Is hypnosis a religion, scientific, or medical?"

"The reader should not be confused by the supposed differences
between hypnosis, Zen, Yoga and other Eastern healing methodolo-
gies. Although the ritual for each differs, they are fundamentally the
same." (William Kroger and William Fezler. *Hypnosis and Behavior*

Modification: Imagery Conditioning. Philadelphia: J.B. Lippincott Co., 1976, p.412)

Kroger tries to down play the religious aspect of hypnosis and Yoga by the following statements, but only goes on to contradict his own words. "The fundamental principles of Yoga are, in many respects, similar to those of hypnosis. Yoga is not considered a religion, but rather a 'science' to achieve mastery of the mind and cure physical and emotional sickness. There are many systems to Yoga, but the central aim—union with God—is common to all of them and is the method by which it achieves cure." (William Kroger. *Clinical and Experimental Hypnosis*, 2nd Ed. Philadelphia: J.B.Lippincott Co., 1977, p.122-123.)

Modern society pastes the title of medical or scientific on many things that are actually neither. Hypnosis is one of these. Paul wrote to Timothy to "...*keep that which is committed to thy trust, avoiding profane and vain babblings, and oppositions of science falsely so called. Which some professing have erred concerning the faith.*" (1 Timothy 6:20-21)

Satan uses many deceptive devices to intrigue people and detour them from the truth of the Gospel. False religious systems and occult practitioners are not above using satanic methods and then attempt to dignify them with the idea that they are acceptable in the name of medicine or science. When they tag them as such, they are able to get them into government, schools and churches with little or no questions on the part of the Christian world.

John Weldon and Zola Levitt say in their book, "An increasing number of practitioners in the healing profession (M.D.'s, nurses, chiropractors, etc.) are being swayed by psychic philosophies and practices, largely due to the influence of parapsychology, psychic healing, and the holistic health movements.

"Patients can no longer afford the luxury of failing to determine the spiritual status of those who treat them. Failure to ascertain that may be more costly than a yearly medical bill. Practices that look entirely innocent...can become the means of occult bondage." (John Weldon and Zola Levitt. *Psychic Healing*. Chicago: Moody Press, 1982, pp.32,7.)

Hypnosis (enchanters, mesmerizers) is an old hidden art of the occultic Chaldeans and was used by people throughout the ancient world. God forbids His people to be involved with any aspect of it and warns of its dangers. The Word of God often lumped a variety of the occult practices together because the source is the same—the power of the devil.

A few of these verses are: Leviticus 19:26,31; 20:6,27; Deuteronomy 18:9-14; 2 Kings 21:6; 2 Chronicles 33:6; Isaiah 47:9-13; Jeremiah 27:9.

QUESTION: "When the police force uses hypnosis to recall abuse or a psychic to locate a missing person or object aren't they using evil for good?"

Bernard Diamond, a professor of law and a clinical professor of psychiatry, says that hypnotized court witnesses "often develop a certitude about their memories that ordinary witnesses seldom exhibit...They graft onto their memories fantasies or suggestions deliberately or unwittingly communicated by the hypnotist...After hypnosis the subject cannot differentiate between a true recollection and a fantasy or a suggested detail." (Bernard L. Diamond, "Inherent Problems in the Use of Pretrial Hypnosis on a Prospective Witness." *California Law Review,*March 1980, p.348 and p. 314.)

Diamond asks and gives the answers to a number of questions:

"Can a hypnotized person be free from heightened suggestibility? The answer is no. Hypnosis is, almost by definition, a state of increased suggestibility.

"Can a hypnotist, through the exercise of skill and attention avoid implanting suggestions in the mind of the hypnotized subject? No, such suggestions cannot be avoided.

"After awakening, can the hypnotic subject consistently recognize which of his thoughts, feelings, and memories were his own and which were implanted by the hypnotic experience? No. It is very difficult for human beings to recognize that some of their own thoughts might have been implanted and might not be the product of their own volition.

"Can previously hypnotized persons restrict their memory to actual facts, free from fantasies and confabulations? No. ...Out of a desire to comply with the hypnotist's suggestions, the subject will commonly fill in missing details by fantasy or confabulation.

"After the hypnotic subject is awakened, do the distorting effects of the hypnosis disappear? The evidence...is that the effect of suggestions made during hypnosis endure.

"During or after hypnosis, can the hypnotist or the subject himself sort out fact from fantasy in the recall? Again the answer is no. No one, regardless of experience, can verify the accuracy of the hypnotically enhanced memory."(Bernard L. Diamond, "Inherent Problems in the Use of Pretrial Hypnosis on a Prospective Witness." *California Law Review,*March 1980, p.348 and pp.333-337.)

With these testimonies in mind, why would anyone want to knowingly put themselves into the hands of a hypnotist?

The Old Testament talks about the days when people would try to make dark light and evil good. *"Woe unto them that call evil good, and good evil; that put darkness for light, and light for darkness: that put bitter for sweet, and sweet for bitter!"* (Isaiah 5:20)

Trying to use something cursed of God for good does not make the occult right. Hypnosis practiced by law enforcement officers, psychiatrists, doctors, witch doctors or occult practitioners is energized from the same power source. It shows how far we've gotten away from relying on God's knowledge.

When anyone looks to the devil for guidance, it is occultic and needs to be forgiven. The pact that was established with Satan's realm through this deed must be repented of and broken audibly. This cuts off Satan's continued harassment and shuts that door to him.

QUESTION: "What should a person do if they are asked by the police, etc. to submit to hypnosis in order to remember forgotten details of a crime or other incident?"

As a Christian you should decline. You can pray in private and ask the Holy Spirit to bring to your remembrance any details that are necessary. *"But the Comforter, which is the Holy Ghost, whom the Father will send in my name, he shall teach you all things and bring all things to your remembrance, whatsoever I have said unto you."* (John 14:26) *"Howbeit when he, the Spirit of truth, is come, he will guide you into all truth: for he shall not speak of himself; but whatsoever he shall hear, that shall he speak: and he will show you things to come."* (John 16:13) Jesus also said that when we appear before the courts, etc. He would give us the correct words to answer. *"But when they deliver you up, take no thought how or what ye shall speak: for it shall be given you in that same hour what ye shall speak."* (Matthew 10:19)

This will require that you spend time in prayer and God's Word so your spirit is receptive to the voice of the Holy Spirit at those times.

Many courts do not accept hypnotic confessions and regressions as evidence because they have been found to be suspect. That gives you a reasonable right to refuse being subjected to this type of interrogation.

When people open up their minds, the devil can feed them information that may sound logical, but are lies and deceptions.

QUESTION: "Can demon spirits live in buildings such as churches, houses or places of business? How do they get there? How does a person get them out?"

Many times people experience poltergeist activity, hear voices or see apparitions in a house that they have moved into. This indicates that a previous occupant has very probably been involved in occult practices of some kind. If not, it is possible that it was a ceremonial ground for ritual practices by indigenous people who may have even shed innocent blood there. If the current occupant is a born-again Christian they have the right to evict those entities from the premises in the Name of Jesus. It doesn't matter if that person is buying or renting; the fact remains that the property is now under new control.

Yes, even churches can have demonic manifestations and controlling spirits harassing their spiritual progress. We have heard instances of people involved in witchcraft who surrounded churches in midnight rituals and released demons to hinder the work of God. They also send people into church congregations to release demonic power and hinder the work of God. If the head of a church, the pastor or leaders, have been involved in immorality, etc. these strongmen take up residence and try to cause others to fall into the same sin.

One pastor told us of a church he pastored that groaned and creaked as though the ceiling was going to fall in whenever he gave an altar call to the point that the service was disrupted and he could not finish. The church had gone through some gross immoral problems in the past and had never had a spiritual breakthrough. The pastor decided to spiritually clean out the church. He started with the prayer tower, that had been nailed shut because it had been the scene of immorality. There were thousands of dead flies on the floor so he cleaned it out and bound the spirits of whoredoms and perversion. Then he went into all the classrooms and the main auditorium and anointed and prayed over the whole area. Never again was the altar call interrupted by the creaking and groaning and revival broke out in the once struggling church.

In private residences, churches, and businesses, people can walk around the property, binding and commanding the enemy to get out/ off and stop his activities. We can use the authority God has given us to stymie the devil's plans. Remember, *"Every place whereon the soles of your feet shall tread shall be yours:"* (Deuteronomy 11:24) *"Every place that the sole of your foot shall tread upon, that have I given unto you, as I said unto Moses."* (Joshua 1:3) *"Neither give place to the devil."* (Ephesians 4:27) Ask God to station His angels around the entire perimeter. *"The angel of the Lord encampeth round about them that fear him, and delivereth them."* (Psalm 34:7)

Look through the rooms of the building to make sure there are no occult objects present. If so, destroy them in the Name of Jesus. If that is impossible, then seal them off spiritually with prayer and tell them they have no authority, power or influence in that place from that time on!

Go into each room of your house, apartment, church or business and bind the power of the enemy in the Name of Jesus. Command that he stop all manifestations and that he leave immediately in the Name of Jesus. Tell him he has no authority or covenant standing in this place anymore. Then loose, or ask, the Holy Spirit to take up residence in each and every room. (Matthew 18:18)

QUESTION: "What is a hallucinaroty problem, one that puts actors 'faces' on the faces of people in the street?"

This kind of manifestation is caused by a familiar spirit, trying to distract or cause fear.

QUESTION: "Is there such a thing as a false prayer language?"

Yes. The devil tries to imitate anything he can get away with. When Christians receive their prayer language they need to be instructed to speak clearly and get past the stammering lip stage and move on to the full language God has for them. If people would use their prayer language more often in their personal devotions they would develop more fluency. Using well formed sounds and phrases from the Holy Spirit comes with use.

You will recognize a demonic language manifestation by the gift of the Discerning of Spirits down in your spirit. You will sense an evilness instead of the normal uplifting, positive presence of the Holy Spirit. Be **very** sure you have read the situation clearly before dealing with the individual.

QUESTION: "Can parents pass along evil spirits to their young children?"

Yes, some children are possessed even at birth. Unsaved parents have no spiritual protection because of their continual sin and involvement in the occult, drugs or false religions which can open their children to demonic possession also. This can come also through inheritance from past generations as far back as the third and fourth generations. (Exodus 20:1-5)

QUESTION: "What about people who receive 'messages' from the spirit world that help people? Should we be involved with them?"

Edgar Cayce would qualify as an example of this type of person. He received prescriptions for drugs, etc. to help people medically and in other ways as well.

Edgar Cayce received his information from a familiar spirit and there is never a time when that is condoned in the Bible. The supposed "good" that they do is off-set by the confusion and entrapment spiritually that comes to people involved with this type of practice.

QUESTION: "How do we cleanse our house spiritually?"

Destroy those things that pertain to worship of other gods from idolatrous cultures such as the zodiac and any other occult objects or pictures. Do it in the Name of Jesus and command that it never again have any influence in your house. Do not sell it and thus pass the curse on to other unsuspecting people.

"The graven images of their gods shall ye burn with fire: thou shalt not desire the silver or gold that is on them, nor take it unto thee, lest thou be snared therein: for it is an abomination to the Lord thy God. Neither shalt thou bring an abomination into thine house, lest thou be a cursed thing like it: but thou shalt utterly detest it, and thou shalt utterly abhor it; for it is a cursed thing." (Deuteronomy 7:25,26)

A mother in Alaska heard Carol teach that we should clean our house of any objects, pictures or statues that have occultic significance. She went home and destroyed a Buddha someone had given her.

She had been having serious problems with her teenage son. He hadn't spoken to her for three weeks. The next morning after she destroyed the Buddha, her son come down to breakfast whistling a tune, gave her a big kiss and told her he loved her!

That was worth getting rid of an ugly, little, fat devil!

A pastor friend of ours and his wife visited a lady in their church. When visiting they sensed a terrible oppression and evilness in the lady's house. They asked permission to anoint the rooms of her house and drive out whatever was causing the problem in the Name of Jesus. The lady readily consented.

As they walked through the house, binding the devil and loosing the Power of the Holy Spirit, they encountered an Indian Sun God hanging on the wall of one of the rooms. They immediately informed the lady that it was a devilish piece of art and needed to be destroyed as quickly as possible.

The lady took it down, leaned it against the wall and promised to throw it away.

A few weeks later they visited the lady again in her home and saw the sun god back up on the wall. The pastor's wife had heard that this woman had made the statement that people shouldn't tell other people to take things out of their house so they weren't surprised that the sun god was back in place.

Imagine this situation. A woman who claimed to be a Christian, openly rebelled against the advice of her pastor. He has shown her in God's Word that it is dangerous to keep devilish art objects in her home. But she refuses to get rid of it.

The pastor and his wife were concerned about the welfare of the lady with good reason. Not long after that time the lady had a terrible, debilitating stroke that left the woman paralyzed and near death.

The pastor's wife and another friend visited the lady many times in the hospital, praying fervently that the woman would not die in the condition she was in. Without doubt, God honored their prayers, but the woman has only partially recovered to this date.

Some people would say there was no connection between the woman's sun god rebellion and the stroke, but why take a chance? No art object or statue is worth more than our health.

QUESTION: "How do I deal with objects I can't remove from my house, it would begin a major revolution if I destroy them or throw them out?"

I recommend that you go to these objects and rebuke and bind the power of the enemy that has tried to use it as an entry place into your home. Seal off all its power and future influence in your home. Loose the Holy Spirit to fill your home and to deal with those persons who own the objects. When they make a commitment to follow the Lord, pray that they will remove the objects themselves.

QUESTION: "Can I sell my occult objects and give the money to the church? I have some very valuable objects."

No. Why pass the curse on to someone else? *"The graven images of their gods shall ye burn with fire: thou shalt not desire the silver or gold that is on them, nor take it unto thee, lest thou be snared therein: for it an abomination to the LORD thy God. Neither shalt thou bring an abomination into thine house, lest thou be a cursed thing like it: but thou shalt utterly detest it, and thou shalt utterly abhor it; for it is a cursed thing."* (Deuteronomy 7:25,26)

QUESTION: "Are totem poles from the American Indians of the occult?"

Yes, each animal face or object on the pole represents a demonic god or spirit that is worshipped in the Indian culture. They may deny it, to appear more modern in their thinking, but it originated that way in their cultural history. These entities are still reverenced today in their rituals and dances.

QUESTION: "How do we discern between a Word of Knowledge and E.S.P.?"

We will sense the moving of the Holy Spirit in our spirit when there is a Word of Knowledge and it will never contradict the written Word of God. (Refer to chapter 6)

E.S.P., on the other hand, will have no such indication in our spirit because it is energized by a spirit of divination. People who learn to fine-tune themselves to receive information from a spirit of divination are very proud of their ability. But you will note that they aren't always correct, which indicates that God is not involved and that the devil is behind it. E.S.P. is a snare to "hook" people on the occult so they can be further induced into the satanic.

Premonition or "Deja-Vu" is a similar activity. Usually the devil uses it to "soften" people up, through fear of some tragedy, to get a door open in their life so he can do to them what he couldn't do if the door had remained shut. When we experience such things, we rebuke and bind it in the Name of Jesus and command that it will **not** take place. Then we "loose" or ask the Holy Spirit to protect the people involved in the premonition so that nothing evil will transpire.

Of course God can also warn us of danger through the Gifts of the Spirit, but we will note it is God because we sense it in our spirit, not our mind, as is always the case with the satanic and it will not induce fear in our heart. (Refer to chapter 24)

QUESTION: "Is TM a religion or a science?"

TM is another passive-mind control method that Satan uses to get a foothold in people's lives. When they are told to repeat words for relaxation, etc. they are calling in a familiar spirit guide and giving him the authority to rule their minds and bodies.

A judge in New Jersey declared TM a religion and therefore prohibited teaching it in the public school system because it would violate the guaranteed separation of church and state. (*TM in Court.* Berkeley: Spiritual Counterfeits Project, 1978.)

QUESTION: "Is conversing with demons dangerous even when doing spiritual warfare?"

Yes, it is. Necromancy is carrying on a conversation with the dead, which are nothing more than demon spirits masquerading as people who have died. The more anyone converses with demons, under any circumstances, the greater the opportunity for them to trick and deceive the individual with their lies. There is a fine line between talking to demons in a spiritual warfare setting and one that is necromancy.

It is not uncommon for some Christians to spend large amounts of time conversing with the demons in people. They ask the demons their names and other information they feel is important to learn so they can cast demons out in the future. That is bad enough, but then they turn around and teach what the demons have told them as truth and claim that this is how everyone should do spiritual warfare. What they don't realize is that this is a form of channeling—they are speaking out messages from demons! The fact that they call themselves Christians does not change the fact that they are being a channel of demonic information.

We have noticed that people involved in this kind of activity are continually under attack and wonder why they are always being harassed. To make matters worse, they spiritualize the situation by telling people the reason they are under attack is because they are so deeply involved in spiritual warfare. The truth is, they have opened a door through their channeling activities and are in danger of deep deception that could lead them far from God.

People have informed us of such activities and told us of having to withdraw from groups doing the above in order to maintain a healthy relationship with God and not be drawn into something that had turned demonic. What a deception that people start out doing spiritual war fare and end up being involved with demons because they don't follow God's Word. Although the error may appear ever so insignificant to begin with, it is still error. That is why we must be sure we are doing **Biblical** spiritual warfare.

Jesus, "...*suffered not the spirits to speak to Him.*" and we should follow His example. (Mark 1:34)

Spirit of Jealousy 17

QUESTION: "Is there a spirit of bitterness?"

There is a root of bitterness mentioned in Hebrews 12:15. I believe the Bible is correct and when seeds are planted, roots develop and grow. Possibly a seed of hurt, contention or some other work of the flesh was sown and a root of bitterness grows out of that and becomes jealousy, heaviness, etc. It must be repented of and uprooted spiritually by using the Power of the Holy Spirit to keep it from springing up again.

QUESTION: "Can jealousy have secondary effects in a person's life?"

Any of the strongmen spirits can have secondary effects. Once they are established they make room for others to also get a foothold.

A lady told us that during one of our seminars she wasn't too interested in hearing about the spirit of jealousy because she didn't feel she had any problem with that area so she spent the time thinking about other things until we changed to another topic. The next morning during her devotions the Holy Spirit pointed out to her that she had been jealousy of her younger sister since the day she had been born. It had made them very competitive and had ruined their relationship even as adults.

The lady knelt down and confessed her problem immediately and shut the door that had been opened early in her life. Then she released God's power to heal the rift between her and her sister. She immediately called her sister on the phone and asked her forgiveness which resulted in a renewed relationship.

This same lady had been suffering from a chronic back disorder for many years she had tried chiropractors and doctors without any alleviation. But when she repented of jealousy and asked her sister for forgiveness, the back pain went away and she was completely healed.

Not everyone that has back pain has a problem with jealousy. But in this case Satan took advantage of that open door to afflict her. Sometimes we don't associate the cause and effect. But if the enemy is "whipping up on us," we can be almost certain that we need to ask the Holy Spirit to show us where the open door is in our life and then get it taken care of right away. We might be surprised at what clears up or gets out of our life as a result!

QUESTION: "Is jealousy really a serious problem among Christians?"

Yes it is!

We used to make fun of "Hallelujah" John when I was growing up. Woe to the unsuspecting people who sat directly in front of him in church. Without warning this silver-haired, quiet man would shout out, "Hallelujah," clapping his hands together rapidly. That would be about the extent of it, but my pastor father could always count on a wide-awake congregation for the rest of the service.

I stopped laughing at John the night I was sitting where I could observe him more closely after one of his patented outbursts. Tears streamed down his face and I knew that this was not just a performance—it was his particular way of reacting when the Holy Spirit touched his heart.

From such early experiences I learned that there is a vast diversity of members in the Body of Christ. *"Some of us are Jews, some are Gentiles, some are slaves and some are free. But the Holy Spirit has fitted us all together into one body."* (II Corinthians 12:13 Living Bible)

Paul says, *"But God has so adjusted (mingled, harmonized, and subtly proportioned the parts of) the whole body, giving the greater honor and richer endowment to the inferior parts which lack [apparent importance], So that there should be no division or discord or lack of adaptation [of the parts of the body to each other], but the members all alike should have a mutual interest in and care for one another. And if one member suffers, all the parts [share] the suffering: if one member is honored, all the members [share in] the enjoy-*

ment of it. Now you [collectively] are Christ's body and [individually] you are members of it, each part severally and distinct [each with his own place and function]." (I Corinthians 12:24-27 Amplified Bible)

Wouldn't it be wonderful if we could honestly say today that the Body of Christ is functioning perfectly, with each member working in 'harmony?'

The fact is that a vicious disease is spreading through the Body causing some cells to devour other healthy cells. The name of the disease is Jealousy.

It is almost politically correct today for Christians to attack their fellow Christian brethren over the least little thing. We get more angry and vicious with each other over some theological disagreement than we do with the devil who is the one we are supposed to be fighting.

Rumors and innuendos are spread—at times by just the tone of voice or the uplifted eyebrow. Books are written and sermons are preached, castigating the offending brother. Half truths become lies because man is not equipped to read men's hearts as God does. In a short time we hear of a great church in trouble, another ministry threatened, new converts disillusioned and the news media has a field day.

Paul the Apostle knew from first-hand experience the devastating effects of being shot down by his fellow brethren. Paul's conversion scared the other disciples and believers. Ananias told God what a terrible risk Paul was, but the answer came back, *"But the Lord said to him, Go for this man is a chosen instrument of Mine to bear My name before the Gentiles and kings and the descendants of Israel:"* (Acts 9:15 Amplified Bible)

Later, Barnabas and Paul went into the evangelistic work. The longer they traveled together the more successful Paul became, but Barnabas didn't seethe with jealousy or express fear about how this would affect his own future ministry. Paul made a mistake concerning Mark, but rather than jeopardize Paul's ministry, Barnabas quietly took Mark and went on preaching separately while Paul and Silas continued the missionary journeys.

Barnabas could have torpedoed Paul concerning Mark. But because Barnabas maintained a correct attitude, his original judgment concerning Mark was vindicated. Paul realized he had been wrong and acknowledged his error.

This illustrates that it is possible to be correct in our assessment of an individual or situation, but dead wrong in what we do about it. Baby chicks notice that one of the chicks is smaller or different in appearance from the rest and will literally peck the little fellow to death. Don't you think God expects us to use more than "bird-brain" intelligence when dealing with our fellow members?

Before attacking them, just remember that God is the only One who has ALL the facts about the person or situation. Wouldn't it be wiser to tilt toward the merciful side rather than the harsh? God's Word says that if we are merciful in our treatment of others we will receive mercy also. *"But if you bite and devour one another [in partisan strife], be careful that you [and your whole fellowship] are not consumed by one another."* (Galatians 5:15 Amplified Bible)

How many souls have been lost **forever** because some of God's people were critical and jealous of another's ministry or position and in effect crucified him as surely as the Pharisees crucified Jesus.

The usual copout is to call it a personality conflict, but it is much more than that. When we limit another's ministry or sphere of influence, for whatever reason, we are affecting the Body's total outreach to the lost souls of this world. Christ is going to judge not only for what we did or did not do, but also for whether we were a **hindering factor** in limiting our brother from doing what God had specifically called him to do.

God commands us, *"Judge not, that ye be not judged."* (Matthew 7:1) Instead, we are to pray for one another. James 5:16) We are dependent upon each other to survive in this treacherous day.

Some use the hypocritical excuse that they are "protecting" the Word of God when they censure those who appear to be wrong in their eyes. But the parable of the tares illustrates that there are some situations and problems in which God does not want or expect us to intervene for fear that we'll do more damage to the Harvest than good. The householder commanded his servant not to gather up the tares lest they uproot the tender sprouts in doing so. *"Let them grow together until the harvest: and in the time of harvest I will say to the reapers, gather ye together first the tares and bind them in bundles to burn them: but gather the wheat to my barn."* (Matthew 13:30)

If we really believe God is in control of this universe we must trust Him to discipline His own Body and keep His Kingdom in running order. This is not to say that we should allow everyone freedom to do as they please and expect God to do all our dirty work for us. Even our natural bodies have white corpuscles to search out harmful diseases and fight them. But keep in mind that **all the cells of the body aren't called to be white corpuscles!**

Even those who are specifically responsible for dealing with the failures of others must be careful not to believe they are infallible. There are times when we would do well to follow the advice Gamaliel gave to the Pharisees when they wondered about what to do with Peter and the apostles after the resurrection of Jesus. *"...stand off (withdraw) from these men and let them alone. For if this doctrine or purpose or undertaking or movement is of human origin, it will fail (be overthrown and come to nothing): But if it is of God, you will not be able to stop or overthrow or destroy them; you might even be found fighting against God!"* (Acts 5:38,39 Amplified Bible)

We must bind the spirit of jealousy in our midst and loose the Love of God. It will take perceptive, Spirit-led Christians to apply the "antibiotic" of God's Word to the Body so that we can return to spiritual health and defeat the enemy who is attempting to destroy the Body and keep it from accomplishing God's Will on this earth.

QUESTION: "Why is anger under the spirit of jealousy?"

The spirit of jealousy is the strongman that energizes anger in a person's life. *"For jealousy is the rage of a man: therefore he will not spare in the day of vengeance."* (Proverbs 6:34)

Unrecognized anger is very dangerous in a person's life. It can cause damage in relationships. *"Whose hatred is covered by deceit, his wickedness shall be showed before the whole congregation."* (Proverbs 26:26) Anger is often covered by deceit. We bury it, swallow it, stuff it, store it and ignore it. But it comes back and then we try to rationalize it, analyze it, explain it away and still feel guilty.

Sometimes we need to listen to the words we speak, they can reveal amazing amounts of hidden anger. Most physicians say that swallowed anger contributes to episodes of depression, headaches, backaches, ulcers, colitis, hypertension and a host of other physical ailments.

When anger is stored, it grows into a green-eyed fantasy monster. Remember, God has the Holy Spirit who specializes in green-eyed monster control!

QUESTION: "Is envy normal?"

Envy should not be normal for a Christian who is living a victorious life in Jesus Christ. We should never be envious of anyone else. We are blessed by God for our faithfulness to Him, not by luck or special favor.

Envy causes people to gossip and make cruel remarks. Envy is really very hostile even though it sometimes comes disguised as admiration, respect or flattery. Envy many times really shows resentment towards others and a desire to bring them down.

Lying Spirit 18

QUESTION: "What causes us to doubt our salvation and prayer language?"

A lying spirit and a spirit of fear will try to deceive the believer into thinking that they are really not saved and that their prayer language is not valid and as a result they are powerless.

When we pray in the Spirit, making sounds directed by the Holy Spirit, (1) He is interceding for us or someone else, *"Likewise the Spirit also helpeth our infirmities: for we know not what we should pray for as we ought: but the Spirit itself maketh intercession for us with groanings which cannot be uttered. And he that searcheth the hearts knoweth what is the mind of the Spirit, because he maketh intercession for the saints according to the will of God."* (Romans 8:26,27), (2) We are praising God, *"...we do hear them speak in our tongues the wonderful works of God."* (Acts 2:11), (3)He is helping us witness in the Power of the Holy Spirit, *"But ye shall receive power after that the Holy Ghost is come upon you and ye shall be witnesses unto me both in Jerusalem, and in all Judea, and in Samaria, and unto the uttermost part of the earth."* (Acts 1:8), (4) We are being edified, *"He that speaketh in an unknown tongue edifieth himself; but he that prophesieth edifieth the church."* (1 Cor.14:1-4) No wonder Satan tries to talk you out of this wonderful experience!

QUESTION: "What causes people to cheat?"

Cheating is a form of deception. Satan is the deceiver in this world. Cheating and deception has become epidemic throughout our society today and as such costs taxpayers billions of dollars each year.

"Hattye Liston of North Carolina Agricultural and Technical State University told the annual convention of the American Psychological Association that cheating has become an American pastime:
- About $100 billion a year is lost through tax cheating.
- Extramarital affairs are at epidemic proportions.
- Fraudulent telephone charges cost millions annually.

• Department stores lose over $4 billion a year from pilferage.

• 14 percent of students have defaulted on federal education loans.

• About 60 percent of employees improperly use company post age meters." (Salem, OR Statesman Journal, Aug 29,1982)

It is easy to understand why unbelievers fall into this trap of the enemy, but the terrible truth is that many Christians are cheating and lying also. These areas create an open door for the enemy to get a foothold in people's lives and turn their life into a nightmare.

QUESTION: "Can a lying spirit be influencing our churches?"

A pastor friend of ours related that he had finally figured out what was happening in the church he pastors as well as many other churches across the U.S. He had just experienced what is becoming an all too familiar crisis in congregations today. A group of people had gotten upset over something that didn't really amount to all that much and had left the church. The remaining members were in a state of shock from the bitter infighting that had preceded the split. This pattern of behavior had happened a number of times in his stay as pastor and, to say the very least, he was frustrated by his seeming inability to prevent it from happening.

As he sought the Lord over the matter, the Holy Spirit showed him that the cause of this spiritual insanity was a lying spirit. He further revealed that the same lying spirit was sweeping through many churches today causing untold damage to the pastors and congregations and as a result to the Work of God.

A Word of Knowledge was given by a noted person in this regard which said, "There is a wave of deception flooding into the church and My people do not know the difference between truth and error anymore."

How do we stop this kind of thing from happening in our churches?

(1) It is necessary to guard our own tongues. Don't get involved in helping spread the lies.

(2) Double-check what you hear before believing it. We are engaged in combat with the enemy and one of the important rules of war is: **be careful where you get your information!** The enemy will do everything possible to feed false information into our lines of communication which cause us to mistrust our commanders and fellow soldiers.

Many Christians are fighting each other more than they fight the devil. This spiritual fratricide is not only debilitating to the Body of Christ, but also sidetracks us from our main purpose on this earth which is to preach the Gospel to every creature. Our attention is so focused on our problems **within** that we forget the lost world that is all around us.

(3) Be on guard for enemy agents who have infiltrated our churches and are doing everything possible to sabotage God's program for His Church. These enemy agents come in two classes:

(a) Carnal "Christians" who, because of their carnality, are used unconsciously by the devil to cause chaos in the church.

In the carnal "Christian's" eyes nothing is ever right, good or spiritual in the church. They can always do it better, but somehow they never seem to get around to actually doing anything spiritual themselves, much less do it better. They are vicious backbiters, gossips and character assassins.

(b) New Agers and Satanists are infiltrating Pentecostal churches, even to the point of giving messages in tongues, interpretations, prophecies and getting elected to church boards and other positions of authority. Can you imagine the havoc this causes in churches where the members are so blinded spiritually that they are unable to distinguish between a Satanist and a true child of God?

Paul speaks of people in both of the above classes as enemy agents in II Timothy 3:3&5, *"[They will be] without natural [human affection (callous and inhuman), relentless (admitting of no truce or appeasement); [they will be] slanderers (false accusers, troublemakers), intemperate and loose in morals and conduct, uncontrolled and fierce, haters of good...For [although] they hold a form of piety (true religion), they deny and reject and are strangers to the power of it [their conduct belies the genuiness of their profession]. Avoid [all] such people [turn away from them]."* (Amplified Bible)

We must realize that we aren't just talking about personality conflicts here, we are talking about dealing with the devil and his imps who are influencing and using these people to accomplish <u>his</u> will in the situation.

A word of caution—**don't** suspect that everyone who disagrees with us in the church is of the devil. We will not always be in agreement with our fellow Christians, but there is a **Godly way to disagree** which is light years away from the devilish way.

You will know the difference between the two because God is never involved with the works of the flesh or sinful methods which carnal "Christians" and New Agers-Satanists invariably use in church disputes. When you observe such behavior in church people, **Do not become involved in their evil plots and fleshly manipulations!** Come against them in the Name of Jesus and bind the strongmen who are working through them and continue to do so until they are exposed for who and what they are. Be sure you conduct your warfare on a **spiritual** level.

Not all strongholds of the enemy are located in topless joints, dope houses and crime-saturated neighborhoods. There are some huge strongholds right in front of our noses—in the very churches where we worship each week!

How can we hope to conduct God's business in our churches when the devil has the **veto power** over what we know to be God's Will?

Paul tells us, *"For though we walk (live) in the flesh, we are not carrying on our warfare according to the flesh and using mere human weapons. For the weapons of our warfare are not physical [weapons of flesh and blood], but they are mighty before God for the overthrow and destruction of strongholds, [Inasmuch as we] refute arguments and theories and reasoning and every proud and lofty thing that sets itself up against the [true] knowledge of God;"* (II Corinthians 10:3-5 Amplified Bible)

The "knowledge of God" is always our standard to judge whether something is of God or the devil. Anything that rises up against God's knowledge or Word is to be dealt with on a spiritual level and utterly refuted for what it is—an evil tactic of the devil—something which must be overthrown and destroyed in the spirit realm.

Therein is the problem, however. As the message from the Lord stated, **"My people do not know the difference between truth and error anymore."** The reason why they don't, by-in-large, is because they don't read, listen to or know God's Word as they should. If we have any hope of judging between a lie and the truth we must know what the Truth is.

I am told that bank tellers are taught to recognize the difference between good and counterfeit money by studying the good bills so that they instantly recognize the errors in the counterfeit ones when they see them.

We must be able to cut through the deception of this age if we are going to survive these perilous days. Thank God the Spirit of Truth is present within us to guide us into all truth. (John 16:13)

Let Not Your Heart Be Troubled

Jesus instructed the disciples, *"Let not your heart be troubled, neither let it be afraid,"* which is good advice today. (John 14:27) As we walk in the Spirit, the Holy Spirit will warn us and give us the Power to destroy the devil's strongholds. Only then will we be able to operate in Power and accomplish God's Will for these last days!

QUESTION: "How can people do such horrible things these days; the killings, the terrorists, the violence? How can we be sure we will be protected from them?"

Let's look at this from a different perspective to see why these things are happening and how we can be sure God will protect us from them.

A sweating figure struggles, fighting through the maze of jungle vegetation with his machete. He has been lost for days. His strength is ebbing fast as insects and tropical heat have done their deadly work.

When he feels he can go no further, off in the distance a sound floats to him on the heavy, stifling air currents like a hammer clanging on an anvil in a bell-like tone. Surely civilization isn't too far off if the sounds of life can be heard so clearly. So he follows the tolling of the bell with his last bit of strength.

He strains to catch a glimpse of the village, but it is not to be. All he actually does is wander in circles as he seeks the illusive sound. Finally, he falls to the ground, exhausted, never to rise again. The mysterious bellbird, a bird that actually exists, has claimed another victim.

Many a lost traveler in the rain forests of Central and South America has been led to his death by the call of the bellbird—a call that promises so much, but delivers only death.

The major mistake the victim makes is that he gets into terrain where he doesn't belong.

The jungle is without conscience and its deceptive sounds are only illusions that lead the lost soul more deeply into the jaws of the jungle maze. *"There is a way that seemeth right unto a man, but the end thereof are the ways of death."* (Proverbs 14:12)

Multitudes by the millions are being lured by a spiritual "bellbird" into a jungle of sin and death. Its call promises so much, but it only leads them deeper into the "jungle" of misery and confusion.

Deception

Deception is one of the chilling characteristics of the last days of this Age of Grace. Jesus clearly warns, *"Take heed that no man deceive you."* (Matthew 24:4) He describes the terrible scenario as the world arrives at this time in history. *"And many false prophets shall rise, and shall deceive many."* (Matthew 24:11,5)

Paul continues the description of the end-times by telling Timothy, *"But evil men and seducers shall wax worse and worse, deceiving, and being deceived."* (II Timothy 3:13)

We see who is behind this program of trickery when John describes the scene in which the devil was ousted from heaven. *"And the great dragon was cast out, that old serpent, called the Devil, and Satan, which deceiveth the whole world:"* (Revelation 12:9)

People who take drugs, get drunk, have abortions, kill people, get involved with false religions, have illicit sex and commit suicide have been **deceived by the devil**. On the other end of the spectrum, Christians also believe the deception of the devil when he tells them God isn't going to heal them or supply their needs or protect them or a thousand and one other things that God has specifically promised them in His Word if they will only believe and receive them by faith. They have been tricked into believing what the devil says about the situation in their lives as surely as the man in the jungle was deceived by the bellbird.

Do you think a mother would let a stranger invade her body and kill her defenseless, unborn baby if she wasn't deceived into believing that what she was doing was the correct and intelligent thing to do under the circumstances?

But millions upon millions of mothers around the world are allowing the murder of their babies because they are under a thick cloud of deception and cannot see the truth of such a terrible, vicious act against their own flesh and blood. Thankfully, mothers who have had abortions can come to Christ and receive forgiveness for this sin, just like any other sin, when they acknowledge that they have sinned against God and receive the healing they need from this act.

Do you think homosexuals would do the perverse things they do if they weren't deceived?

The terrorist feels he is justified in killing people because the devil has tricked him into believing the end justifies the means.

People do evil things because they have been duped by the evil devil.

The Bible warns, *"Let no man deceive you by any means; for that day (Rapture of the Church) shall not come except there come a falling away first..."* (II Thessalonians 2:3) We are seeing this in an unprecedented manner today as Christians are being led down the primrose path by the deception of the devil because it **looks and feels so good**. But trust God to tell you the Truth—everything the devil offers you is a **lie** to deceive you and take you into unfamiliar terrain where demons will lead you in circles, suck the life out of you and then kill you. Don't listen to the "bellbird"—to your emotions and desires, to this world, to the devil. Listen to God's Word and Holy Spirit.

Simulated Flights To The Moon

A few years ago we visited the Kennedy Space Center and observed how the astronauts are trained for space flights. Inside the Flight Crew Training Building are machines run by computers, called simulators, which enable the astronauts to experience simulated flights to the Moon in every detail.

The Command Module Simulator is modeled to appear exactly like the inside of the real Command Module. When the hatch door slams shut, the astronauts feel like they actually travel to the Moon. This is possible because every step of the mission is programmed on computers. T.V. monitors are placed in the windows so the Earth, Sun, Moon and stars are located exactly where they will appear during the actual flight. When the astronauts complete the many months of accelerated training, for all intents and purposes they will have already traveled to the Moon and back, even though they have never been higher than 15 feet off the floor of the Flight Crew Training Building!

As the tour guide explained this to us, I thought, *Isn't that an example of how deceptive things can appear in our life and yet not be real at all?* Christians must have faith in God and His Word more than in what the devil says or how he manipulates the situation to appear in the natural realm. What we see and feel in the natural realm isn't true if it conflicts with what God's Word says about the situation. *"While we look not at the things which are seen, but at the things which are not seen: for the things which are seen are temporal; but the things which are not seen are eternal."* God's Word is what is real and **reality** is believing God more than anything else.

The Man Who Almost Died Of Nothing

Missionary-evangelist Richard Jeffery is the man who taught us how to conduct open-air crusades and he illustrates what we are talking about here with the testimony of a man named, Craig, who was a member of a church he pastored a number of years ago.

"Craig had a very unusual problem when he came to the platform to be prayed for during our Wednesday evening service. The muscle or valve between his esophagus and stomach would not open properly when he ate or drank something. Over a period of 14 years it had gotten to the point that he had difficulty getting even liquids to enter his stomach. As a result he was slowly starving to death.

"I remember having dinner at his home some months before these events occurred and the only food he could eat was soft food that had been mashed and run through a strainer. If he took a drink of water and then laid down, the water would start running out of his mouth and choke him.

"He had been to the doctor the day before we prayed for him, on Tuesday, for X-rays and after looking at them his doctor had decided the only option left was to operate. The X-rays showed the wall of the esophagus, just before entering the stomach, had been herniated by the weight of food over the years which could not enter the stomach. A large pouch had formed as a result of the muscles of the esophagus being stretched all out of shape.

"The doctor informed Craig there was a 50/50 chance he would survive the operation. Of course this took place a number of years ago when they didn't have the modern techniques available today. The operation needed to be done immediately, but there wasn't a bed available in the small hospital. So the doctor sent Craig home, telling him he would phone as soon as a bed was vacated and asked him to come back for more X-rays on Thursday.

"After we prayed for him on Wednesday, he didn't feel anything special and he went home to all appearances the same as ever.

"The next day he went back to the doctor for more X-rays. He was informed that it appeared a hospital bed would be available the next day and that the doctor would phone him immediately when that happened.

"But the doctor didn't call Friday and after the church service Craig's daughter, Betty, asked me to stop by and see her Dad.

"Craig told me that this was the end. 'The doctor hasn't called so there still must not be any beds in the hospital. I can't even get liquids down. I'm all dehydrated. It looks like I'm going to die.'"

"On Saturday he was worse. I tried to cheer him up but he told me it was the end—that he was going to die. To be quite frank, he was discouraging me too.

"On Monday I stopped by in the morning and Craig's wife informed me that her husband was so weak he couldn't get out of bed. When I saw him it was clear that he was starving as well as becoming very dehydrated. He looked like a dead man. After talking with him for awhile he persuaded me that this indeed was the end.

"But suddenly the thought struck me, 'If that isn't the devil!' I gathered the family around Craig's bed and told them, 'Now there is to be no praying, not even one prayer. We're going to rebuke the devil and we're not going to stop until Craig is well again."

"By this time I was angry with the devil because I had seen through his deception. Craig had received healing nearly 2000 years ago, '...by whose stripes ye were healed.' (I Peter 2:24) And we had almost allowed the devil to talk us out of it.

"I began rebuking and binding the devil in the Name of Jesus and told him he wasn't going to talk us out of what God had already given us. 'Craig was healed on Calvary and you are a liar, Satan.'

"When I opened my eyes 15-20 minutes later, Craig was sitting on the edge of the bed, dressed, and asked his wife to fix him something to eat. After he ate a hearty meal we could visibly see him blossom out. Everything went down and stayed down and in a matter of a few hours he was like a new man! He told us he wanted to go to the doctor's office so he could tell him to forget about the operation.

When we arrived, the doctor came out with two X-rays in his hands and said, 'What happened to you, Craig? Look at these X-rays. The one on the left was taken last Tuesday and shows the hernia in your esophagus as usual. But look at the one we took on Thursday. Your esophagus is as normal as it can be. I just can't figure it out. I didn't see any reason to operate on a normal esophagus so I canceled the operation.'

"Now, the truth is that he was healed when we prayed for him on Wednesday night, but Satan almost succeeded in tricking him out of his life! **CRAIG ALMOST DIED OF NOTHING!**"

If the devil can convince us by false symptoms that we are sick, he will do so. There is no honor code in the jungle. We **must** believe what God says about the situation more than what the devil tells us. I

149

know this illustration also belongs in the chapter on the spirit of infirmity, but the same truth applies to anything God has promised us—finances, protection, eternal life—whatever.

"The just shall live by faith." (Hab. 2:4, Rom. 1:17, Gal. 3:11, Heb. 10:38) *"For we walk by faith, not by sight:"* (II Corinthians 5:7) *"And Jesus answering saith unto them, Have faith in God."* (Mark 11:22)

The Moses Sole

Even in the world of nature we can see the Truth of God's Word illustrated by a little, delicate flatfish or flounder called the "Moses sole." (Pardachirus Marmoratus) It abounds in the Red Sea, as do vicious shark, who would like nothing better than to eat these seemingly helpless, naive, unsophisticated fish. (those are also adjectives people use to describe Christians who live by faith in God's Word)

The November, 1974 issue of National Geographic Magazine, page 718, reports on a team of researchers who went to the Israel to study this amazing little fish which has an impressive, God-given defense system.

The article shows actual pictures of the shark swooping in to kill and destroy the "Moses sole"—in fact, the "Moses sole" is shown, **tethered** in one picture so that there is no hope of escape—half-way in the shark's mouth! I believe anyone would call that a "worse-possible-case-scenario." Was the little fish frightened, even in the shark's mouth? Did it struggle, trying desperately to get away from the savage, saw-toothed, sea demon? Did its blood pressure rise even one degree. Did it wonder why God had allowed it to be in such a terrible, precarious situation? Absolutely not!

It had total faith in the defense system God has given it—more faith in God than many Christians have in fact. The little "Moses sole" just kept up its easy, undulating motion, as if nothing out-of-the-ordinary was happening. It was secure because it secretes a lethally toxic, milky poison from two glands that literally stops the shark in its tracks. **The little fish was surrounded by a halo of God-given protection!**

The researchers watched in amazement as the deadly predator jerked away from the "Moses sole," its jaws **"frozen open!"** Isn't that great—it couldn't shut its big mouth! "Vigorously shaking its head from side to side, the shark dashed around the pool in the marine laboratory at Elat, Israel, before at last succeeding in closing its mouth.

The captive 'Moses sole' kept up its easy undulating motion as if nothing had happened."

Isn't that a beautiful picture of what happens in the spirit realm when the devil tries to mess with us, and we truly believe God and His Word more than anything else? There really **wasn't** anything for the little fish to get excited about, was there. And there is no reason for us to be fearful of the devil either, because we have a special, built-in defense system called the "whole armour of God."

"Finally, my brethren, be strong in the Lord, and in the power of his might. Put on the whole armour of God, that ye may be able to stand against the wiles (tricks, deceptions, illusions)*of the devil."* (Ephesians 6:10,11) He tries to make us believe things exist that really are nothing but shadows and false impressions. **He is a master illusionist who manipulates circumstances to appear contrary to God's Word**. *"We know [absolutely] that anyone born of God does not [deliberately and knowingly] practice committing sin, but the One Who was begotten of God carefully watches over and protects him [Christ's divine presence within him preserves him against the evil], and the wicked one does not lay hold [get a grip] on him OR TOUCH [HIM]."* (I John 5:18 Amplified Bible) Jesus also said, *"Behold, I give unto you power to tread on serpents and scorpions, and over all the power of the enemy: and nothing shall by any means hurt you."* (Luke 10:19)

Oh yes, the devil puts on a real "show" for us, raging and ranting around as he tries to bluff us into believing he can overpower us. But when he comes for the final death thrust, all he gets for his trouble is our "shield of faith" jammed between his jaws! The shark can eventually shake off the effects of the "Moses sole's" toxic, milky poison, but the devil can never get rid of our shield of faith between his jaws as long as we continue believing God more than the devil, the world and our flesh.

Be Prepared For The Final Showdown!

As the world approaches the final showdown, be prepared for an influx of demonic propaganda from every side. You'll hear of scary and powerful exploits of the occult, New Agers and Satanists. **BUT DO NOT BE ALARMED! Satan is a defeated foe**! He is doomed and what we are seeing now is just the last crescendo before this age is wrapped up and Satan is cast into the pit for a thousand years. (Revelation 20:1-3)

Isaiah gives a glimpse of just how far Satan has been stripped of the power he had before he fell into sin and his final destination. *"How art thou fallen from heaven, O Lucifer, son of the morning...For thou hast said in thine heart, 'I will ascend into heaven, I will exalt my throne above the stars of God:' Yet thou shalt be brought down to hell, to the sides of the pit. They that see thee shall narrowly look upon thee, and consider thee, saying, 'Is this the man that made the earth to tremble, that did shake kingdoms;'"* (Isaiah 14:12-16)

Christ's death and resurrection broke the power of Satan's dominion once and for all over the human race. No longer do we have to put up with being pushed around. *"We are more than conquerors through him that loved us."* (Romans 8:37) We appropriate or receive into our life everything Christ has won for us and then we live like God wants us to live—as children of God, joint heirs with Christ Jesus and overcomers. God has provided for our every need if we will live by faith in His Word and not by our natural sight.

We must understand that it makes no difference whether the devil tries to kill us in the form of a disease, an accident or a gun. He must obey us when we live a righteous life, speak in the Name of Jesus, according to God's Word, with our heart filled with faith in God's ability to deliver us.

The most dangerous situation we can be involved with today is not to be trapped in a mall with a crazy gunman running loose. It is to allow sin, fear and doubt into our heart, because that is what will come out, instead of faith, when the pressure is on—when the doctor says the disease is incurable; a gun is pointed at our head; an earthquake strikes or a hurricane is headed in our direction. If our shield of faith comes down, we will be totally vulnerable to the devil.

Live In A Constant State Of Faith

GOD'S PEOPLE MUST LIVE IN A CONSTANT STATE OF FAITH IN GOD'S PROMISES. We may not **feel** like Superman, physically—ready to leap tall buildings in a single bound—but if we believe God more than anything else, when the crisis comes, the Holy Spirit will have the faith available in our heart to work with, to bring about our deliverance from the wicked one.

Don't allow the enemy to trick you into believing your natural senses instead of God's Word. The little "Moses sole" doesn't believe what it sees, even when the very jaws of the shark are closing over it.

It has complete faith that its God-given protection will not fail in the crisis, and it never does. The researchers reported that there was not one case when the shark ate one of the "Moses sole." And neither will your protection fail because God keeps His Word to you and me!

However, when the researchers removed the "faith" glands, the shark were free to close their jaws and destroy the little fish. So only as we look at this life in the light of what God says about it in His Word and keep our shield of faith operational, will we keep from being tricked out of God's Promises.

"The Lord is the strength of my life; of whom shall I be afraid?" (Psalms 27:1)

"No weapon that is formed against thee shall prosper; and every tongue that shall rise against thee in judgment thou shalt condemn. This is the heritage of the servants of the Lord, and their righteousness is of me, saith the Lord " (Isaiah 54:17)

Just keep spreading the "milk" of the Word around you—it will stop the devil dead in his tracks!

Treat The Devil Like A Dog

I'm becoming more and more convinced that we must maintain an attitude of dominance and authority over the devil much like we have over our dog. Personally, I've never allowed any of the many dogs we have had in our household dictate to me how our family would live. If the dog couldn't adjust to the way we did things in our family the dog was history.

It didn't matter how big the dog was, he and I had an understanding, "Either do it my way or else!" I didn't check with the dog every morning to see if he was in a good mood or not—he checked with me.

There is a mind-set, which actually must become a heart-set, that we carry over into the spirit realm if we are going to have the victory we've been talking about here. We don't look out for the devil, he looks out for us. The **devil** was the one who was defeated by Christ and because I believe in Christ's victory more than anything else, I am also victor over the devil. When it appears in the natural realm that things aren't working out, I don't stop believing God and start believing the devil's lie that it isn't working this time. I command the devil, "**IN THE NAME OF JESUS SHUT UP AND HEEL, DEVIL!**" He has no alternative—he must obey.

Hallelujah!

Rienhard Bonnke has the habit of shouting, "Hallelujah" when he takes the microphone and walks to the pulpit of his gigantic crusades in Africa.

In one of his crusades, a top witch in the world was flown in by people who opposed the crusade to curse him and the crusade. He didn't know that she and four of her henchmen were sitting in the audience the first night of the crusade.

When he stood to take the microphone that particular night, he shouted his customary, "Hallelujah!" The witch immediately started coughing and said, "Get me out of here! I'm dying! Get me out of here!" and ran out of the crusade area.

After the service, one of her warlocks come up to Reinhard and told him what had happened. He said, "Today I have seen that Jesus is stronger than my Lucifer. I want your Jesus!"

Reinhard cast the devil out of him and he accepted Jesus as his Lord and Savior and was baptized in the Holy Spirit! (Christ For the Nations Magazine, November, 1991, page 2,3)

Let's believe God and live Christ's victory in our life!

(For information on why bad things happen to Christians please refer to chapter 26—the spirit of infirmity.)

Micholobe Beer

A pastor friend of ours related a true story about an elderly lady who was unhappy with what some of the church members were doing. She told them they should change their ways, but they wouldn't listen to her.

She told her pastor about it and he didn't get excited about it either.

So she decided to take care of it herself. The next Sunday morning she got up and gave a prophecy. She laid the situation out and stated what she thought was the solution to the problem.

To be sure the people would pay attention to what she had said she added, "If you don't do what I tell you, thus sayeth the Lord, I will write the word, 'Micholobe' across the front of this church!" Unfortunately, the word she should have said was, "Ichabod," which means, "the glory has departed from this place."

Perverse Spirit 19

No, it is not. This question is usually asked in conjunction with homosexuality because in the U.S. AIDS is a disease that affects mostly homosexuals. While we realize that the sin of homosexuality is an evil, gross sin, yet the Bible clearly teaches that if we have committed one sin we have committed them all. *"For whosoever shall keep the whole law, and yet offend in one point, he is guilty of all."* (James 2:10) Sin is sin with God and if the homosexual accepts Christ as his Savior, repents of his sin and receives the change of lifestyle that God wants him to live, he can be saved like any other sinner.

If it was the habit of God to kill certain people because of their wicked sin, how many of us would not have lived long enough to be able to accept Christ as our Savior because of **our** wickedness? The fact is that God is in the saving business today. *"The Lord is not slack concerning his promise, as some men count slackness; but is longsuffering to usward, NOT WILLING THAT ANY SHOULD PER-ISH, BUT THAT ALL SHOULD COME TO REPENTANCE."* (II Peter 3:9) It would be counterproductive for God to kill sinners before He has a chance to save them. God will not act against His own Will. So we can be sure God did not invent AIDS to punish the homosexuals.

AIDS is simply the wages people receive for sinning. *"For the wages of sin is death; but the gift of God is eternal life through Jesus Christ our Lord."* (Romans 6:23) People get paid for their sin whether they want to or not. The difference with AIDS is that the cause (sin) and the effect (AIDS) is so clear and takes place relatively fast. The majority of people who die with AIDS in the U.S. have committed homosexual acts or have had secondary contact with them, such as tainted blood transfusions, sharing needles with infected drug addicts or babies born of infected mothers. Once these people contact AIDS there is no hope—they die. The sinners see God's warning about the wages of sin played out before their eyes and it scares them because if it is true that sin kills like that, they are going to die, too, because of their sins. In fact, the threat of AIDS has caused more people to change their way of living than much of our preaching. They haven't believed the Bible, but they **have** to believe the death statistics concerning AIDS.

So now there is a frantic race to find the cure for AIDS. Of course the major reason is to stop the terrible loss of life from this plague, but another reason is an unconscious desire to wipe out this graphic illustration of what sin does to them so they can continue their sin in peace.

So who is actually doing the killing through AIDS? Jesus says it is the devil. *"The thief (devil) cometh not, but for to steal, and to kill, and to destroy: I (God) am come that they might have life, and that they might have it more abundantly."* (John 10:10) God isn't the killer—He is the Life-giver—**in abundance!**

More information about what God does and doesn't do can be found in Chapter 6.

QUESTION: "How does a perverse spirit get started in a person's life?"

Every sin that mankind commits begins as a thought. Satan drops an evil thought into our minds and if it is not rejected, it grows and becomes the catalyst for that sin to take place. *"Let no man say when he is tempted, I am tempted of God: for God cannot be tempted with evil, neither tempteth he any man: But every man is tempted, when he is drawn away of his own lust, and enticed. Then when lust hath conceived, it bringeth forth sin: and sin, when it is finished, bringeth forth death."* (James 1:13-15)

Sin and evil begin in the mind as a result of inner desires or inclinations in our heart that are not subjected to the Word of God and the Holy Spirit. *"For out of the heart proceed evil thoughts, murders, adulteries, fornications, thefts, false witness, blasphemies."* (Matthew 15:19) Whenever we note that an evil thought or desire is forming in our minds we must immediately pull it into captivity and ask for cleansing from it. *"Casting down imaginations, and every high thing that exalteth itself against the knowledge of God, and bringing into captivity every thought to the obedience of Christ;"* (II Corinthians 10:5) The Holy Spirit will help us dominate our minds as we determine to think on things that are clean and praise worthy. *"Finally, brethren, whatsoever things are true, whatsoever things are honest, whatsoever things are just, whatsoever things are pure, whatsoever things are lovely, whatsoever things are of good report: if there be any virtue, and if there be any praise, think on these things."* (Philippians 4:8)

If these evil thought patterns are not interrupted and cast down, there is a conception (or willful acceptance) of the thought or deed that begins to take on a life of its own until it becomes a sinful action that eventually causes the person to be spiritually lost.

The necessity to continually cleanse our minds with a daily washing of the water of the Word must be adopted by believers of all ages. There is never a time when we won't have to put a guard on our thought life.

When Judas betrayed Jesus, the Bible says, *"the devil, having now put into the heart of Judas Iscariot, Simon's son, to betray Him."* (John 13:2) It started with a thought and ended in death for Judas. He could have stopped the thought and the devil would have had to use someone else.

When Simon the Sorcerer came to Peter and requested to buy the power of the Holy Spirit, Peter rebuked him and said, *"Repent therefore of this thy wickedness, and pray God, if perhaps the thought of thine heart may be forgiven thee."* (Acts 8:22) Simon's problem began with a thought from the devil. He knew of Simon's lust for power and attention. He convinced him that the power of the Holy Spirit could be bought and used, even as he had used sorcery and gained large crowds and fame. He wanted to pervert the power of God and Peter instantly rebuked him for it.

Any twisting or perverting of something good is energized by a perverse spirit. It will drop a thought into someone's mind and encourage them to act on what is already in their heart. Jesus said, *"But those things which proceed out of the mouth come forth from the heart; and they defile the man."* (Matthew 15:18)

Any thought that is not cast down and brought into subjection to the Word of God will immediately begin to build a stronghold in the mind. The imaginations and fantasies that are allowed to remain begin to build walls stronger and taller each day until there is a rationalization that these things aren't perverse or wrong at all. In fact the person feels very comfortable with them and enjoys reviewing them in private. These thoughts can take the form of perversion, sickness, fears, poverty or any other direction that is contrary to God's Word. As long as they are permitted and accepted, they will stay.

The day must come, though, when each individual makes up their mind that they don't want the harassment of the devil in their minds any longer and they, themselves, through the power of the Holy Spirit, begin pulling down each and every stronghold the enemy has built. *"For though we walk in the flesh, we do not war after the flesh: (For the weapons of our warfare are not carnal, but mighty through God to the pulling down of strong holds;) Casting down imaginations, and every high thing that exalteth itself against the knowledge of God and bringing into captivity every thought to the obedience of Christ;"* (II Corinthians 10:3-6)

We have been given mighty weapons! Our weapons arc the Word of God, the Blood of Jesus, the word of our testimony, and the Name of Jesus! But they will only help us if we learn how to use them. There aren't any easy victories in warfare—they all have a cost. We must be willing to discipline ourselves and become victorious in the mighty Name of Jesus.

When our areas of disobedience are taken care of, then we can fight against the disobedience of the world that surrounds us. Until we take care of the strongholds that have built up in our own minds, we are not ready to do battle with the pornography industry, etc. Ask the Holy Spirit to show you if there are areas that you have been secretly hiding and enjoying or being tormented in that need to be taken care of once and for all. He is our Counselor and will gently lead us through restoration and healing in that area. *"Wherefore seeing we also are compassed about with so great a cloud of witnesses, let us lay aside every weight, and the sin which doth so easily beset us, and let us run with patience the race that is set before us, Looking unto Jesus the author and finisher of our faith; who for the joy that was set before him endured the cross, despising the shame, and is set down at the right hand of the throne of God."* (Hebrews 12:1,2)

"Wherefore he is able also to save them to the uttermost that come unto God by him, seeing he ever liveth to make intercession for them." (Hebrews 7:25)

QUESTIONS: "What is a reprobate mind mentioned in Romans 1:28? Is there hope for such people?"

"And even as they did not like to retain God in their knowledge, God gave them over to a reprobate mind, to do those things which are not convenient:" (Romans 1:28)

Reprobate in the Greek language means; castaway, rejected, unapproved, void of judgment.

The reprobate mind of the sexually perverse or abortionists for instance, is a stronghold of Satan. Satan delights in seeing how far he can swing mankind away from the original plan and creation of God. When people insist on doing the unnatural, God lets them have a mind that is void of judgment. In other words, they become so twisted they actually begin to believe their life style is normal. It's not normal to have sex with a partner of the same sex. It's not normal for a mother to kill her unborn child. It's not normal for people to abuse their living children or any other person. *"Unto the pure all things are pure: but unto them that are defiled and unbelieving is nothing pure; but even their mind and conscience is defiled. They profess that they know God; but in works they deny him, being abominable, and disobedient, and unto every good work reprobate."* (Titus 1: 15,16)

Psychologists and sociologists have found that there are steps to perversion that invariably occur in people who are overcome by sin: first, addiction; then escalation; next desensitization; and finally, the acting out of the role.

But the light of the Gospel of Jesus Christ can completely free any person from a reprobate mind. It can be exchanged for the mind of Christ that is offered to all who come to the Lord and ask for His help. *"For who hath known the mind of the Lord, that he may instruct him? But we have the mind of Christ."* (1 Corinthians 2:16)

Romans 12:1, admonishes each believer to present their bodies as a living sacrifice, holy and acceptable to God. Anything short of that isn't a sacrifice that is acceptable! In verse 2, Paul stresses that we can't afford to conform to this world's ideas and shifting standards. We need to continuously reprogram our minds with God's Word so we will know what is God's good, acceptable and perfect will for our life.

QUESTION: "Are the homosexuals really trying to take over or are they just misunderstood because of their sin?"

Let me answer that by giving you a quotation from some of their own writings, you can then decide what you think about it.

"...We shall sodomize your sons, emblems of your feeble masculinity, of your shallow dreams and vulgar lies. We shall seduce them in your schools, in your dormitories, in your gymnasiums, in your locker rooms, in your sports arenas, in your seminaries, in your youth groups, in your movie theater bathrooms, in your army bunkhouses, in your truck stops, in your all-male clubs, in your houses of Congress, wherever men are with men together...

"...The family unit—spawning ground of lies, betrayals, mediocrity, hypocrisy and violence—will be abolished. The family unit, which only dampens imagination and curbs free will, must be eliminated...

"...All churches who condemn us will be closed. Our only gods are handsome young men." First printed in *Gay Community News*, February 15-21, 1987 and later published in *Gay Revolutionary*, and entered in The Congressional Record.

QUESTION: "Does homosexuality effect lifespan?"

The following information is from Family Research Institute, P.O. Box 2091, Washington, D.C. 20013:

Effects on the Lifespan

"Smokers and drug addicts don't live as long as non-smokers or non-addicts, so we consider smoking and narcotics abuse harmful. The typical lifespan of homosexuals suggests that their activities are more destructive than smoking and as dangerous as drugs.

"6,516 obituaries from 16 U.S. homosexual journals over the past 12 years were compared to a large sample of obituaries from regular newspapers. The obituaries from the regular newspapers were similar to U.S. averages for longevity; the median age of death of married men was 75 and 80 percent of them died old (age 65 or older).

For unmarried or divorced men the median age of death was 57 and 32 percent of them died old. Married women averaged age 79 at death; 85 percent died old. Unmarried and divorced women averaged age 71 and 60 percent of them died old.

"The median age of death for homosexuals, however, was virtually the same nationwide—and, overall, less than 20 percent survived to old age. If AIDS was the cause of death, the median age was 39. For the 803 gays who died of something other than AIDS, the median age of death was 42 and 9 percent died old. The 133 lesbians had a median age of death of 45 and 23 percent died old.

"2.8 percent of gays died violently. They were 116 times more apt to be murdered; 24 times more apt to commit suicide; and had a traffic-accident death-rate 18 times the rate of comparably aged white males. Heart attacks, cancer, and liver failure were exceptionally common. 20 percent of lesbians died of murder, suicide, or accident—a rate 487 times higher than that of white females aged 25-44. The age distributions of samples of homosexuals in scientific literature from 1858 to 1992 suggests a similarly shortened lifespan.

"Percentage-wise, nine times as many married males live to age 65 than gays; 3.5 times as many married women live to be 65 than lesbians. Homosexuality, in both men and women, is indeed an alternative **death**-style; it is not an **alternative** life style."

"For this cause God gave them up unto vile affections: for even their women did change the natural use into that which is against nature: And likewise also the men, leaving the natural use of the woman, burned in their lust one toward another...Who knowing the judgment of God, that they which commit such things are worthy of death" (Romans 1:26-27,32)

QUESTION: "Do Sins of the Body Effect the Whole Being?"

We held a seminar in a Pentecostal church that had seen a number of homosexuals exposed, some of them board members. When the pastor asked them how they could possibly think they could engage in such activity and still be leaders in the church they responded, "Oh that's just something we do with our bodies. In our spirits we are still living for God."

But the Bible says our bodies are temples of the Holy Spirit and what we do with them has a direct bearing on where we will spend eternity. *"What? know you not that you body is the temple of the Holy Spirit which is in you, which ye have of God, and ye are not your own? For ye are bought with a price: therefore glorify God in your body, and in your spirit, which are God's."* (I Corinthians 6:19,20)

Spirit of Haughtiness (Pride) 20

QUESTION: "Why is your teaching on spiritual warfare so simple? It almost seems too good to be true."

It is not an insult for people to ask us this question. In fact, it is a compliment because that is exactly what we want it to be. We have noticed that some theologians seem to deliberately hide what they say behind confusing theological terms that only the insiders understand. It seems to be a matter of pride that if it is important, it has to be complicated.

We find that people want the "gobble-de-gook" deleted these days so they can understand what the Bible is really saying. Spiritual warfare does not have to be complicated to be effective. It is the same for Salvation, the Baptism of the Holy Spirit, Healing and many other things God has provided for us in His Word.

In fact, nearly everything God has promised us can be received by a four-year-old child. *"And Jesus called a little child unto him, and set him in the midst of them, and said, Verily I say unto you, except ye be converted, and **become as little children, ye shall not enter into the kingdom of heaven.** Whosoever therefore shall **humble himself as this little child, the same is greatest in the kingdom of heaven.** And whoso shall receive one such little child in my name receiveth me. But whoso shall offend one of these little ones which believe in me, it were better for him that a millstone were hanged about his neck, and that he were drowned in the depth of the sea."* (Matthew 18:2-6)

I remember a four-year-old boy named, Hayden Kessler, from our second crusade church in San Jose, Costa Rica. His parents, Carlos and Anna, never missed a service and his father is one now of the assistant pastors of the great crusade church there in the suburb of

Moravia that has a great congregation of several thousand people.

One day Anna told Carol about what was happening during the day with Hayden. He had listened to us pray for the sick in every service and had heard us tell the people that it didn't matter who was doing the praying, if they had faith in God's Word, they could receive what the Bible promised them. One day he saw that his mother wasn't feeling good, so he told her, "Let me pray for you, mommy."

She said the first couple of times she thought to herself, isn't that cute! He would put his hand on her forehead and bind the devil in the Name of Jesus and command the sickness to leave his mommy alone, among other things, just like we did in the Crusade.

She said the strange thing was that every time he prayed for her, she was healed! After that she began looking for Hayden whenever she didn't feel good because his child-like faith was just as powerful as Jesus said it would be.

For those who think the devil is some awesome force that we should watch out for, look at this situation—a four-year-old commanded him to take his sickness and go in the Name of Jesus and the devil **had to obey him!** If a little child can put the devil to flight, don't you think you can too if you have the same kind of faith in Jesus Christ?

Go for it!

QUESTION: "Why is a spirit of pride so hard to see in ourselves?"

Pride is something we usually observe in others first. We really don't believe we are capable of having it until we fall on our faces spiritually. People who are proud stumble around and fall over things because spiritually their eyes have been blinded by the god of this world's system, the devil. He comes in many disguises to entrap people with his pride. He offers them status, knowledge, spiritual experiences that no one else has, etc. He appeals to whatever it is that they desire.

When people see others faltering and coming under attack because of the door they've opened to pride, it is so often said that God is trying to humble them—that's why they are having such a hard time.

The truth of that is found in James 4:10, *"Humble **yourselves** in* *the sight of the Lord, and he shall lift you up."* **The humbling process is initiated by us.** When we realize that our protection has evaporated because we are walking in pride and humbly ask God to forgive us, He does just that. Then God immediately begins to lift us back up and restores us as His children.

God's greatest desire is for each one of us to realize and enjoy all the gifts and talents He has placed within us, but we'll never know them until we humble ourselves and put our lives in His hands.

QUESTION: "What does I John 2:16 mean when it talks about 'The pride of life?'"

"According to I John 2:16, three aspects of the sinful world create open hostility to God: (1) 'The lust of the flesh': this includes impure desires, sinful pleasures, and sensual gratification (1 Cor. 6:18; Jas 1:14; cf. Phil. 3:19). (2) 'The lust of the eyes': this refers to coveting or lusting for things which are attractive to the eye but forbidden by God, including the desire to watch that which gives sinful pleasure (Ex. 20:17; Rom. 7:7). In the present modern age this includes the desire to entertain oneself by viewing pornography, violence, ungodliness, and immorality in the theater, television, movies, or magazines (Gen. 3:6; Josh. 7:21; II Sam. 11:2; Matthew 5:28). (3) 'The pride of life': this means the spirit of arrogance, pride, and self-sufficient independence that does not recognize God as Lord or His Word as final authority. It is seeking to exalt, glorify, and promote oneself as the center of life (Jas. 4:16)." (Donald Stamps, *The Full Life Study Bible*, Zondervan Publishing House, pgs.2004-2005)

QUESTION: "What is 'rebellious pride?'"

"Rebellious pride, which refuses to depend on God and be subject to Him, but attributes to self the honour due to Him, figures as the very root and essence of sin." (*The New Bible Dictionary,* Eerdmans, pg. 1027)

We see the best illustration of rebellious pride in the story of Lucifer found in Isaiah 14 and Ezekiel 28. He boasted that he would place his throne above the very throne of God in total independence of Him.

In the Garden of Eden we see Lucifer as the fallen devil persuading Adam and Eve that they could be like gods themselves. Today we see this idea widely promoted by the devil among people of all cultures who are striving to become as gods in themselves and dominate the world.

Haughtiness appears as a root cause of atheism in Psalm 10:4. *"The wicked, through the pride of his countenance, will not seek after God: God is not in all his thoughts."*

Jesus said, *"Take my yoke upon you, and learn of me, for I am meek and lowly in heart: and ye shall find rest unto your souls."* (Matthew 11:29) Jesus provided for our eternal salvation when He humbled Himself and took on the form of man. If we take His advice, we will learn how to walk with a humble heart before the Lord.

Throughout the Old and New Testaments the quality of humility is praised and God pours out His blessing on those that possess it.

Spirit of Heaviness 21

QUESTION: "How would you define the difference between a spirit of heaviness and natural grief?"

Whenever natural grief turns into **abnormal** or excessive grief it is an indication that something is wrong because the Bible says that Jesus has, "...*borne our griefs, and carried our sorrows:*" (Isaiah 53:4) There is a normal period of grief when we miss the one who has died or departed, but we must give it over to the Lord and allow Him to heal the pain of separation so we can go on living. This involves faith on our part, because it is easier to give in to our natural desires and "throw in the sponge" than to battle it out with the Word of God. But if we truly believe and allow God to help us out of our grief, He will do it .

This rule can also apply to all areas of activity of the strongmen. We know there has been a failure of faith somewhere in our life, and usually a need for repentance on our part, when the problem has pushed us beyond the point of normality into abnormality. The devil always pushes us to accomplish his will. When the problem pushes us more than we want to be pushed, then we know the problem has entered the area of the operation of a strongman. And, according to how abnormal or out-of-control it gets, it will require that degree of deliverance for us to get back to the normal, Christian, "child of God" way of life that we should be living.

(1) If the failure is handled immediately, a simple, "Please forgive me of that sin," may be all that is necessary. (2) But if a habit pattern of behavior is developed, we may need other Christians to pray with us to break the bondage. (3) It could get to the point that we may allow it to choke out our faith in God to the point that we stop serving Him and return to a life of sin. (4) Finally, the condition could lead to demonic possession that involves major deliverance.

As we say in "Strongman's His Name, What's His Game," it is better to take care of the problem when the tree is just a seedling instead of waiting until it has grown into a tree and a chain saw has to be used.

QUESTION: "Is there a spirit of rejection?"

It is not mentioned by name in the Bible as a strongman. Therefore we can conclude that it is a symptom or the result of an attack by a strongman, such as jealousy or heaviness, that causes deep inner hurts.

The emotional damage done by rejection can follow us around for many years and give the enemy an opportunity to get a foothold in our life. The one thing that will close the door to Satan in this area is to forgive those who despitefully use us and that includes those who have caused us feelings of rejection. Parents, teachers, siblings, friends and even Christians can do or say things which cause us to experience rejection and be totally unaware of what they have done to us. But in spite of the fact that we are the one who suffers the anguish of rejection, **we** must diagnose the cause and put an end to it by forgiving those who have caused it. When we do, God is then released to help us get free of the rejections and be healed in our mind and spirit.

QUESTION: "Is attempted suicide unforgivable?"

No. People need to understand John 10:10 better. *"The thief cometh not, but for to steal, and to kill, and to destroy:"* Satan has pushed them to the point of suicide because he wants them dead and he uses a spirit of heaviness, death, jealousy, fear, or a dumb and deaf spirit to get them there.

Suicide is one of the three leading causes of death between the ages of 5 and 44 years old. Over 28,000 people take their own lives each year. A teenage suicide occurs every 90 minutes in the United States according to the National Institute of Mental Health. Suicide ranks eighth among the major causes of death.

A suicidal person has both a side that wants to live as well as a side that wants to die; a suicide attempt is a cry for help expressing that ambivalence. But they can be freed of that harassment of the devil and live in victory if they repent of their sins, get into the Word of God and make a sacrifice of praise to the Lord.

"To appoint unto them that mourn in Zion, to give unto them

beauty for ashes, the oil of joy for mourning, the garment of praise for the spirit of heaviness; that they might be called trees of righteousness, the planting of the Lord, that he might be glorified." (Isaiah 61:3)

QUESTION: "At what age are people most vulnerable to depression?"

It appears from studies done about depression that people are at peak risk for major depression between the ages of 45 and 55 years old.

"During childhood and adolescence, and to an extent young adulthood...there are others to buffer the effects of adverse life events," says University of Oregon psychologist Peter M. Lewinsohn. "But at middle-age, most of us start getting exposed to major set-backs—the loss of our parents, career problems—and we don't have such strong buffers anymore."

At all ages, women are at greater risk for depression than men, he found. Lewinsohn's team studied 6,742 Oregon adults, tracking first bouts with serious depression lasting at least two weeks. For women, the risk rises steadily after age thirty, reaching the lifetime peak—25 in every 1,000—between the ages of 45 and 55. For men, the risk remains about 10 per 1,000 until the ages 45 to 55, where it becomes 15 in 1,000. After 55, the rate for both sexes drops steadily. (USA TODAY, Marilyn Elias)

What does the Word of God say about this? *"I will say of the Lord, He is my refuge and my fortress: my God; in him will I trust. Surely he shall deliver thee from the snare of the fowler, and from the noisome pestilence. He shall cover thee with his feathers, and under his wings shall thou trust: his truth shall be thy shield and buckler. Thou shalt not be afraid for the terror by night, nor for the arrow that flieth by day; nor for the pestilence that walketh in darkness, nor for the destruction that wasteth at noonday."* (Psalm 91:2-6)

Our trust must be in the Lord when the destroyer tries to bring destruction on us in the "noon day" of our life. We must bind the spirit of heaviness in the Name of Jesus and believe that God's Word will take us through the desert places of our life. Be sure to read the Word and praise God for all His provision.

Studies have found that bipolar depression (manic-depressive or extreme mood swings) tends to run in families and experts believe it may be inherited. Remember, each one of the strongmen try to cause generational problems in families. (Jane See White, Statesman Journal, Salem, OR, Feb. 3, 1981) Bind the strongman that activates depression (the spirit of heaviness) and loose the Comforter (the Holy Spirit), the garment of praise and the oil of joy to flow back into your life.

God's children should be continuous praisers. The words of our mouth are very important and will cause us to change our thinking. Paul told us not to be shy about what we say, *"Be careful for nothing; but in everything by prayer and supplication with thanksgiving let your requests be made known unto God. And the peace of God, which passeth all understanding, shall keep your hearts and minds through Christ Jesus. Finally, brethren, whatsoever things are true, whatsoever things are honest, whatsoever things are just, whatsoever things are pure, whatsoever things are lovely, whatsoever things are of good report; if there be any virtue, and if there be any praise, think on these things. Those things, which ye have both learned, and received, and heard, and seen in me, do: and the God of peace shall be with you."* (Philippians 4:6-9)

QUESTION: "Should a person experience grief when a loved one dies?"

Grief is a God-given emotion that allows us to empty out the deep feelings that must not stay in us. It is estimated by some that the normal healing period for grief is from 6 months to 2 years. If grief is continued over a long period of time without healing, it becomes neurotic and opens the door for the enemy to take advantage of the situation.

Isaiah 53:4, says that Jesus will bear our griefs and carry our sorrows, but the key is to turn them over to Him quickly so that He can heal us of them. Jesus also said in John 14,15 and 16 that He would send the Comforter (the Holy Spirit) to be with us and live in us at all times. He will accelerate the healing process as we give Him the liberty to do so.

QUESTION: "How can I forgive people if I don't feel like it? Does it do any good?"

Jesus made forgiveness a prerequisite for receiving His promises. In Matthew 18:21-22, Peter came to Jesus asking how many times he needed to forgive a brother that was sinning against him.

Jesus told him to forgive 70 times 7 or 490 times! He didn't tell him to wait until he felt like it or until his attitude was right. He just said to do it.

After the Lord's prayer, Jesus told his disciples to forgive. When we stand praying, we are told to forgive anyone that has done something against us. In the beatitudes, Jesus said we were not to judge or condemn, but we were to forgive and we would be forgiven. After the parable of the debtor, Jesus told of the unforgiving man who was put into torment because of unforgiveness.

We have a clear choice, we can either have compassion and forgive those who have wronged us and have peace about it, or we can choose not to forgive them and be tormented until our mind and bodies break down.

"If we confess our sins, he is faithful and just to forgive us our sins, and to cleanse us from all unrighteousness." (1 John 1:9) If Jesus could forgive us of all our sins, we should be able to forgive others of their sins against us.

How can we forgive the husband who left us for another woman, the scheming co-worker who cost us our job, the parent or relative who abused us? "Rage toward the person who hurt you, can consume your life," warns psychologist Lewis Smedes, a professor of ethics and theology at Fuller Theological Seminary in Pasadena, Calif. "Much time and energy may be spent brooding about the past, internally curing the wrongdoer or plotting ways to get even." (Dianne Aprile, Gannett News Service, Statesman Journal, Salem, OR, June 7,1988, p.6B)

Psychologists say that one of the most destructive emotions is bottled up rage. Among its side effects are poor self-esteem, withdrawal, difficulty maintaining friendships and sexual dysfunction. It can even lead to severe depression and suicide.

There are physical manifestations too. People who nurse deep hatred are prone to migraines, chronic stress, anxiety, colitis, ulcers, high blood pressure and alcohol and drug abuse.

"Forgiveness isn't primarily for the one forgiven, who may not want to be absolved," explains Smedes. "It's the forgiver who benefits. By putting his hurt behind him, he resumes control of his life and is able to move on. When you release the wrong-doer from the wrong, you cut a malignant tumor out of your inner life." (ibid)

First, recognize your anger, then make a decision to abandon the luxury of revenge and refuse to dwell on past wrongs. Decide as an act of your will and in obedience to God, to forgive the person involved in the hurt. Begin steps to reconcile with the person without any move on their part to correct their wrong-doing. This last step may be impossible if the person who hurt you is already dead, but don't worry, the forgiveness is complete as long as you're reconciled in your mind and heart.

David Seamands, a Methodist minister who teaches pastoral counseling at Asbury Theological Seminary in Wilmore, Ky., says, "Forgiving is often a one-way street. Even when the people who hurt you are still active in your life, it is not always possible to confront them with your decision to forgive.

"In cases of sexual trauma, it is not always the wisest thing in the world to go back to the abuser and tell him you forgive him. His defenses are up, and he may just throw the guilt back on you," Seamands said. (ibid)

The Inverness Lady

After service one Monday night a lady approached Carol in tears and told her of the emotional and spiritual pain she had been in for several years.

"Tonight," she said, "the depression was unbearable and I told my husband there was no changing my mind, I was going to take my own life. He convinced me to take a ride in the truck with him and think it over. He had talked me out of suicide several times before but tonight living was unthinkable.

"At one time I had been a regular telephone counselor at one of the largest national television ministries, but so much had happened since then that an incurable ache had replaced my joy of serving Jesus.

"As we were driving around we passed by the church and saw a meeting was in progress. We decided to go in and see what it was about and you were talking about people who were fighting depression and suicidal tendencies. You were speaking to me!

"The Holy Spirit spoke to me and for the first time I realized I was fighting a real enemy called a spirit of heaviness found in Isaiah 61:3.

"I prayed with you and felt such a spiritual release as peace flooded over my whole being. Thank God you were there tonight! I believe God has set me free and I know I can find my place in God's work again."

Spirit of Whoredoms 22

Being critical is accusing, judging or questioning the motives of others. Revelation 12:10 says that Satan is the accuser of the brethren. *"...for the accuser of our brethren is cast down, which accused them before our God day and night."*

When we accuse, question or criticize a brother in Christ, we are actually siding with the enemy. A lying spirit can use that to open up a door the devil can take advantage of to neutralize us spiritually. Only God knows the intents of man's heart and therefore He is the only One who can truly judge what is going on in the hearts of others. Also, judging people is a sin. *"Judge not, that ye be not judged."* (Matthew 7:1) Paul tells us how to direct our thoughts in Philippians 4:8, *"Finally, brethren, whatsoever things are true, whatsoever things are honest, whatsoever things are just, whatsoever things are pure, whatsoever things are lovely, whatsoever things are of good report; if there be any virtue, and if there be any praise, think on these things."*

QUESTION: "Why can't I overcome a critical spirit? I have been through deliverance."

There is a lack of knowledge here about the responsibility this person has in addition to being delivered. Deliverance is not the cure-all—it is just getting free from the devil's deception and resulting problems so this Christian can now do what he/she **should have been doing in the first place to stay free from a critical spirit**.

He/she must discipline their mind so that each time they are tempted to be critical they will note it, and choose **not to be** critical by the Power of the Holy Spirit. They must get into God's Word and have a working knowledge of the scriptures they need to reject the devil's temptation in this area of their life so they can stay free. They must be filled with the Holy Spirit so they have the Power they need to not only be free from a critical spirit, but to be the person God wants them to be.

It doesn't just come automatically. He/she has to establish a track record by living a disciplined life of obedience to God and His Word over a period of time until a habit pattern is developed that is normal and wholesome.

This advice will basicly serve for any area of breakdown in our spiritual life. Just change the "critical spirit problem" to your problem and follow the above steps because sin is sin. It may have different symptoms, but it is still the same old sin that must be dealt with in the same way God's Word has laid out for us.

Don't be discouraged just because a button can't be pushed that does it instantly. It took time to get where you are and it will require time for you to become what you would like to be in your heart. But the very fact that you desire to be different is a great sign that you are on your way already!

QUESTION: "What can I do about a husband who abuses me?"

God has given us all the Power we need to defeat the devil in our life. Your husband is allowing the devil to use him in this way, so you are going to have to stop the devil in the spirit realm. Pay particular attention to chapters 3, 25 and 26 in this book.

When you realize that your husband is yielding to the devil for whatever reason, it will help you realize that his attacks aren't necessarily personal—he is just following orders—he is under deception. When the deception is taken away, he will act different. So you must bind the devil in the area that he is deceiving your husband and then loose or come into agreement with what the Holy Spirit wants to accomplish, which is the salvation of your husband. So do this whenever the Holy Spirit leads you to do it because your husband is opening up the doors all the time.

Then, be careful to follow the Holy Spirit's direction. A lady who attended our seminar had a similar problem. One day her husband began choking her. In a loud voice she commanded, "I bind you spirit, and she named the spirit that was deceiving her husband, in the Name of Jesus."

Her husband immediately looked shocked, stopped choking her, backed up and never tried it again.

This approach isn't recommend for every situation unless the Holy Spirit rises up in your spirit with authority and power and you find it flowing out almost automatically. But whether the change takes place quickly or over a period of time, the Power of God is greater than the power of the devil, so be faithful to do your part and God will be faithful to do His.

QUESTION: "How can fasting help us?"

It subjects the physical body to spiritual discipline and weakens its carnal voice. Our bodies are quite determined to rule over our spirit and souls, therefore, we have to decide that we will put our bodies in submission to the Word of God and rule over it. When our flesh is in subjection, it is much easier to hear the voice of the Holy Spirit who lives within us.

QUESTION: "How do I 'shut doors' in my life?"

Shutting a door usually involves repentance. We have done something that displeases God because we have disobeyed His Word when we believed the deception of the devil or yielded to the lust of our flesh and sinned.

(1) We ask God to forgive us of the jealousy, fear, lying, occult, infidelity, pride or whatever the Holy Spirit has convicted us of doing.

(2) We bind the devil and the spirit he has used to hook or trick us and command it to get out of our life and stay out in the Name of Jesus.

(3) We loose or allow the Holy Spirit to work in our life with complete freedom so that we can please God in every part of our life.

We use the free will that God has given us to **reject** the devil's plan for our life and **accept** God's plan.

As long as we don't get back into the sin and deception of the devil, the door remains closed. We don't have to keep binding and binding—we just remind the devil that we aren't falling for his tricks anymore and thank the Holy Spirit for delivering us from the tricks of the devil. We **chose** to follow God's Will for every part of our life. Some people do not understand this and get into bondage to "binding." **The door stays shut as long as we don't allow it to open again by choosing to sin.**

(4) If your old lifestyle has contributed to your weakness to deception in a certain area, **it is necessary to change that lifestyle with the help of the Holy Spirit.** Don't go back to the activities or friends or practices that got you into trouble in the first place. If the person is a husband or wife, pray for them and do spiritual warfare on their behalf. Bind the strongman that deceives them and loose the Holy Spirit to convict them of sin and then pray that the Lord of Harvest will send out laborers that they respect and listen to, so they will accept Christ as their Savior.(Matthew 9:38, Luke 10:2) It will require that you bind the strongman each time the Holy Spirit brings them to your attention because they are continually opening the doors to the devil.

If you do your part, God will do His. It may not happen as quickly as you would prefer, but it will happen if you are faithful and believe God more than what you see and hear physically. It is true that you can't make them get saved, but you can make it a lot easier for them to finally see the light by limiting the effect of evil in their life in the spirit realm.

Your Ears Are Your Spiritual Mouth

(5) **It is necessary to build up your spiritual defense system so you aren't tricked by the devil anymore.** You do that by listening to God's Word. *"So then faith cometh by hearing, and hearing by the word of God."* (Romans 10:17) Your ears become your "spiritual mouth," so to speak, and the spiritual food (God's Word) enters your ears and goes down to your heart or spirit to give you spiritual nourishment which then becomes spiritual strength and wisdom. Read your Bible out loud when it is possible. Listen to the preaching of the Word of God. **Make sure** that the preaching is truly what the Bible says by checking it out in your Bible. Remember, **"...greater is he that is in you, than he that is in the world."**

Spirit of Infirmity 23

QUESTION: "How can you be so sure it is God's Will to heal everyone?"

We are so thankful for the life and ministry God has given us. We spent 20 years as missionaries to Latin America, where we were involved in open-air crusades that resulted in the birth of large, new churches. During that time we saw the demonstration of the Power of God like we had never seen it before. People were saved by the thousands, healings took place from every kind of disease we had ever heard of and deliverances from demonic power were normal whenever we were confronted by the devil. We are absolutely convinced that **what** God's Word promises will happen, if we believe, meet the conditions God demands and receive by faith what God promises us.

The reason we know it is God's Will to heal everyone is because **He has already done it!** The work of Redemption is complete— there is nothing more God can do to make us whole—body, soul and spirit. Peter shows that healing is part of the Atonement when he says, "*Who his own self bare our sins in his own body on the tree, that we, being dead to sins, should live unto righteousness: by whose stripes ye were healed.*" (I Peter 2:24) How can we **not** be healed when the Bible says that we **were** healed?

Even in the Old Testament we see the confirmation of this declaration, "*Who forgiveth all thine iniquities;*" "ALL" in percentage means 100% of our sins have already been forgiven and paid for on the cross by the sacrifice of Jesus. I don't believe any true Christian would dispute that statement. Yet, when we come to the second part of the same verse, there are all kinds of controversy, "*...who healeth all thy diseases;*" (Psalms 103:3) How can Christians believe that

100% of our sins have already been forgiven and not believe that 100% of our diseases have already been healed? How can ministers tell their people that sometimes God allows them to stay sick so they can learn something from it? If that's true they should also teach their people that sometimes God tells sinners, "I think you need to sin more so you can learn something from the sin." They can't teach that because they know it is not true—God is, "*...not willing that any should perish, but that **all** should come to repentance.*" (II Peter 3:9) Neither is it true that God hasn't provided healing for humanity.

We choose to accept Christ as our Savior and we must choose to be healed. Because Salvation and healing are accomplished works, we have to personally come to Christ and **accept** what He has done for us on a personal basis. Many people do not meet God's requirements to be saved, so as much as God wants them to receive salvation, they remain unsaved because God will not violate man's will.

I've heard people say, "Everything that happens in my life is because it is God's Will for it to happen." But is it God's will for them to sin? No, and neither is it God's will for them to be sick. Many times the reason Christians are not healed is because there has been a breakdown somewhere in their knowledge of what God's Will is about healing.

God cannot be used as our cop-out. In this time of no-fault divorce, no-fault accidents no-fault violent actions because it is supposedly society's fault, we must not let that kind of thinking spill over into the responsibilities we have in this matter of receiving healing and all the other things God has promised us.

The truth is that it doesn't matter whether everyone believes it or not, the Bible confirms that it is so and those who realize that it is available, believe it, meet the conditions God has specified and receive it, are the ones who experience the healing that God has made freely available to them.

The incredible fact is that the traditions, teachings and prejudices of men and denominations have robbed millions of Christians of this tremendous blessing from God. I have talked with people who came from such backgrounds and they said that when they read the Bible, the words in those particular passages just didn't seem to register in their thought processes. A revelation of God's Word had to be experienced and, all at once, they saw it! Then they wondered why they had been blind to it for so long. The list of areas this phenomenon occurs in not only includes healing, but the Baptism of the Holy Spirit with the evidence of speaking in an unknown language, faith, protection, the casting out of demons and many other legitimate things which Jesus put His stamp-of-approval upon while on this earth. In these last days the blindfolds are coming off because there is a world full of people who are looking for the reality of the Power of God in their lives and we are the ones God has chosen to reach them!

Sin Isn't Always The Cause

We want to be clear about the fact that it is **not** our belief that **every** time a Christian gets sick it is because he has sinned or left a door open in his life. No, the human race has been tainted by Sin and sickness is a resulting evidence of the degenerating process of dying that automatically takes place in the bodies of every member of the human race. **But** that doesn't obligate a child of God to continue suffering the results of Sin in his/her body. Jesus took the stripes on His back that gives us the right to reject, rebuke and bind the spirit of infirmity so that we do not have to suffer the results of Sin any longer. Jesus has delivered us from the curse of Sin. *"Christ hath redeemed us from the curse of the law, being made a curse for us: for it is written, Cursed is every one that hangeth on a tree: That the blessing of Abraham might come to the Gentiles through Jesus Christ; that we might receive the promise of the Spirit through faith."* (Galatians 3:13) He paid for our freedom from sickness and now it is up to us to receive our birthright as a child of God by faith in His Promises. We don't have to live like a sinner lives and we don't have to die like a sinner either. *"For the law of the Spirit of life in Christ Jesus hath made me free from the law of sin and death."* (Romans 8:2)

On the mission field we saw what happens when people are saved and do not have prejudices—they just believe what they are shown in the Bible. The sky is the limit! In fact, before long we had a difficult time keeping up with them, which was just fine because we needed to stretch out our belief system too.

The Boy With No Ear!

Miguelito was a good example. On the second night of the first crusade we had in San Jose, Costa Rica with the Richard Jefferys, we saw an incredible miracle take place, among hundreds of others. This eight-year-old boy had been born without an ear on one side of his head—no eardrum, no ear canal, just a small part of the outer ear. **After prayer he could hear perfectly out of the side of his head that had no ear!** He still didn't have the necessary organ to hear— every word he heard and still continues to hear is a miracle of faith.

Before prayer he had to sit in the front row in class at school and turn his head so that his good ear was more in line with the teacher so he could hear what was said. The next day, after attending the Crusade, he sat in the back row to show what God had done.

A medical doctor who didn't believe in miracles came to the crusade to examine Miguelito. When he realized the miracle that had taken place he began attending the crusade.

Miguel didn't understand a word of English, but he could repeat English words perfectly with his good ear plugged in a variety of ways to show it wasn't a trick. I never heard him ever make a mistake repeating words.

When the Jefferys left and I was leading the crusade, I remember backing off the platform numbers of times and slowly walking half a block away, repeating words in a loud voice to Miguel, and he would repeat them back perfectly, without hesitation. I would end up going across a busy street, with buses and trucks roaring by, standing in the dark, where there was no possibility he could read my lips which he did not know how to do anyhow, speaking any word in Spanish or in English that came into my head and he heard them all and repeated them into the microphone. One pastor from the U.S. was standing beside Miguel while I did this and he told me later, "I have two good ears and I could barely hear you when you got across the street."

We demonstrated this miracle on our television programs, along with many, many other miracles, to show the Power of God to the citizens of Costa Rica and that miracle was probably one of the major ones God used to shake the country and begin a tremendous revival that is still sweeping across the country of Costa Rica today.

20 Years Bent Over Double

A miracle in the first crusade in Managua, Nicaragua was almost an exact duplicate of the scripture in Luke 13:11-13 that we use in our first Strongman book to show one of the places the spirit of infirmity is mentioned by name in the Bible. In Jesus' day the lady had been bent doubled for 18 years and had not been able to straighten up in all that time. For the lady in Managua, Nicaragua it had been 20 years.

I'll never forget that night—I can still see her coming out of the shadows onto the crusade lot as I stood on the platform waiting for the service to start. She was probably 50-55 years-old. I had never even seen such a condition before. But at the conclusion of the service she was completely delivered and walked home as straight as any other person!

Healed Of Cancer

Maria de Arrieta was listening to our daily radio broadcast in San Jose, Costa Rica one day. She knew she was dying. The doctors had already operated twice and they offered little hope that it would help this time. The cancer had slowly developed in her mouth and face since she was thirteen years old before it reached the rapidly developing, fatal stage.

I'll let her tell the rest of the story in her own words. "After the doctors began the last treatments available, I was sure I would never return to my family again so I sat down at the table to compose my last letter to them.

"The pain had been one long nightmare for the past few months. I was continually hungry because it hurt my head to drink even a cup of coffee. My four children disturbed me when they came home from school because even the slightest movement was agonizing.

"As I began writing the letter your radio program came on the air. I said to myself, 'This is my last opportunity to be healed.' I was desperate as I listened attentively to the message of faith. I was a dead woman if I didn't receive a miracle from God!

"At the end of the program I put the part of my face that was affected by the cancer close to the radio and prayed with you and the other pastors. Instantly, the pain left me and I knew I had been healed. The next day I began eating every three hours and by the second day I was beginning to feel normal.

"I also had suffered from heart trouble for three years, but the cancer had been so much worse that I hadn't paid too much attention to my heart condition before receiving healing from cancer.

"Later I went back to the doctor to be examined to prove God had done a miracle in my body. The doctor took three sets of X rays and became quite agitated because he thought the technicians were making mistakes. Finally he had to admit that the cancerous lumps that had been growing larger every day had completely disappeared and that I was free from cancer. Not only that, but they found that the damage to my heart had been healed also. Today I am really a new creature in Christ Jesus, both physically and spiritually!"

It got to the point that I had to factor in extra time whenever I went downtown because people would stop me for prayer, advice or counseling because they had seen us on television or heard the radio programs. The incident that follows is comical now, but at the time it got my attention quite effectively.

A Miracle I Was Happy To Hear About!

I was hurrying to my next appointment in downtown San Jose, Costa Rica when, without thinking, I jaywalked across a busy main street. I hadn't noticed the stern-looking policeman standing on the corner, but he noticed me. He waved me over with that look that says, "You've had it buddy!" The thought flashed through my mind as I walked over to him, "They must have passed a law against jaywalking yesterday and I'm the first one in Costa Rica to get a ticket."

With dark thoughts swirling through my head I arrived at where the policeman stood, eying me every step of the way. I was ready to plead "habeas corpus" all the way to the Supreme Court.

Just as I opened my mouth to begin my defense the policeman leaned over and said, "Brother Jerry, I just had to tell you that God has healed my wife. She has suffered terribly from stomach ulcers. She could hardly eat anything, but now she's completely healed after praying with you on your television program and in the Crusade."

I successfully curbed my desire to break out into slightly hysterical laughter and then began rejoicing with the policeman over the miracle God had preformed in his wife. All her neighbors knew about her condition and it created quite a sensation in her neighborhood when she was healed so dramatically.

The Wheel-Bed Man

The last healing miracle we want to mention illustrates that sometimes it requires time for some people to finally act on their faith in God's Word to receive healing. It took place in Minus, Uruguay, South America and it was told to me by Richard Jeffery.

"In the first Minas Crusade the wife of a cripple brought her husband to the services in a home-made wheel chair. For nearly 20 years this man had been a hopeless cripple and the wheel chair, or actually a wheel-bed, had been made to accommodate his condition. The man's back had been locked by arthritis which made it impossible for him to bend over so the wheel-bed was on a slant for him to lie on. The rest of his body that wasn't frozen in place by arthritis shook constantly with Parkinson's disease. As a result, he suffered terrible pain as one disease acted as an irritant to the other. He was in constant motion and had been that way for many years. The only time he calmed down at all was when he slept.

"When they began attending the crusade, they heard me say what I tell everyone wherever I have crusades: 'If you will be faithful to be in the services night after night to hear the Word of God and accept the Lord as your Savior, I can promise you by the authority of God's Word that He will heal your body.'

"They attended the crusade for months and every night they heard me make that same declaration and every night he left in the same painful condition. Every night he would lie in the audience, shaking and hurting, while hundreds of other people were being healed.

"We had to return to the U.S. to rest after many months in the Crusade and I left it in the hands of a pastor who continued on with the services.

"The following year we returned once again. In the first service we had, the wife wheeled her crippled husband into the service just like she had done for months, seven months previously.

"I asked the pastor privately if this couple had been attending the services in our absence and he assured me that they had been very faithful. The devil didn't miss the opportunity to point out to me that God's Word wasn't going to work this time for the crippled man.

"Satan would mock me as I told the people night after night that if they would be faithful to hear God's Word they would receive the faith they needed to be healed. He would say, 'But look at that crippled man. He's been faithful to be in the services almost a year now and he is exactly the same as when he started.'

"I'd rebuke the devil in the Name of Jesus and inform him that God cannot lie, that God had already healed the man when Jesus took the stripes on His back and to be quiet.

"The time came for us to have a water baptismal service and I began instructing the people about the need to follow the Lord in this act. Of course, the crippled man's wife informed me that her husband wanted to be baptised in water and that I was the one he wanted to do it.

"It is awful to confess, but I really didn't want to baptize him. How do you baptize someone like that? I thought maybe we could tie him onto the contraption and turn the whole thing upside down and then flip it back over, but we were just as liable to drown him as not.

"The morning of the baptismal we had all the people meet at the church where we formed a procession and marched down to the river where the event would take place. Just as we were leaving the church, they rolled the crippled man up on his wheel-bed.

"There were probably 800 people who were going to be baptized so it made quite a parade as we marched through town. I was taking pictures of the people as they marched by, but I would stop my 16 mm camera whenever the crippled man came by. I had come to the point within myself that I thought that because of the man's pitiful condition he was somehow incapable of opening up his heart to receive the faith he needed to receive his healing. It was a good lesson for me in how the devil can deceive us into believing there are exceptions to God's Word. I had arrived at my conclusion from a logical point of view and logic has nothing to do with the life of faith—faith is not logical in the natural, physical realm.

"When we arrived at the river, those who were going to be baptized crossed over to the far side and the spectators stayed on the city-side of the river. Four of us were doing the baptizing and I still hadn't figured out how we were going to baptize the crippled man.

"I was facing the spectators as I baptized when a great shout went up from that side of the river. Somehow they had gotten the wheel-bed with the crippled man over to the far side of the river with the rest of the baptismal candidates. The bank was rather steep and not a safe place for him to be, but I don't think wild horses could have kept him from that baptismal service.

"I looked up and all the spectators were pointing over behind me and shouting, 'Glory to God, hallelujah!' When I looked back over my shoulder the crippled man was out of his wheel-bed, walking and running around on the bank of the river! He was a little unsteady at first, but no one was helping him either. As soon as he calmed down a little, he ran down to the water and I baptized him without having to worry about the wheel-bed!"

That man's testimony points up the fact that **as long as there is life, there is hope!** In spiritual warfare, as long as there is life the battle is never over. Keep on believing God's Word more than anything else because God's Word outweighs any other circumstances no matter how bad they may appear.

How To Keep Your Healing

It is very important to understand that we must **maintain our healing, or any other victory we have received from the Lord, by believing Gods' Word more than anything else**. One of the enemy's tricks is to steal what God has given us. That is why Christians sometimes lose their healing or salvation or anything else God has given them. You can always be sure the devil will return to see if your spiritual defenses are adequate to protect all that God has given you. It may be a week or a month or a year or five years, but he will eventually be back and you must have your shield of faith and sword of the Spirit ready to drive him off again. The symptoms will return, the fear will appear again, the finances will fall off, the marriage problems will return to make you think that God really didn't do what you thought He did when you received it originally.

What do you do about it? The same thing you did at the beginning. State what God says in His Word, thank Him for giving it to you and bind the lying devil in the Name of Jesus who is trying to rob you. Stay with it until he backs off and leaves you alone which he **has to**

do. If you have gotten into sin or doubt or unhealthy spiritual practices, repent of them as quickly as possible. In fact, that is probably the open door which has given the devil the opportunity to attempt this take-back what God gave you. The just **live** by faith. When you get out of faith you are vulnerable to the devil's traps and tricks. It isn't intelligent to leave yourself open like that!

Is There A Death Wish?

Because the subject of "why Christians have difficulty receiving healing" is so difficult for many to understand, it is necessary to talk about things that we would really prefer not mentioning. But because it may help some people understand the situation better, we'll mention another reason we have found that helps explain why some Christians die, despite the fact that everyone appears to have done what God's Word commands them to do.

The truth is that some Christians have a death wish or really prefer to die and be with the Lord rather than continue living on this earth for whatever reason they may have. Paul admits that this thought crossed his mind. *"For I am in a strait betwixt two, having a desire to depart, and be with Christ; which is far better; Nevertheless to abide in the flesh is more needful to you."* (Philippians 1:23,24)

We have seen cases when Christians have chosen to die rather than continue living, for instance, with an unsatisfactory marriage partner. Because of their religious beliefs they feel they cannot divorce their partner, who shows no sign of changing his/her lifestyle that is continually abrasive to them. They are apparently unaware of the possibilities of spiritual warfare as a means of changing the situation, so they just check out.

Or the individual has lived a full life and is tired of putting up with the problems of physical existence. Heaven looks better to them every day so they decide to die. Understand that we are not talking about suicide here. The Bible does tell us we have to **choose** life if we desire to live. *"I call heaven and earth to record this day against you, that I have set before you life and death, blessing and cursing: therefore choose life, that both thou and thy seed may live."* (Deuteronomy 30:19)

It is important to ascertain whether the person truly wants to live. Don't just assume they want what your desires are. In some cases, when the individual has lived a full life and has passed the amount of years that God has promised them and wants to go to be with Him, it may be more merciful for the family to release them to the Lord and let them go where they want to be—with the Lord. Be sure they are not making this decision because the devil has deceived them into cutting their life short, but because God has revealed to them that it is time for them to come home to be with Him.

Hidden Desires To Be Sick

There are also people who enjoy being sick. Doctors Marc D. Feldman and Charles V. Ford have written a book called, "Patient or Pretender: Inside the Strange World of Factitious Disorders," that tells about these people.

"People with factitious disorders are not hypochondriacs, who think they are sick but are not. Nor are they malingerers, who fake illness to get money or get out of work. Instead, Feldman says, 'These are people who fake illness or even induce disease with the goal of assuming the patient role. They get some emotional satisfaction out of being sick.'

"People with the most extreme patterns of faked illness rarely are capable of normal lives. In such cases—dubbed Munchausen syndrome, after a famous storytelling duke—people make a career out of faked illness. They usually are men and often are hostile to society, with no concern for the harm they cause others.

"A related syndrome, Munchausen by proxy, usually involves women who induce illness in their children to get attention for themselves." (USA Today, 12/20/93, page 4D)

Of course, looking at these cases in the light of God's Word, the individuals involved need deliverance not only from the spirit of infirmity but also a lying spirit and spirit of bondage, among other things. But this does clarify the fact that just because Christians do not get healed does not mean God's Word is not true—there are many different reasons why some Christians have difficulty receiving healing.

Missionary-Evangelist, Franklin Burns told us of a man in a wheelchair he prayed for. The man half rose up in his wheelchair and sat back down with the comment, "I can't get up—I'll lose my disability pension."

This doesn't infer that all people in wheelchairs think like that, but this one did.

Consequently, **we cannot form our doctrine on healing according to what happens to other people**. It doesn't matter if every Christian in the world dies in a car accident or of cancer, we still believe that it is God's Will to heal and protect us because His Word is our ultimate point of reference in the matter. "...*let God be true, but every man a liar.*" (Romans 3:4)

When the promise of God does not happen in our life, we do not blame God—we examine our life and faith to make sure we are not the cause. After asking the Holy Spirit to reveal any failure in our life that might be blocking the healing, we can assume the devil is trying to include us in the Curse of Sin if the Holy Spirit has not convicted us of any sin or failure to believe or receive the healing. Then it is a matter of commanding the devil to take his sickness and go because he has no right to put it on us.

It is easier to stand against the devil when he has no right to do what he is doing, than when we have opened a door to him in our life. For instance, it is easier to run a thief off your property with a 12 gauge shotgun, who is trying to steal your furniture, than it is to deal with the sheriff when he comes with a written document that gives him the right to repossess your furniture because you haven't made the payments. The sheriff has a right to take the furniture because you left an opening, but the thief has absolutely no right to take your furniture if your house is locked up.

So keep those doors shut!

QUESTION: "If we believe in healing, why do we accept headaches, wearing glasses, etc.?"

Why indeed? We've been programmed to do so by the society we live in. There's nothing wrong with wearing glasses, but we can also believe God can give us perfect eyesight. He provided healing for whatever we need. It is up to us to build up the faith we need to receive it by hearing God's Word. "*So then faith cometh by hearing, and hearing by the word of God.*" (Romans 10:17) So reach out and believe.

QUESTION: "Can demons really prosper or heal people?"

Demons cannot heal people. They afflict people. There are times when they can withdraw their affliction and it seems like people are healed. They usually do it just to get their attention or allegiance and then backhandedly put something worse on them. (See *Strongman's His Name...What's His Game?* manual, page 31.)

This world's system is run by Satan. He is the god of this world. He can make people prosper under his system, but he always extracts a price for everything he does. It may be alcoholism, divorce, sickness, mental illness, or estrangement from children, but he will collect his dues either through that person or his descendants. Someone always pays a handsome price for getting wealth from the devil.

God helps His people prosper in spite of this world's system and He only asks that we give back 10% to the work of God as tithe and then offerings on top of that and He will rebuke the devourer on our behalf. *"And I will rebuke the devourer for your sakes, and he shall not destroy the fruits of your ground; neither shall your vine cast her fruit before the time in the field, saith the Lord of hosts."* (Malachi 3:11)

Our Daughter's Healing

Our youngest daughter, Debbie, was born prematurely and had hyperactive problems. Her attention span was very short and she couldn't contrate properly in school so that her school work suffered as a result.

When Carol realized what was happening, she began praying over Debbie at night while she slept. She would put her hand over Debbie's head and release the Power of the Holy Spirit. Within a week Debbie had improved so drastically that her teacher called and asked what kind of program was being used to help her. She had promoted Debbie several levels during one week because her reading abilities had improved so much.

In the case of adults or teen-agers, pray over their pillow while they are at work, etc. Command the devil that he must withdraw his forces while the person sleeps and ask the Holy Spirit to work as their head rests on the pillow. That pillow is an anointed place as you lay hands on it and interceed for them in the Spirit.

Dumb & Deaf Spirit 24

QUESTION: "How did Jesus do spiritual warfare?"

Mark 9:17-27:*17.*"*And one of the multitude answered and said, Master, I have brought unto thee my son, which hath a dumb spirit;*
8.   And wheresoever he taketh him, he teareth him: and he foameth, and gnasheth with his teeth, and pineth away: and I spake to thy disciples that they should cast him out; and they could not.
19.   He answereth him, and said, O faithless generation, how long shall I be with you? how long shall I suffer you? bring him unto me.
20.   And they brought him unto him: and when he saw him, straightway the spirit tare him; and he fell on the ground, and wallowed foaming.
21.   And he asked his father, How long is it ago since this came unto him? And he said, Of a child.
22.   And ofttimes it hath cast him into the fire, and into the waters, to destroy him: but if thou canst do any thing, have compassion on us, and help us.
23.   Jesus said unto him, If thou canst believe, all things are possible to him that believeth.
24.   And straightway the father of the child cried out, and said with tears, Lord, I believe; help thou mine unbelief.
25.   When Jesus saw that the people came running together, he rebuked the foul spirit, saying unto him, Thou dumb and deaf spirit, I charge thee, come out of him, and enter no more into him.
26.   And the spirit cried, and rent him sore, and came out of him: and he was as one dead; insomuch that many said, He's dead.
27.   But Jesus took him by the hand, and lifted him up; and he arose."

This incident concerning a boy with many demonic manifestations illustrates the fact that it is not necessary to cast out every minor spirit, one by one, as many do today.

As we have mentioned a number of times, it is important to follow how Jesus did spiritual warfare and this is a prime example.

There were many symptoms or **minor** spirits that can be identified in this case from just a casual look at the demonic manifestations. A spirit of suicide caused the boy to attempt to kill himself in fire and water. We believe a spirit of suicide exists, but it is a minor spirit under the leadership of the dumb and deaf spirit (It can also be under the control of a spirit of heaviness or a spirit of death). There were mental symptoms which manifested themselves as actions that are not normal in a healthy child. We believe a spirit of insanity exists, but it is also a minor spirit under the leadership of the dumb and deaf spirit.

Jesus didn't cast out a spirit of suicide or a spirit of insanity. He looked into the spirit world and saw that the dominate spirit, or strongman, was a dumb and deaf spirit. **When He cast the dumb and deaf spirit out—all the minor spirits left with it.** Even in physical warfare, when the General surrenders, all the troops under his command surrender with him. In the spirit world the minor spirits know that if the stronger demon has been bound and cast out, they don't stand a chance because they are weaker than it and so **they must leave with the strongman.**

This cuts the whole process down to a minimum. Instead of working His way up from the bottom, He started at the top. How long did it take Jesus to cast the demons out? Was it a long, drawn-out procedure? No, when He "nailed" the strongman the battle was over!

That is the reason we feel it is important to stick to what the Bible calls a spirit. We realize there are all kinds of other minor spirits out there, but why deal with underlings? Why take up space in our memory by memorizing long lists of minor demons? We can keep it down to a minimum with just the 16 strongmen mentioned by name in the Bible.

Notice something else here, Jesus spent time asking the boy's father some questions about the boy. He wasn't just making conversation. Part of the boys problems involved his father's lack of faith.

When Jesus straightened that out, the deliverance took place.

And finally, Jesus didn't allow the deliverance to turn into a circus. When He saw the crowd of people running toward them to see the action, He quickly dispatched the strongman and it was all over. I'm afraid Jesus would have been a great disappointment for many people today who throng to deliverance services to see evangelists interact with demons.

It is important to follow the example of Jesus!

QUESTION: "How does God teach His children?"

The way He prefers is by His Holy Spirit, out of His Word. That is the normal way.

People will testify that if they hadn't gotten into a mess, they would never have learned what they learned, but that's not true. God wanted to teach them what they learned **before** they got into the mess, without having to go through the mess. But because they didn't listen to God and went their own way, they got into the mess. When they cried out to God for help, God helped them. But they learned something God wanted to teach them out of His Word, by His Holy Spirit without having to go through the mess. Then to top it off, they blame **God** for the mess because that makes them sound so spiritual!

A fellow told me one time, "I just know God caused me to be in a car wreck to teach me what I needed to know, because when I was in the hospital, after the wreck, I had so much time to pray and read my Bible. My, I learned so much. I know if it hadn't been for the car wreck, I would never have learned all that I learned."

I thought to myself, "He didn't have to be in a car wreck just to be able to read the Bible and pray—He could have done that anytime he wanted to."

We must be careful not to blame God for our shortcomings. Just as we would rather our children would learn life's lessons without having to go through what we went through, God wants to save us from the hidden pitfalls too.

QUESTION: "Are demon-possessed children under the age of accountability automatically lost and will they go to hell?"

We know God has mercy and grace, but only eternity will determine His decisions. My personal opinion would be that because they are children without any understanding, God will not hold them responsible for their condition. The Bible says that children have angels that watch over them so we know that God cares for them and will always treat them with loving care.

QUESTION: "Are all mentally ill people demon possessed?"

No. There are chemical imbalances, birth defects, accidents, etc. that can also cause mental problems. The good news is that God has provided healing for all these problems also. Those who are mentally ill because of demonic activity can find restoration through deliverance if they so choose.

QUESTION: "Are words that we speak really important?"

Yes, other wise the Bible would not warn us over and over again to choose our words carefully. Read the following example:

Our missionary-evangelist friend visited with his sister last year and observed the new large screen television she had just bought. His sister said to him, "Do you know why I bought it? Because next winter when we all get sick and the kids get colds, flu and everything, we'll be ready for it. We can just sit in front of the T.V. and get over it."

Sure enough. It happened just like she said. Our friend would call her on the phone and she would say, "Don't come over here because we've all got fevers."

"The sad thing is," our friend said, "her husband died of cancer during this last year also."

"The words of a man's mouth are as deep waters..." (Proverbs 18:4)

"A man's belly shall be satisfied with the fruit of his mouth; and with the increase of his lips shall he be filled. Death and life are in the power of the tongue: and they that love it shall eat the fruit thereof." (Proverbs 18:20-21)

"But I say unto you, That every idle word that men shall speak, they shall give account thereof in the day of judgment. For by thy words thou shalt be justified, and by thy words thou shalt be condemned." (Matthew 12:36-37)

Spirit of Bondage 25

QUESTION: "Can you bind spirits for others?

Yes, but it is only for a season that the enemy will depart from them or draw back his symptoms. After Jesus resisted the devil during his wilderness temptation, Satan "departed from him for a season."(KJV Luke 4:13) *"...he [temporarily] left Him [that is, stood off from Him] until another more opportune and favorable time."* (Amplified Bible Luke 4:13) We don't know how long a season lasts, but the Holy Spirit does, so when the Holy Spirit impresses you to pray again you will need to reinforce your stand on their behalf again. As soon as they become believers they should be taught to recognize areas of temptation or attack on their own so they can shut the doors and stop the deception of the devil once and for all.

QUESTION: "Can you bind when people don't cooperate?"

Only for a season and then they will willfully, out of ignorance or rebellion, open doors and let the enemy control their life again. For permanent relief, they need to cooperate completely by giving their lives to Christ and learning to resist the enemy for themselves.

QUESTION: "Should you tell people you are binding the devil?"

It generally does not serve any purpose to tell them you are binding spiritual enemies. Before they become a believer their spiritual understanding is dead. They wouldn't understand what you mean and it might only cause them to turn a deaf ear to the minister of the Word. *"But the natural, nonspiritual man does not accept or welcome or admit into his heart the gifts and teachings and revelations of the Spirit of God, for they are folly (meaningless nonsense) to him; and he is incapable of knowing them (of progressively recognizing, understanding, and becoming better acquainted with them) because they are spiritually discerned and estimated and appreciated."* (Amplified Bible I Corinthians 2:11,12)

QUESTION: "Must Christian keep binding the same spirits?

As a born-again believer we have a covenant standing with God. Jesus won the war over the devil and made an open show of him. *"And having spoiled principalities and powers, he made a show of them openly, triumphing over them in it."* (Colossians 2:15) Then He destroyed the works of the devil according to 1 John 3:8, *"For this purpose the Son of God was manifested, that he might destroy the works of the devil."* When we close the doors to the enemy and bind his works in the Name of Jesus it is an accomplished fact. We don't need to continue binding him; just remind him of it if you recognize him skulking around you again.

If you fall into sin and open up the door once more to the enemy, then repent and repeat the process of closing the door. It's very important that we continue to hear a good diet of the Word and consistently read the Word. It will build spiritual strength for each day and give us a desire to fellowship with the Lord through prayer.

Satan always tries to come back and retake the ground he once had. In any area of spiritual battle, we take the ground and then stand, praying in the Spirit to hold that ground. *"Praying always with all prayer and supplication in the Spirit, and watching thereunto with all perseverance and supplication for all saints;"* (Ephesians 6:18)

Too many times we win a victory and then forget to hold our ground, thus losing a healing, etc. When Satan tries to move in with old symptoms, immediately rebuke him and let him know he's still bound. *"Cast not away therefore your confidence, which hath great recompense of reward. For ye have need of patience, that after ye have done the will of God, ye might receive the promise."* (Hebrews 10:35,36)

QUESTION: "How often do you bind and loose for another person? Is it done just once or until you see the manifestation of the answer?"

Be persistent in binding and loosing as the Holy Spirit nudges you to pray for them until you see or hear of the results. You don't need to be in bondage to pray every day, just do it when the Holy Spirit reminds you of them.

"Let us draw near with a true heart in full assurance of faith, having our hearts sprinkled from an evil conscience, and our bodies washed with pure water. Let us hold fast the profession of our faith without wavering: (for he is faithful that promised;)" (Hebrews 10:22,23)

QUESTION: "Can a demon possessed person ask God for help?"

God has given each person a free-will so they are able to call out to him as they desire. Even the Gadarene demoniac came and fell at the feet of Jesus seeking help from the demons that possessed him. *"But when he saw Jesus afar off, he ran and worshiped him."* (Mark 5:6) *"When he saw Jesus he cried out, and fell down before him,"* (Luke 8:28)

We have seen many possessed people who have called out to God for deliverance and we have also seen those who refused, but it was an act of their own will. They made up their minds to accept or reject the freedom. Some people become so comfortable with the bondage that they don't want to give up the attention and the feeling of being different. It sounds sick but deception will do that to anyone who believes the lies of the devil. They feel the price is too high.

The Bible says that *"whosoever shall call upon the name of the Lord shall be saved."* If a demon-possessed person has a desire to be free, he can call on the Lord and be set free.

QUESTION: "Why don't I see results in my family? I have been binding spirits in their lives daily for the past 2 years and still I don't see anything happening. Why not?"

Even though we walk by faith and not by sight it is still encouraging to see some results. Sometimes people who are fighting God sense the Holy Spirit working on them and almost go out of their way to drown out His voice. They drink more, do more drugs, use viler language than ever before and generally give signals that things are getting worse instead of better.

Don't get weary in doing the right things or as Paul said, "faint not." When we bind the enemy he is bound in the spirit world and things are happening. Also it is very important to remember to loose the power of God to draw them to Christ and loose Truth so they begin to hear and see truth at every turn. Then as Ephesians 6 says, when we have done all we are to stand, praying in the Spirit. God is faithful, *"...he which hath begun a good work in you will perform it until the day of Jesus Christ."* (Philippians 1:6)

QUESTION: "Can we bind the spirits from a distance or do we have to be with the person for our prayers to be effective?"

There is no distance in prayer of any kind. Whether you are beside the person or 5,000 miles away, the prayer is carried out by the Holy Spirit and the hosts of heaven are set into motion by your binding and loosing according to the teaching of Jesus. *"And I give unto thee the keys of the kingdom of heaven: and whatsoever thou shalt bind on earth shall be bound in heaven: and whatsoever thou shalt loose on earth shall be loosed in heaven"* (Matthew 16:19) and, *"Verily I say unto you, Whatsoever ye shall bind on earth shall be bound in heaven: and whatsoever ye shall loose on earth shall be loosed in heaven."* (Matthew 18:18)

QUESTION: "Is drug and alcoholic addiction a disease?"

We have always been led to believe that disease is something that is spread by germs and viruses or inherited because of family weaknesses. But because drugs and alcohol abuse is so prevalent it has become more politically correct to call it a disease. Whether it is a spirit of infirmity or bondage, it is still the devil who is behind it and as such can be bound in the Name of Jesus. Whether it is sickness or bondage, when the devil is dealt with biblically the patient becomes well.

Teen Challenge has led the way in showing that when addicts get saved and filled with the Holy Spirit they successfully stay free a greater percentage of the time than in any type of government program.

One of our readers wrote us: "I don't see people problems anymore. I see the driving spirit causing them to act as they do. You can't get angry at folks in bondage—you can't hate a victim. I **do** get angry at the spirit causing the problem."

When the spirit is bound in the Name of Jesus according to God's Word, the people have an opportunity to accept Christ as their Savior and become the kind of person they should be.

QUESTION: "Should Christians drink alcoholic beverages?"

Absolutely not! Why should we take the chance of becoming hooked by a deception that has destroyed millions and millions of lives? True, some people appear to be able to control alcohol, but who knows what could happen if these same people are exposed to a stressful situation they are not able to cope with? Why give the devil an opportunity to open a door in our life that would not be available if we weren't already drinking occasional alcoholic drinks. Isn't it better to just not start? And if a person has started, wouldn't it make good sense to stop and get that door of temptation closed?

Spirit of Fear 26

QUESTION: "Can fear cause negative events in my life? Do I actually have control over catastrophes and disease to a certain extent by whether or not I fear them?"

Job reveals to us that, "...*the thing which I greatly feared is come upon me, and that which I was afraid of is come unto me.*" (Job 3:25)

I remember talking with a fellow minister some years ago who was in the final stages of cancer. He had been a strong, vital young man, but the ravages of cancer had taken their terrible toll on his body.

While we were conversing he revealed something I will never forget. "Jerry, the thing that I greatly feared has come upon me." A short time later he died. I believe that if I would have known then what I know now about fear, I could have helped him close the door to the spirits of fear and infirmity and he could have returned to health..

Natalie Wood was said by her close friends to have a lifelong fear of drowning in dark water. In the early morning hours she drowned in darkened waters around her yacht.

Film star, Linda Darnell, had a terrible fear of fire and died when the couch she was sleeping on caught fire, apparently from a lighted cigarette she had dropped.

Carole Lombard intensely feared flying and died in a plane crash.

Jayne Mansfield feared that her face would be disfigured. She was decapitated in a car accident.

Singer-actor Jack Cassidy had an overwhelming fear of fire and died when his apartment burned.

Sal Mineo spoke on many occasions of his fear of violence and was killed of multiple stab-wounds.

Comedian Freddie Prinze was extremely frightened of firearms, but took his own life with a gun.

According to the Hebrew writer, people who have an obsessive fear of death are in bondage to Satan and must be freed from his clutches before he accomplishes what he has set out to do in their life. For that reason Jesus came to deliver those, "...*who through fear of death were all their lifetime subject to bondage.*" (Hebrews 2:15)

QUESTION: "Can fear kill?"

Yes, fear can kill if we allow Satan to penetrate our spiritual defenses!

When we speak of fear we must understand that there is both a negative and a positive kind of fear.

The positive helps us preserve our life. We don't do dumb things like play football on a busy freeway because we know the terrible damage a speeding semi-truck can cause when it crushes the human body. So out of respect for the semi-truck, we play football in other places.

Positive fear could also be categorized as a "profound respect or reverence." For instance, "*the fear of the Lord is the beginning of wisdom:*" (Psalms 111:10) Because we have a deep respect for God, we obey His Word and give Him the place in our life that He deserves.

The negative kind of fear rips, tears, paralyzes and torments. It destroys our faith in God and His Word and opens us up to further harassment of the devil.

Paul tells us that, "...*God hath not given us the spirit of fear;*" (II Timothy 1:7) Negative fear is satanic in origin. The enemy uses it like a club to beat people into submission to his will, much as a bully terrorizes a weaker boy as he walks home from school.

The disciples suffered from this kind of fear as they cowered behind closed doors after Jesus was crucified. Not only had their dreams been terminated, along with their Teacher, but they feared they would also be killed. Jesus had taught them both in Word and deed for three years that fear was not something they had to accept, so it was not from a lack of knowledge that the disciples allowed themselves to be neutralized by fear behind closed doors.

Their major problem was that they really didn't believe that Jesus would back-up His Word at crunch time if they totally confided in His Promises. Jesus even asked them after calming the wind and the storm on the Sea of Galilee, *"He said to them, Why are you so timid and fearful? How is it that you have no faith (no firmly relying trust)?"* (Mark 4:40 Amplified Bible) And that is usually the root cause for fear in our own lives. For whatever reason, we don't believe God will keep His Word in our particular case for our particular problem.

But the fact is that God **does** keep His Word. *"Heaven and earth shall pass away, but my words shall not pass away."* (Matthew 24:35) *"...for I (God) will hasten my word to perform it."* (Jeremiah 1:12) *"...how much more shall your Father which is in heaven give good things to them that ask him?"* (Matthew 7:11) *"There is no fear in love; but perfect love casteth out fear."* (I John 4:18) Love involves trust. If we truly believe that God loves us, we will trust Him with our lives and know that we are absolutely safe if He says so.

QUESTION: "Do Christians have to suffer bad luck?"

What about people who have bad luck? Christians who are living according to God's Word and who believe and apply that Word to their life situations **do not have** either good luck or bad luck—they have faith in their Heavenly Father's ability to take care of them in any kind of situation. God says we stay alive by having faith in God, not in whether we are lucky or not. *"The just shall live by faith."* (Hab. 2:4, Rom. 1:17, Gal. 3:11, Heb.10:38) How can we believe that a God, who runs His Universe on a split second time-table, who knows how many hairs we have on our head and who knows where we are every second of our life, can't keep track of us and protect us according to His Word?

The first thing the devil tells us in a fearful circumstance is, "Think of all the good Christians who have been killed in terrible accidents. God didn't protect them. You aren't nearly as good a Christian as they were so you are probably the one God will allow to slip through His fingers."

Why Did My Mother Die In A Car Accident?

We had just finished giving our Strongman seminar in the church of some dear pastor friends and we were driving together to a restaurant to get something to eat. I teach on the spirit of fear the last night and I suppose the pastor's wife was still thinking about that when she asked me, "Why did my mother die in an automobile accident? She was a wonderful Christian woman."

This was not the first time I had heard a question like that and I answered her by asking a question which usually reveals the answer if the people are honest with themselves. I asked, "What was your mother's greatest fear?"

The pastor's wife responded in a shocked manner as she took a quick breath, "I never thought of that. My mother's greatest fear was to die in a car accident!"

Of course this does not mean that fear caused every Christian who has ever died in a car accident or any other kind of accident to be killed. But in this case the cause and effect was very suspicious and as far as I'm concerned if there is just a 5% possibility that fear can cause bad things to happen in our life, it is worth getting rid of the fear. Why allow fear in our life anyhow? But it is surprising how many Christians protect their right to be fearful!

Later, we learned that the mother of the pastor's wife had dreamed three times before it happened that there would be a terrible car accident. Another member of the family was also killed at the same time. I asked the pastor's wife what the dreams had produced in her mother. She testified that her mother had become even more fearful. The other person who died also gave strong indication that he sensed he was going to die soon.

The reason we can be sure this was a premonition from the devil, which helped open up a door in the mother's defenses so he could do what he wanted to her, is the fruit the dreams produced—a work of the devil—fear. This is not to say that the mother didn't go to be with the Lord when she died. Her faith in Jesus as her personal Savior was no doubt still strong, but she went to heaven on the devil's timetable and in a very traumatic way for her and her family.

If the dreams had been from God or through a Word of Knowledge of the Gifts of the Spirit the reaction would have been different. She would have recognized the warning for what it was, bound the devil in the Name of Jesus and broken the plans of the devil by speak ing and believing what God's Word says about her protection as a child of God. *"I will say of the Lord, He is my refuge and my fortress: my God; in him will I trust. Surely he shall deliver thee from the snare of the fowler, and from the noisome pestilence. He shall cover thee with his feathers, and under his wings shall thou trust: his truth shall be thy shield and buckler. Thou shalt not be afraid for the terror by night; nor for the arrow that flieth by day. Nor for the pestilence that walketh in darkness;* **nor for the destruction that wasteth at noonday***."* (Psalms 91:2-6)

She would have pleaded the protection of the Blood of Jesus and would have released or asked the Holy Spirit to protect them from harm. The sad truth is that she probably didn't know she had the right to do that. She probably didn't know that it was the devil who was deceiving her into opening the door to fear so hc could do to her what he couldn't have done if the door had been shut.

We have found that this is a common problem in our churches today. Instead of informing people to be on the lookout for this kind of deception of the devil, they are told everything under the sun but the truth to try to calm their grief, which only creates other problems. Now they are angry at God for taking their loved one from them in such a horrible manner. That makes it a double robbery—the loved one is gone and the family's relationship with God is damaged or even destroyed.

The pastor's wife was supposed to have gone on the trip with her mother, but the Holy Spirit spoke so forcefully, telling her not to go, that she refused to make the trip, in spite of strong pressure from her family. So the Holy Spirit was present in the situation, trying to save those who were involved from being swept away. But people who are in fear do not think correctly because their perception is clouded by the deception of the devil. He will tell them that it is their time to go and even convince them that it is God speaking to them if they are unaware of his tricks. *"Lest Satan should get an advantage of us: for we are not ignorant of his devices."* One of the abilities God gives us to combat fear, if we will listen to Him and believe His Promises, is a sound mind. (II Timothy 1:7)

The pastor's wife was not necessarily more spiritual than the other family members, she just listened to what the Holy Spirit probably spoke to all of them and obeyed God's voice instead of the devil's.

It is so easy to make a mistake at this point because the Holy Spirit usually speaks to us in a still small voice and the devil uses a PA system. For that reason we must know how to distinguish between what God says and what the devil says to us. For more information concerning what God does and does not do, please read chapter 5.

QUESTION: "Do ministers and missionaries battle fear?"

Both Carol and I had to learn how to dominate fear in our lives before we could accomplish anything of an eternal nature on the mission field. In our STRONGMAN'S HIS NAME WHAT'S HIS GAME book Carol told about her bout with fear in Managua, Nicaragua. I call my last major bout with fear the "Shoot-out at the OK Corral" and it happened in San Jose, Costa Rica.

I had suffered from a stomach ailment for a number of months that had resulted from a combination of overwork, tension and fear. At first I assumed it was an occupational hazard of living in a foreign culture with all the accompanying hassles of life, but that was just the lie of the devil that I believed.

It got to the point that it was affecting my effectiveness as a missionary. I would wake-up in the middle of the night in a state of panic with terrible abdominal pains. My weight was falling and my patience was minimal.

One night at 4 o'clock in the morning I woke-up with my nerves screaming and my stomach on fire. The devil shrieked that I was having a nervous breakdown and that my fellow missionaries would "send me home in a basket." The terror I felt in that half-awake, half-asleep state had **ALL** the symptoms of being the start of a nervous breakdown. It **FELT** like I was doomed to suffer a horrible fate.

All of this took place in a few seconds of time and just when it seemed like everything was lost, I sensed the Holy Spirit come to my rescue in a great surge of faith in my spirit. I didn't feel any better physically, but I **KNEW WITHOUT A DOUBT** that the devil's plan was not going to succeed. In a flash I saw the reason for the devil's attack was to force me to leave Costa Rica and destroy the ministry God had given to me.

It made me angry that he would try such a trick and I began rebuking the devil in the Name of Jesus and quoting the scripture,

"*...and with his stripes we (I am)are healed.*" (Isaiah 53:5) "I was healed, devil," I cried inwardly, "and you can't do this to me. I'm a child of God doing the Will of God in my life and you have no right to torment me like this. I rebuke you in the Name of Jesus."

Physically the symptoms got worse and worse. But I absolutely knew in my spirit that the devil wouldn't win this all-out attack. I continued battling in the spirit, using the Word of God.

Then the devil informed me in as helpful a voice as he could muster under the circumstances, "Take your medicine, Jerry. It will soothe you."

By now I was so mad at what he had done to me that I wasn't about to accept any advice from him and I answered, "I'm not taking any medicine because according to God's Word I am healed." And I continued claiming the Promises of God and binding the devil in the Name of Jesus.

Finally, the devil told me something which almost made me laugh out loud in spite of the seriousness of the situation because I knew this was his last trick. My nerves were still stretched like piano wires and my stomach was in terrible shape, but I knew the devil was whipped because he said in a whinny kind of voice, "Well, at least take a drink of milk."

"I'm not even drinking any milk," I retorted, "because I'm healed. Now you get out of here in the Name of Jesus!"

When I said that, the pain and nerve attack **instantly** disappeared! From one moment to the next, I went from what **appeared** to be a nervous breakdown to complete, absolute peace like I had not known for some time and I immediately dropped off into a deep, restful sleep.

That taught me a graphic, important lesson. **The devil will torment us with fear or anything else just as far as we will allow him to go.** When I recognized by the Holy Spirit what was going on and began using the Word like the two-edged Sword that it is, the devil was defeated in my life. And to this day he cannot use that to intimidate me any more because now I know the Truth and the Truth has set me free! All praise be to God!

QUESTION: "How do we dominate fear in these last days?"

We are living in the days the apostles and Early Church followers dreamed about reaching before they died—the time when Jesus returns to rapture His followers to Heaven. What an added bonus it will be not only to take part in this blessed event but also to miss having to taste of dead! *"Then we which are alive and remain shall be caught up together with them (those who have died previously) in the clouds, to meet the Lord in the air; and so shall we ever be with the Lord."* (1 Thessalonians 4:17)

Many Christians are experiencing great fear and anxiety as they observe what is going on in our world today. From one day to the next they could be faced with everything from nuclear war to stock market failure, shortages of every kind, attacks from drug-crazed addicts, terrorists or just people who have flipped out, job loss, major physical problems, family stress and breakups and threats, pressure and even harassment from every side. How much more can the world and the human race stand before everything unravels with a vengeance?

Anyone with a basic knowledge of Bible prophecy can sense that we are headed for the final wrap-up of this Age of Grace. THESE are the perilous times Paul warned would come in II Timothy 3:1-9. How do we as Christians expect to navigate through such dangerous waters?

Jesus had much to say about these days and it would be wise to pay attention to what He reveals about them. In Matthew 24:6 He commands, *"And ye shall hear of wars and rumors of war;* **see that ye be not troubled.** *"* The word, "troubled" means: "To clamor, wail, to be frightened." In modern terms that would be, **"Don't panic** when these terrible things begin happening. It doesn't matter how bad it gets, **you will make it IF you keep your eyes on me and your feet planted in my Word."**

The reason many Christians are having trouble, as they watch the awful things that are happening today, is because **they are looking at the wrong things**. Jesus tells us that in the last days men's hearts will fail them for fear. (Luke 21:26) Why? Because they are, *"...looking after those things which are coming on the earth:"*

Where are you looking? Are you looking at what is happening on the earth or at Jesus? The rest of the verse says, *"...when these things begin to come to pass, then* **look up, and lift up your heads;"** Why? Because that is where your **redemption** is coming from.

Hebrews 9:28 also adds, *"Unto them that LOOK FOR HIM*

shall he appear the second time without sin unto salvation." The word, "salvation" is the Greek word, "soteria" which means: "To rescue, to bring to safety, to deliver from danger, to save or to preserve." So if we will place our "eyes" or "faith" in Jesus, He promises to bring us victoriously through these terrible days with a shout on our lips instead of a whimper.

Don't Look At The Snake's Eyes

A farmer was on his way to work in the field when he heard a shrill, squeaking noise. He looked over and saw a field mouse acting strangely. The little mouse was trembling and quaking, frozen with fear. Then the farmer saw the reason for the actions of the mouse—a huge snake was slithering toward the mouse, coming closer and closer. The snake's eyes had locked on to the eyes of the mouse and had hypnotized it with fear.

The kind farmer decided to help the poor, helpless mouse so he took his handkerchief out of his pocket and held it in front of the mouse. Immediately the mouse turned and scampered off to safety because when the mouse stopped looking at the snake's eyes, the power of fear was broken.

That is why Jesus tells us to stop looking at the "snake's eyes" today. **When we break our vision away from the fearful things of this earth and place our faith and trust in Jesus, the devil's deception is broken and we are freed from the paralyzing results of fear!**

After giving us the order in which things will take place when Jesus returns for those who are looking for Him, Paul adds at the end of 1 Thessalonians 4, *"Wherefore comfort one another with these words."*

This world is NOT out of control nor will its destiny be decided by the devil! God is Supreme and HIS WILL SHALL BE DONE! If we stay within His Will, we will also overcome the enemy and be the more than conqueror that Paul says Jesus has made us. (Romans 8:37)When we really understand the world situation today in the light of God's Word it will be clear that the devil is just mimicking the roar of the lion—HE IS ONLY A RODENT WITH A MEGAPHONE! The Good News is that Jesus has given us the Power to take the

Strongman's His Name . . . II

devil's megaphone away from him and drive him out of our lives, PROVIDED we live according to His Word and Will. I think that's a fair exchange, don't you?

So use the Sword of the Spirit, which is the Word of God, on that fear when it attacks you. Command it to go and leave you alone from this moment on. If you will consistently resist fear it will flee from you. (James 4:7) Then don't forget to receive the power, love and sound mind He has promised us. (II Timothy 1:7) We must treat fear as a recovered alcoholic must treat liquor—he avoids it at all costs. Whenever he is tempted to drink, he has to bind the spirit of bondage and take authority over it in the Name of Jesus. That is what "fearaholics" must also do. If fear has dominated you in the past, you must not let it get started again. Each time you are tempted to be fearful you must bind the spirit of fear in the Name of Jesus and then allow the Holy Spirit to give you the Power you need to keep fear defeated in your life.

QUESTION: "What are some of the power tools God has given us to keep the devil in his place and maintain victory in our life?"

1. The Word of God — Hebrews 4:12
2. The Name of Jesus — Philippians 2:9-11
3. The Blood of Jesus and the Word of our testimony — Rev.12:11
4. The Holy Spirit within us. — John 16:13
5. The Armour of God that comes with the Sword of the Spirit. — Ephesians 6:11-18
6. The keys of Binding and Loosing. — Matthew 16:19 and 18:18

208

QUESTION: "Is 'Christian Rock and Roll' something we should have in the church today?"

This is a prime example of the deception of the devil. Listen to what Tex Marrs has to say about the subject.

"About a year ago, I spoke out against this satanic style of music on major national radio talk shows. I also did a small piece in my newsletter, Flashpoint. The response from the devil's crowd was like nothing I had ever seen before. The hornets of hell—literally! came after me!

"I have gone head-to-head with witches, the devil worshipers and the New Agers. But never had I experienced the hatred and acidic meanness that was thrown against my ministry and me personally by these pro-rock and roll people who claimed to be 'Christian.'

"Viewing the devil's ferocious counterattack against the Truth, I was both amazed and intrigued. It struck me that this was one area where the devil must be making fantastic headway in capturing souls. Otherwise, why had he launched such an unparalleled offensive to shut me up, the likes of which I had never before seen?" (Living Ministries letter, June/July, 1990)

The Russian Letter

Here is an urgent letter from the Persecuted Church in Russia which expresses grave concern over the subject of "Christian" Rock and Roll music.

"For thirty years we have suffered intense persecution, and now freedom is bringing another great harm to our churches. This damage is coming from the Christians in America who are sending rock music and evangelists accompanied by rock bands.

"Our young people do not attend these meetings because we have all committed not to participate in secular entertainment.

"This is a great burden on our hearts. Many come with Bible in hand and rock music. We are embarrassed by this image of Christianity. We do not know what words to use in urging that this be stopped. We abhor all Christian rock music coming to our country.

"Rock music has nothing in common with ministry or service to God. We are very, very against Christian Americans bringing to our country this false image of 'ministry' to God. We need spiritual bread, please give us true bread, not false cakes. It is true that rock music attracts people to the church, but not to Godly living.

"We were in prison for fifteen years and eleven years (respectively) for Christ's sake. We were not allowed to have Christian music, but rock music was used as a weapon against us day and night to destroy our souls. We could only resist with much prayer and fasting.

"Now, we have a time of more openness, and we are no longer taken to prison. However, now it is Christians from America who damage our souls. We do not allow this music in our church, but they rent big stadiums and infect teenagers and adults with their rock music.

"We, the leadership and congregations of the Unregistered Union of Churches, the former Persecuted Church, have made an agreement to not allow rock music in our Church. We urge you to join us and advise you to remove rock music from America, and certainly do not bring it to our country.

"Do not desecrate our teenagers with it. Even the unbelievers recognize it is unholy music and they cannot understand how American Christians can be so much like the world. We can give you the conclusions that after Russian unbelievers have attended these rock concerts where Christ's Word was preached, the people were very disappointed and disillusioned with Christianity.

"We call this music from hell. We urge all Americans to stop giving money for the organization of such concerts in Russia. We want only traditional Christian music in our churches. This is the unanimous decision of all our leaders." **signed**, Peter Peters, Head of the Unregistered Union of Churches, Moscow, Russia and Vasilij Ryzhuk, Elder, Unregistered Union of Churches, Moscow, Russia. How can we justify the use of such music in our churches and then wonder why we don't see revival?

The Ann Landers Letter

Here is a look at the roots of "Christian" Rock and Roll music— Rock and Roll music in all of its degenerated glory as witnessed by a mother who attended a secular Rock and Roll concert a number of years ago. She wrote to Ann Landers of the shock she experienced. The rock group was not named and we would hope that all such concerts are not as bad, but the history of Rock and Roll music

Seducing Spirits

SHOWS that it has progressively worsened from the days of the Beatles and Elvis Presley down to the demonic heavy metal and acid rock of today and who knows what else in the future.

"DEAR ANN LANDERS: A few days ago I took my 15-year-old daughter and three of her friends to a rock concert. I decided on the way out that instead of fighting the traffic both ways I would buy a ticket and see the show.

"I consider myself fairly open-minded, but I was shocked senseless by what I saw and heard.

"The language of the kids around me was unreal. Every other word started with F or S. When one of the rock stars appeared in a G-string, the crowd went wild. The fellow was 99.9 percent naked.

"The audio was turned up and the audience went crazy. My eardrums began to pop...Then the kids around me started to light up joints.

People all over the place began to toss firecrackers...I have never been so petrified in my life, not only for me but for every person in that building. There were broken bottles all over the place and several fights going on. The police were nowhere to be seen.

"I lost track of the number of people who had to be carried out...I saw two couples having sex right out in the open. Others were taking off their clothes all over the place.

"When the concert ended, there was an incredible stampede. I was afraid if I fell I would be stomped to death. I prayed for strength to stay on my feet.

"On the way home (still shaking) I told my daughter that she would not go to another rock show as long as she lived in my house...And I am going to stick to it.

"Here is some advice to every parent who is reading this. Don't ask your kids what goes on at these performances. Go see for yourself...—Madison, WI."

"DEAR MADISON: I am at a loss to comment on your letter. ...I do know...that last December two teenagers were crushed to death and 29 were hospitalized following a show in Nashville..." (Sunday Oklahoman, February 7, 1988, reprinted, Bible in the News, May 1988, pages 21,22)

Now we have "cross-over" Christian musicians and singers who have their music albums for religious people and other music albums for the sinners. Where is it going to stop?

It is difficult these days to distinguish between the music of some "Christian" contemporary music stations and the ungodly Rock and Roll stations. The "beat" is the same and the words are indistinguishable so what is the difference? Oh, but that is the point, we are told. By having "Christian" Rock and Roll, we will attract the unsaved

211

young people to Jesus who are deceived by Rock and Roll.

Let's just carry that over to other sinful practices. Should we also have "Christian" taverns and "Christian" houses of prostitution and "Christian" crack houses so we can appeal to sinners who are attracted to those areas of sin? What does the Bible say our methods should be in attracting sinners to the Gospel of Jesus Christ? *"And I, if I be lifted up from the earth, will draw all men unto me."* (John 12:32) It is the crucified Christ, who died for the sins of the world, that is going to get the unsaved person's attention, not some sugar-coated form of sin which is still sin no matter how it is packaged.

Let's get real about this. Who's trying to kid who? When the lines between Christianity and the world become so blurred that we can't distinguish the difference between the two, then Christianity is no longer Christianity—it has become the world! *"...choose you this day whom ye will serve; whether the gods which your fathers served that are on the other side of the flood, or the gods of the Amorites, in whose land ye dwell; but as for me and my house, we will serve the Lord."* (Joshua 24:15)

"Out of the same mouth proceedeth blessing and cursing. My brethren, these things ought not so to be. Doth a fountain send forth at the same place sweet water and bitter? Can the fig tree, my brethren, bear olive berries? either a vine, figs? so can no fountain both yield salt water and fresh." (James 3:10-12)

"No servant can serve two masters: for either he will hate the one, and love the other; or else he will hold to the one, and despise the other. Ye cannot serve God and mammon." (Luke 16:13)

We are **supposed** to be different from the world. In our society today there is such an aversion to being different that it, unfortunately, is affecting the Church in a very negative way. The truth is that if there is no difference between Christians and sinners, why would the sinners want to be Christians? The theory that we have to have music that is borrowed from the world to attract the unsaved is flawed from the beginning. There must be more than just a change of words—there has to be a change in the **spirit of the music** to do any lasting, eternal good in an individual.

The basic problem with "Christian" Rock and Roll is that it still retains the "spirit" of the world and that is dangerous to individuals and to our churches. God help our young people and churches if they continue to buy-in to this gigantic deception of the devil!

QUESTION: "Are my family prayers effective against drugs, rock music, etc. in the lives of my family?"

Your prayers can bind the powerful influence Satan has enjoyed in their lives. His work is hindered when you consistently bind him and loose the Holy Spirit of Adoption and Truth into their lives. The Holy Spirit is released to draw their attention to His Word from every available source. *"For ye have not received the spirit of bondage again to fear; but ye have received the Spirit of adoption, whereby we cry, Abba, Father."* (Romans 8:15) They are part of the harvest and according to Luke 10:2 Jesus will send out laborers to bring them in. *"The harvest truly is great, but the laborers are few: pray ye therefore the Lord of the harvest, that he would send forth laborers into his harvest."*

If we are consistently faithful with our part, the Lord of the harvest will be faithful with His.

QUESTION: "Will Satan try to attack us again?"

Satan will try to attack **any** moment he finds an entry into our life through either sin or neglect. He tries to catch people asleep and not focused or actively working for God.

However, when we ask for the things of the Holy Spirit...we can be assured that is what we will receive. *"And I say unto you, Ask and it shall be give you; seek, and ye shall find; knock, and it shall be opened unto you. For every one that asketh receiveth; and he that seeketh findeth; and to him that knocketh it shall be opened. If a son shall ask bread of any of you that is a father, will he give him a stone? or if he ask a fish, will he for a fish give him a serpent? Or if he shall ask an egg, will he offer him a scorpion? If ye then, being evil, know how to give good gifts unto your children: how much more shall your heavenly Father give the Holy Spirit to them that ask him?"* Luke 11:9-13

CHILDREN
(WARNING-ARTICLE EXPRESSES A STRONG OPINION BY THE AUTHORS)

It is time for Christians to get angry at what the devil is doing to people in this world. John 10:10 tells us that it is the devil who steals, kills and destroys. If you need an example, just look at what he is doing to our children these days.

1- He is butchering them by the millions around the world through abortion.

2- He is using children for satanic ritualistic abuse that involves terrible sexual activities that leave them scarred physically, mentally and spiritually for life.

3- He is using them for child pornographers to photograph and

213

abuse for the sake of evil adults who feed their twisted sexual appetites by viewing such degenerate behavior.

4- He is killing children in wars around the world by using them, for instance, as human mine detectors; blowing them to bits so troops can pass safely through the mine fields.

5- He is starving babies and children by the millions because of devilish political bureaucracy that allows food to rot in ships because of red tape chicanery.

6- He is condemning innocent babies and children to the demon of drug addiction; savaging their minds, ruining their bodies and making them spiritual zombies.

7- He is using movies, television, music and humanism in the public schools to destroy a generation of children and rob them of their moral fiber to stand against or even recognize the dismantlement of their life of all that is decent, Godly and good.

What will happen when this generation of children, who somehow survive the brutal, animalistic, ravaged, abusive time called "childhood," do when they, in turn, treat their own children as their parents have treated them, creating an even more vile, oppressive scene for their offspring than they experienced themselves?

When this younger generation of demon possessed, rebellious, Rock and Roll addicts, drugged, sex-crazed, alcoholic, abused, teenyboppers hit the world scene in full force, we will have something with which to reckon. We just think things are bad now, but we haven't seen anything yet if Jesus tarries a few more years.

It is true that there are still MANY, MANY good, decent kids left for which we are so thankful. We know the Holy Spirit is working actively among those who will stand and be counted for God. But even so, some of our Christian young people are being brainwashed by the demonic lifestyle that is sweeping the earth. And the terrible, sad fact is that they don't even know they are being brainwashed.

It is time to get mad at the Devil!

Are we going to sit around as people did in Germany while Hitler butchered the Jews and let the devil get away with what he is doing? We are in this world as followers of Christ to STOP the devil's activities in the spirit realm and win this world to Christ.

Part of the problem is that many Christian parents are so messed-up spiritually themselves that it will be a miracle if they are able to keep themselves on track long enough to make it to heaven. There are "Christians" today who lie, steal, swear, drink alcohol, cheat on their spouses—in short—live like sinners and then wonder why their homes and lives resemble padded cells in a mental institution.

IT IS TIME FOR GOD'S PEOPLE TO GET BACK TO THE

BASICS OF CHRISTIAN LIVING! We are in a battle with the devil. He is cruel, fierce, without mercy, totally evil and in large part, winning the war on this earth because God's people have become CONSCIENTIOUS OBJECTORS or even OUTRIGHT DESERTERS FROM THE ARMY OF THE LORD.

God's people have got to quit playing games while the devil runs loose, chopping up babies through abortions, brainwashing children and turning teenagers into spiritual illiterates who have never felt the Power of God.

We know there are many hurting people in our churches these days who are in great need. We would not want to minimize this fact in any way. But we should be honest with them about what has gotten them into that condition so that they can be helped. Some of the reasons many are hurting is because they have been playing around with the devil, sucking up the demonic corruption of this world, believing the lies of this world's system that says money, pleasure and power is what life is all about; neglecting the basic things God says we must do if we are to survive these last days. The devil is having a heyday beating on them because they have opened doors to him in their lives by the way they live.

IT IS TIME CHURCHES START PREACHING THAT SIN KILLS, that people are going to hell if they don't get right with God, that prayer and God's Word are more important than anything else, that it is ABSOLUTELY NECESSARY to have the moving of God's Spirit in our lives and churches, that our purpose here on earth is not to pile up treasures on earth, but to reach this world with the Gospel through our finances, prayers and lives. When that happens we will start seeing a turn-around in people's lives and, as a result, in the world.

The truth is that God has given us the victory over the devil, the world and the flesh, but **we must APPLY that victory to the circumstances of our life on a daily basis.** (for some it may be an hourly basis) The Church of Jesus Christ must be ready for the flood of evil that is saturating this earth. When these abused, twisted children and teenagers hit our churches as young adults it will take more than gimmicks, counseling and programs to straighten them out. It will take a blast of the Power of the Holy Spirit to break through the shell of sin, scars and deception that Satan has used to imprison them, and set them free spiritually, heal their minds and bodies and put them on the road to heaven.

We will HAVE to know how to cast out demons and provide the kind of spiritual atmosphere in our churches and homes that is needed so the Holy Spirit can accomplish the necessary work in their lives to restore them to normalcy.

215

Jesus said, *"Behold, I give you power to tread on serpents and scorpions, and over all the power of the enemy: and nothing shall by any means hurt you."* Luke 10:19) Don't be afraid of these last days if you are living a life that is according to the Word and pleasing to God.

This is our day to show this world the power of God's Holy Spirit so His Truth and Power can set people free!

QUESTION: What signs indicate your child may be into satanism?

"Social worker Dale Trahan said that Satanism is a growing problem among teens. He has been researching satanic beliefs for three years and was contracted to organize the program for Hartgrove's new Center for the Treatment of Ritualistic Deviance.

"We don't know the percentages because so much is secretive, but we do know...it is beginning to show up throughout the country, Trahan said.

"Youngsters involved in Satanism often exhibit unusual behavior, which can include suicide attempts, violent rages, rejection of family, drug use and sexual promiscuity.

"Other signs might include a drastic drop in grades, intensified rebellion, a strong interest in heavy-metal music, role-playing games or horror films, and the use of occult symbols such as '666' or upside-down crosses.

"They usually are intelligent, creative and bored with traditional pursuits...and generally have a feeling of being different and not belonging, are often underachievers and generally have a feeling of being powerless." (Statesman Journal newspaper, Thursday, Sept. 7, 1989 section B, page 2)

But there is power in the Name of Jesus. Do battle in the spirit realm if your child is caught in this deception. Don't let the devil steal them. It is God's will that your children be saved!

Spirit of Anti-christ 28

QUESTION: "Are all out-of-body experiences good?"

No, they aren't. Some are from God and the individuals involved are actually transported in the spirit to heaven. Others are shown what Hell is like in all of its horror.

But other experiences project a giant deception of the devil on the victim to trick them into believing, for instance, that everyone is going to heaven whether they accept Christ as their Savior or not. The people who experience these deceptions talk about the tremendous "love" and "light" they feel emanating from a magnificent "being." Many of them even feel it is Jesus Christ, but the message they receive from the "being" is not supported by God's Word. For example, they are told: (1) "Love is the most important thing—we are to love everyone." It is true that love is very important, but love is not enough to get us to heaven. We must repent of our sins, accept and receive Christ as our Savior and live according to all the teaching of the Bible **as well as** love everyone. Another one is:(2) "All religions eventually lead to heaven." Not true. *"Enter ye in at the strait gate: for wide is the gate, and broad is the way, that leadeth to destruction, and many there be which go in thereat: because strait is the gate, and narrow is the way, which leadeth unto life, and few there be that find it."* (Matthew 7:13,14)

Can you see the deception of the devil? He wants to convince people that Christ and the Bible aren't important. There are even cases of people, who are clearly not believers in Jesus Christ, who experience very positive out-of-body activity after death and come back to tell everyone that they no longer are afraid to die—that there is nothing to worry about because it will all work out in the end. Once again it doesn't matter how awesome the experience may be—it must be something which God's Word supports or it is a lie.

217

Satan can appear very God-like, but he always unmasks himself by what he says. Just because there is light and love and a beautiful city does not prove that God is involved in the experience. *"And it is no wonder, for Satan himself masquerades as an angel of light: so it is not surprising if his servants also masquerade as ministers of righteousness."* (II Corinthians 11:14,15 Amplified Bible)

We don't accept everything that comes down the road even when it has all the "appearance" of being something from God. *"Beloved, believe not every spirit, but try the spirits whether they are of God:"* (I John 4:1) If the devil comes to you as an angel of light, ask him where you can find what he is telling you in the Bible. Then check it out carefully. Don't be surprised, though, if he tries to bully you into accepting what he has said as truth when you try to pin him down by asking for Bible references. Just command him to shut-up and go in the Name of Jesus.

If it is really from God, He will not mind in the least if you ask Him to give you two or three scriptures from the same context as He has been speaking from which support what He is talking about.

God's Word must be our point-of-reference in every part of our life!

QUESTION: "Is *Embraced by the Light* a good book?"

"Mormon author Betty J. Eadie claims to have a message from Jesus—one she personally received in heaven. That's where she discovered that we all assisted God with Creation, we chose our mission in life before we were born, and we're all destined to go to heaven when that mission is fulfilled.

"Those are among the revelations described in *Embraced by the Light*, Eadie's best-selling account of her near death experience." (*Mormon Book Lures Christians,* Christian Retailing, 6/18/1994)

Some of the "truths" that were supposedly revealed to the author were:

1. Pre-mortal existence.
2. God and Jesus are separate beings.
3. Everyone will be saved.
4. We select the illnesses we will suffer.
5. We, not God, determine when we come to earth.

Eadie is a former hypnotherapist which is also significant.

Although the author may truly believe she received these "truths" from God, the Bible does not support that conclusion. This is an illustration of the fact that any experience must be measured by whether it is supported by God's Word which is the final authority for us.

QUESTION: "Is it true that satanists and New Agers are infiltrating our churches, trying to cause problems and destroy them?"

Yes they are.

I appeared twice on the same TBN television program with a man who had been a channeler, allowing demons to speak through him, since he was three-years-old. He told on the program that it had been his job to infiltrate churches and try to steer the people into New Age doctrine and activities. He would study the people in the congregations to pinpoint their areas of weakness so he could exploit that part of their life and bend them into the New Age philosophy and life.

He even gave prophecies or "words from the Lord" in the churches he infiltrated, that were in reality messages from demons. He said he and others, who also did this, found that it wasn't necessary to speak in the guttural, evil-sounding demonic voice that usually comes out of a demon possessed person. That would have given away their real identity to the church people they were dealing with. So they stopped that and spoke in a natural voice because they found that the evil sounds were only theatrics anyhow.

This kind of thing went on for many years and apparently no one ever suspected that he was a demonic plant in the churches. Can you imagine this scene—demon possessed people actively involved in churches to the point that they were giving messages from "God" and **no one knew the difference!**

No one, that is, until a Spirit-filled Christian "nailed" him through the Gift of Discernment and labeled him as a source of evil in the church. It so impressed him that God's Spirit was superior to the devil's that he got saved and delivered from demon possession. Now he is doing all he can to expose the New Agers for what they are.

The Bible tells us, *"no weapon that is formed against thee shall prosper."* (Isaiah 54:17) The original Hebrew of this verse could read,

"No plan, no instrument of destruction, no satanic artillery shall push you or run over you, but it will be done away with." Isn't that a great promise? We are hearing these days about animal and human sacrifices, that the witches and warlocks are fasting to bring about the downfall of pastors, ministries and churches and many other demonic activities, but there is nothing to fear if we are living lives that are pleasing to God, according to His Word. The New Agers can intimate that the Christians and Jews will be the first ones to be killed when they take over the world, but I believe they will be in for a great surprise because the Greater Power lives within us. (I John 4:4) God says we are the ones who are the more than conquerors. (Romans 8:37) And I believe the New Agers and the Satanists won't be able to get their plans off the ground until God's people are taken out of this world in His secret rapture of the saints. There may be persecution, but that will only free us to show the Power of God in an even greater way! (see chapter 3, The Three Hebrew Children)

Many Christians are terrorized by the threats of the New Agers and satanists when, in reality, it should make them angry that the devil is so brazen as to try that kind of stuff on our turf, in our nation! **The devil can only take what we give him.** Let's not only stop giving him any ground, but let's take back what he has gained through fear and ignorance.

Raul Vargas, pastor of the large crusade-church in San Jose, Costa Rica where Carlos Kessler and his family attend, told me of a witch doctor who came to his Sunday night service with the express purpose of creating a disturbance. Before Raul began to preach, he prayed, binding the devil in the Name of Jesus and loosing the Holy Spirit to do His Work in the service that night, as we always do in the crusades. **From that point on, the witch doctor said he could do nothing—he could not talk or move—and at the close of the service he accepted Christ as his Savior!**

The Bigger They Are, The Harder They Fall!

Don't let the blasphemous Goliaths of the devil fake you out in these last days. They must bow their knees to the Name of Jesus. Be like David when he shouted at Goliath, "*...thou comest to me with a sword, and with a spear, and with a shield: but I come to thee in the* *name of the Lord of hosts, and the God of the armies of Israel, **whom thou has defied.***" (I Samuel 17:45) Because God's Power was greater than the devil's, it was the giant who was in danger. People do not defy the God of Israel and get away with it. David knocked Goliath down with a rock and cut his head off with the giant's own sword. To have his head cut off with his own sword is an embarrassment to any giant worth his salt. In a symbolic sense that is what God wants us to do today—shut the devil's mouth with the "rock of faith" right between his eyes and cut off his influence in people's lives and, as a result, in our nation and the world!

I was preaching in the Cartago crusade church in Costa Rica when a young man sitting on the front row jumped up, faced the congregation and shouted, "He's lying, He's lying!"

The Presence of the Holy Spirit was so powerful that I didn't even stop preaching. I just spoke to the demons and commanded, "Shut up and sit down in the Name of Jesus," and went right on preaching as though nothing unusual had happened.

The man shut up and sat down. Later, he got to his feet and tried to do it again, but nothing would come out of his mouth. A couple of the men from the church took him outside the auditorium and dealt with him. Later, after he got cleaned up he became an evangelist and I had the privilege of preaching in one of his outdoor crusades when we returned to Costa Rica for ministry. To God be all the glory!

I've Got To Get Out Of Here!

Before we actually came into the full knowledge of how to do correct, biblical spiritual warfare, Carol had an experience which probably helped push us, as much as anything else, into getting more knowledge of how it should be done.

She had started an English language Bible study of upper-class ladies made up of missionary wives from other missions, Embassy women and upper class Spanish ladies. The meeting was held in a nice conference room in one of the hotels and it was usually a great time of studying the Bible and visiting.

This particular day, however, the meeting was interrupted by a North American woman who began manifesting demonically right in the middle of the chorus time. She cursed and talked out loud in a very course manner which was in stark contrast to the very proper way things were done normally.

Carol looked around for someone to take care of the situation before she realized that **she** was the leader of the group and therefore it was her responsibility to do something about this demon possessed woman.

The lady sitting next to the troubled woman kept repeating over and over again in an audible voice, "In the Name of Jesus, in the Name of Jesus."

The possessed woman told her, "If you don't stop that I'm going to hit you!"

The lady kept repeating it and the possessed woman backhanded her in the mouth.

With visions of her refined Bible study degenerating into a free-for-all, Carol got to her feet and started for the troubled woman, not knowing what she would say and with her knees shaking. When she got to the woman, she stuck her finger under the woman's nose and commanded, "In the Name of Jesus, shut up!"

It wasn't real theological but it got results. One great lesson she learned was that it is necessary to say **what** you want done in the Name of Jesus.

The woman tried to say something, but couldn't. She took deep breaths and still nothing came out.

As Carol and the other ladies sang choruses about the Blood of Jesus the woman became more and more agitated. Finally, she got up, wadded up the chorus sheet and ran through the doorway. Only after she had gotten to the door could she talk again and she shouted, "I've got to get out of here, I can't stand it anymore!"

Then she woman then went to a bar and a drug store and trashed them both, ending up in jail that night.

We prayed with her a few days later and she was helped considerably. Shortly after, she left the country and we lost contact with her.

The sad thing is that we didn't have teaching of any kind to prepare us for dealing with demon possessed people. It should have been a basic part of missionary training or even Bible college or Seminary, but it didn't happen, so we had to learn it on the front lines of the spiritual battle. In fact, we have said many times that if we hadn't learned these principles of spiritual warfare, we would not have survived the mission field. God is faithful and the Holy Spirit became our Teacher for which we will be forever thankful.

How's God Treating You Today?

Carl Johnson, a Missionary-Evangelist, came to Costa Rica with a special ministry of encouraging people to receive the fullness of the Holy Spirit with the evidence of speaking in an unknown language. Our new converts in the Crusade churches were ready to receive anything that was in the Bible and when we began teaching on the book of Acts about the Holy Spirit, they received the message with open hearts. I love new converts! Under Carl's ministry in the Spirit, 2500 people received their prayer language in a period of 5 weeks. What a glorious time that was!

Carl related an experience he had in South America that encouraged us so much. It illustrates that we are not alone in this battle. Just as Elisha demonstrated to his servant in II Kings 6:17, there are more angelic hosts with us than there are forces of the enemy.

While holding a crusade in Surinam he had to battle all kinds of demonic activity, as the case usually is in those circumstances. A man in the crusade had been bothering Carl in a number of ways. One thing in particular he wanted to know was where Carl was staying, and because Carl suspected the man was up to no good, he would never tell him.

One evening he left his hotel room to meet the missionary who was coming to take him to the crusade that night. As he stepped into the hallway, the occupant of the room directly across from Carl's door stepped into the hallway also. He was a giant of a man and Carl greeted him as was his custom, "How's God treating you today?" If the person answered, "Not too good" or a variation of that, Carl would tell him/her about Jesus.

But the giant answered Carl, "Very well, sir, very well!"

They walked together to the elevator and when they reached it, Carl looked through the glass doors where the stairs came up and saw the weird guy from the Crusade running up the steps as fast as he could climb, with a demonic look in his eyes. The man burst through the glass doors and ran smack into the giant. As his eyes traveled up the huge frame he calmed down in a hurry and Carl told him to get

223

back down the stairs and to never come back. The man meekly obeyed him.

Carl and the tall man entered the elevator and descended to the ground floor. Just as they were arriving, Carl glanced down at his watch to see if he was on time to meet the missionary. In that split second the huge, giant of a man instantly disappeared and when the doors opened, Carl was alone! God had sent an angel to protect him!

No wonder he replied when Carl asked how God was treating him, "Very well, sir, very well!"

"Have not I commanded thee? Be strong and of a good courage; be not afraid, neither be thou dismayed: for the Lord thy God is with thee whithersoever thou goest." (Joshua 1:9)

QUESTION: Do miracles happen today?

The miracles became so common in our crusade churches that we didn't realize the full impact of what actually took place in this incident, but in retrospect it was a spectacular happening.

Spiritual warfare also involves the supplying of our physical needs. Many Christians struggle with the deception of poverty. They may have been raised with a poverty mentality in their family and they find it difficult to receive their daily needs by faith. Fear enters the picture and the devil keeps them so strapped financially that they can't enjoy the life God has given them or help spread the Gospel by giving money to their church and missionary outreaches. If that is your problem, just listen as Carol tells about how that we can be sure God is aware of our every need.

There Is Nothing Impossible With God

It started on Christmas Eve in our newest crusade-church in a suburb of San Jose, Costa Rica, called Moravia. After conducting services every night for 10 months, we had planned a program of special music, filmstrips of the Christmas story, and refreshments to celebrate the new convert's first Christmas as believers.

The ladies of the church baked mountains of cakes and I borrowed all the electric coffee makers I could locate among my friends in anticipation of the capacity crowd of new converts we were expecting.

The service began at 9 p.m. on Christmas Eve, and what a wonderful time we had singing Christmas carols and hearing God's Word. At the half-way point, the ladies served cake and coffee to everyone.

Afterward, as we were cleaning up, I noticed there were still 10 double sheet cakes left over. So I suggested that we serve refreshments at the New Year's Eve service the following week. I figured that if we froze the remaining cakes and cut the pieces in half, we would have enough for about 400 people.

You should have seen us trying to get everything into our compact car after the service! Ten sheet cakes on large pieces of plywood, and all our equipment, plus five people, but we made it. That was a sweet little car because there was frosting everywhere!

The following week we loaded the cakes back into the car and drove to church.

When we walked through the front door of the church, one of the girls met me and said, "We already have over 500 people here. Are you sure we will have enough cake?"

I looked at the crowd and said hopefully, "I think if we cut some of the bigger pieces of cake twice, we'll make it."

After the ladies finished cutting the cake in smaller pieces, they counted them carefully. But the people kept coming. Shortly before serving time, the crowd was counted one last time, and we found there were 150 more people than pieces of cake!

"What are we going to do, Sister Robeson? Everyone will take at least one piece of cake, and we don't have enough for everyone."

Silently I sent up an S.O.S. "Lord, you know that most of these new converts have had to walk long distances to be in their first New Year's Eve service as Christians. They've come tonight to hear Your Word and worship You just as the people followed You out into a desert place when You were here on earth and You fed them. Your Word says that You are 'the same yesterday, and today, and forever.' So I'm coming to you now because **we've** got a problem!"

I turned to the ladies who were helping me and asked them, "Do you believe that if we pray the Lord can multiply these cakes as He did when He fed the 5,000 with five loaves and two fishes?"

Heads started to nod in agreement and they said, "OK, **you** pray!" So we joined hands, and I prayed a short prayer asking the Lord to perform a miracle. Then the young ladies picked up the trays of cake and left to serve the large crowd of new believers.

Time after time they returned for more cake; and as they finished serving the people, many of them came back with tears streaming down their faces. Not only had everyone in the church been served one piece of cake, but many had taken two, and there was a mound of cake left over!

What a time we had praising the Lord for this, the first miracle of the New Year. I'm sure none of us will ever forget the time we served real angel cake! *"Man did eat angels' food:"* (Psalm 78:25) Truly we serve a God who will supply all our needs, even if it takes a miracle!

*"But my God shall supply **all your need** according to his riches in glory by Christ Jesus."* (Philippians 4:19)

It would certainly feel better to send them somewhere specific where they will not bother us again, but it isn't scriptural to do so. Jesus never cast demons into the pit or abyss while He was on this earth so it must not have been something He thought should be done. In fact, there is no scriptural precedent to support this practice.

The only place in the Bible that refers to the devil being thrown into a pit—a bottomless pit, is Revelation 20:1-3. But the only one cast in is the devil himself. "*And I saw an angel come down from heaven, having the key of the bottomless pit and a great chain in his hand. And he laid hold on the dragon, that old serpent, which is the Devil, and Satan, and bound him a thousand years, and cast him into the bottomless pit, and shut him up, and set a seal upon him, that he should deceive the nations no more, till the thousand years should be fulfilled: and after that he must be loosed a little season.*"

Notice that it only takes an angel so ordinary that his name isn't even mentioned, to bind Satan with a great chain, throw him in the pit and seal him up for 1000 years. And he does it with just one hand because the other hand is holding the great chain! What an illustration of how far Sin will bring someone down—in this case, Satan. It doesn't pay to disobey God.

It is apparent that demons actually have a right to be on the earth at this time because of the choice that Adam and Eve made in the Garden of Eden when they were deceived and fell into sin. Otherwise Jesus would have been the first to get rid of them once-and-for-all. All He would have had to do was command every one of them to go to the pit at once and they would have had to obey Him—they obeyed every other command He gave them, didn't they? So why didn't Jesus do that? Possibly the answer can be found in the incident when Jesus cast the demons out of the man from the country of the Gergesenes. When Jesus confronted them they cried out, *"What have we to do with thee, Jesus, thou Son of God? Art thou come hither to torment us BEFORE THE TIME?"* (Matthew 8:29) Jesus didn't tell them they were wrong and even honored their request to go into the pigs after being cast out of the man.

It is probably a minor point as to whether or not we should send the demons to the pit, but it points up the fact that it is so easy to get away from the Truth and into something that feels good and appears to make sense—but is wrong. Once we start this kind of thing, where does it stop? This is why spiritual warfare has gotten into trouble and the weird and wacky in the past. Someone grabs an obscure verse that isn't even in the same context as spiritual warfare and says, "Here's our scriptural backing!" and off they go down the road to error. Let's demand that God's Word be the standard for how we teach, minister and conduct our lives.

QUESTION: "What do people mean when they tell us we are unenlightened and are on a lower spiritual plane than they are?"

I John 4:5 says to beware of people that try to apply the terminology of the world to the things of God. *"They are of the world: therefore speak they of the world, and the world heareth them."* Those of the world's system speak in worldly terms.

Paul assures us that we as believers are on the highest spiritual plane possible because of our faith in Christ. *"Even when we were dead in sins hath quickened us together with Christ, (by grace are ye saved;) And hath raised us up together, and made us sit together in heavenly places in Christ Jesus:"* Ephesians 2:5,6

Satan, as an angel of light (II Corinthians 11:14) tells people in the occult they have access to secret spiritual knowledge, but according to Matthew 16:23 and I Corinthians 2:8 they only have the earthly, limited knowledge that Satan has access to. Every believer has access to the hidden wisdom of God and the mysteries of the kingdom of heaven.

"Because it is given unto you to know the mysteries of the king-dom of heaven, but to them (the unbelievers) it is not given." (Matthew 16:23)

"But we speak the wisdom of God in a mystery, even the hidden wisdom, which God ordained before the world unto our glory: Which none of the princes of this world knew: for had they known it, they would not have crucified the Lord of glory." (I Corinthians 2:6,7)

"But the anointing which ye have received of him abideth in you, and ye need not that any man teach you: but as the same anointing teacheth you of all things, and is truth, and is no lie, and even as it hath taught you, ye shall abide in him." (I John 2:27)

QUESTION: "What is gnosticism or "secret knowledge" religion?"

"Gnosticism is a term derived from the Greek, *gnosis,* 'knowledge,' and applied to a body of heretical teaching.

"The Gnostic keynote was knowledge: the possession of secrets which would ultimately serve the soul's union with God. The end of knowledge was thus salvation, comprehending purification and immorality, and it was set in a conceptual framework of contemporary philosophy, mythology, or astrology, different elements prevailing in different systems. In this God's entire separation from matter (conceived, according to Greek dogma, as inherently evil) was assumed, and the drama of redemption enacted within a complex of intermediary beings.

"Almost every cardinal Christian doctrine was revised by such thinking. The mythological setting of redemption had no point of contact with the Old Testament (which was rejected or ignored), and diminished the significance of the historic facts of the ministry, death, and resurrection of Jesus. Indeed, the view of God and man which it implied often led to the denial of the reality of Christ's sufferings and sometimes of the incarnation. Creation was an accident, a mistake, even the malevolent act of an antigod. Resurrection and judgment were reinterpreted to refine their 'crudities.' Sin became a defilement which could be sloughed off: the Church was replaced by a club of illuminati possessing secrets hidden from those uninitiated who claimed the same Redeemer. Ethics centered on maintaining purity: involving in many cases the denial of sex and other bodily appetites, in others (from the same premises) the practice of unrestrained indulgence." (*The New Bible Dictionary*, J.D. Douglas, ed., Eerdmans Publishing Co. p.473.)

Many people who are in the new-age mysticism, witchcraft, unity, secret lodges, etc. get entangled with what they term as secret knowledge. It is the old game of seeking and finding Satanic knowledge which promises all the answers of the Universe, but in reality is limited only to the things that pertain to mankind. (Matthew 16:20)

"The secret things belong unto the Lord our God: but those things which are revealed belong unto us and to our children for ever, that we may do all the words of this law." (Deuteronomy 29:29)

Through the gifts of the Holy Spirit, God has provided us with unlimited knowledge. He gives us what we need, when we need it. *"If any of you lack wisdom, let him ask of God, that giveth to all men liberally, and upbraideth not; and it shall be given him. But let him ask in faith, nothing wavering. For he that wavereth is like a wave of the sea driven with the wind and tossed. For let not that man think that he shall receive any thing of the Lord. A double-minded man is unstable in all his ways."* (James 1:5-8)

QUESTION: "Is it true that many modern translation versions of the Bible are not accurate and are even misleading?"

Yes, it is.

"A devious strategy that seems to be paying off for the New Age is that of revising—or updating—the Bible to make it more 'meaningful' to modern times.

"The New Age truly believes that its current campaign of subtle subversion and quiet undermining of Christian doctrine will result in total victory. It will not be necessary to stage a direct, frontal assault on Christianity...What is planned is an insidious, veiled attack." (*Dark Secrets of the New Age*, by Texe Marrs, p. 212, 205)

As unbelievable as it may sound, Satan is using this method in an attempt to subvert the message of the Gospel of Jesus Christ and prepare the way for the worship of the Antichrist.

Since we stress the fact so forcefully in our books that we must follow and live according to what God's Word says, we felt it was important to make sure the translations we are using are accurate so that we can be sure we are standing on Truth in these last days and not some men's fables. *"For we have not followed cunningly devised fables..."* (II Peter 1:16)

To our horror we have found that many of the modern versions have been translated using purposely corrupted Greek manuscripts that drasticly change the meaning of thousands of strategic passages. Whole scripture verses are deleted. New Age and satanic twists are applied to mislead the reader.

Listen to the anguished words of Dr. Frank Logsdon, the co-founder of the NASB: "I must under God renounce every attachment to the *New American Standard Version*. I'm afraid I'm in trouble with the Lord...its frighteningly wrong; and what am I going to do about it.

"The deletions are absolutely frightening...there are so many...Are we so naive that we do not suspect Satanic deception in all of this?

"[Y]ou can say the *Authorized Version* [KJV] is absolutely correct. 100% correct!" (*New Age Bible Versions,* by G.A. Riplinger, authors recommendation page preceding the table of contents)

At times the process of brainwashing Christianity is not so subtle. The American Bible Society in the past titled its Bibles for worldwide use, *"Good News for a New Age."*

Let's look at some examples of this rape of God's Word.

The Lord's Prayer Luke 11:2

"Our Father which art in heaven" has been reduced to just "Father." "...as in heaven, so in earth" and, "...but deliver us from evil" have been **cut out**. The NIV also **cuts out** "Thy will be done..." The modern versions guilty of this crime against God's Word are: "...the NIV, NASB, Living Bible, NRSV, Good News for Modern Man, New Century Version, The New American Bible, and the New Jerusalem Bible." (Ibid., p. 57)

JOHN 6:69 "...Christ, the Son of the living God," is translated by the NIV and NASB as the, "...Holy One of God." This assault on the Name of Jesus Christ is fully revealed when it is understood that the only other time in the Bible that the title, "...Holy One of God," is used, occurred when the demons addressed Jesus in Luke 4:34 and

Mark 1:24 with this very same title-name. So these translators chose the name the demons called Jesus Christ instead of how the Holy Spirit referred to Him!

DANIEL 11:38 Because the New Age speaks about the devil as "the Force" and "Forces" the NIV and NASB has retooled 11:38 from the KJV, "But in his estate shall he honor the God of forces" into this abomination, "...but instead he will honor a god of fortresses." Apparently their reason for this unscholarly action is to hide the fact that the Antichrist will indeed be under the control of "the God of forces" or the devil, just as is stated in the KJV of God's Word.

MARK 10:21 Jesus' instructions to "...come, take up the cross and follow me" becomes, with the stroke of a computer key, "Then come, follow me" in the NIV and NASB. How easily they would like to destroy the Cross of Jesus Christ, but they will not succeed!

MATTHEW 18:11 The NIV **cuts** this important scripture **out** of the Bible, "For the Son of Man is come to save that which was lost." Both the NIV and the NASB state in the footnotes that most ancient manuscripts do not contain this verse. The truth is that "there are four times as many manuscripts which have the verse than the few that omit it." (Ibid., p. 193)

DANIEL 3:25 In describing the scene when Nebuchadnezzar threw the three Hebrews into the fiery furnace the KJV tells of the appearance of Jesus Christ in the flames with them, "...and the form of the fourth is like the Son of God." Here is how the NIV and the NASB translates it, "...the fourth looks like a son of the gods." Just any old god will do for New Agers, I guess. Their utter gall and arrogance is astounding!

MARK 9:44 The NIV **deletes** this scripture and the one that follows below—they just disappear into thin air! "Where their worm dieth not and the fire is not quenched." and LUKE 17:36 "Two men shall be in the field, the one shall be taken and the other left." The reason for these deletions is that New Agers do not believe in the Judgement—and with good reason!

EPHESIANS 5:9 Both the NIV and the NASB translate, "...the fruit of the Spirit" as, "...fruit of the light." They don't even so much as capitalize the first letter of "light" to signify that the "light" is God. What blasphemy!

ROMANS 1:16 The word, "Christ" is **omitted** here and in the verse that follows this one. "...the gospel of Christ" becomes just plain, "...the gospel..."

PHILIPPIANS 4:13 KJV "I can do all things through Christ which strengtheneth me," is now, "I can do everything through him who gives me strength." At least the NASB has the decency to capitalize the letter "H" in "Him" to show it refers to God.

MARK 13:5,6 Once again the translators attempt to **delete** Christ from the Gospels. KJV "Take heed lest any man deceive you: For many shall come in my name, saying, I am Christ and shall deceive many." Both the NIV and the NASB have it, "Watch out that no one deceives you. Many will come in my name, claiming, 'I am he' and will deceive many." Not only do they have the audacity to make this change, but they do it in the face of the fact that, "[The word 'he' does not appear in any Greek MS (manuscripts) either.]" (Ibid., p. 313)

Another trick of these translators is to insert the word "the" before "Christ" which completely changes the significance of who is being spoken of in the verse. The New Agers believe that Jesus Christ was just one of many Christs so when they say "the" Christ they are actually lowering Jesus to the level of just any god. This slight of hand stunt is done at least 27 times in the New Testament, all the way from Matthew 1:17 to Hebrews 6:1.

In both our books and seminars we hammer away at the fact that we must not form our doctrines on experiences. Another reason we can add for not getting caught in this satanic trap is because the New Agers think that experience is the best way to learn. Marilyn Ferguson in her book *Aquarian Conspiracy*, boasts: "[D]octrine is losing its authority...Doctrine...is second hand experience. Knowing is...the transmission of knowledge through direct experience." (Ibid., p. 328)

ACTS 8:37 The NIV just **wipes** this scripture **out** of the Bible. "I believe that Jesus Christ is the Son of God." KJV

I JOHN 4:3 It is exciting to realize that we are actually living in the last days of this age when we see what these modern translators have done to these scripture, which unerringly pinpoints **them** for who and what they are—**deceivers**! KJV "And every spirit that confesseth not that Jesus Christ is come in the flesh is not of God:" Both the NIV and the NASB translate it like this, "...every spirit that does not acknowledge Jesus is not from God."

Apparently they are so deceived that they don't understand what they are translating because II John 1:7-11 talks specifically about this kind of activity. *"For many deceivers are entered into the world, who confess not that Jesus Christ is come in the flesh. This is a deceiver and an Antichrist...Whosoever transgresseth, and abideth not in the doctrine of Christ, hath not God...If there come any unto you, and bring not this doctrine, receive him not into your home, neither bid him God speed: For he that biddeth him God speed is partaker of his evil deeds."* We must be very careful of these modern translations who are preparing the way for a final New Age Bible that will be acceptable to all of the world's religions.

We have been sold a bill of goods by these people that the King James Version is not as good a translation or as easy to read or understand as their "modern" translations. That is just not true!

"The Flesch-Kincaid research company's Grade Level Indicator [proved that] the KJV ranks easier in 23 out of 26 comparisons." (Ibid., p. 195)

What is the reason for this? "The KJV uses one or two syllable words while new versions substitute complex multi-syllable words and phrases." (Ibid., p. 196)

Here are some examples to show what is meant by this:

MATTHEW 14:24 KJV "But the ship was now in the midst of the sea," The NASB, "But the boat was already many stadia away from the land," The NASB uses "invalidated" for "made" in the KJV of Matthew 15:6, "opportune" for "ready" in John 7:6, "concerning" for "of" in John 16:8, "contemporaries" for "equals" in Galatians 1:14 and "do not exasperate" for "provoke" in Colossians 3:21. That is not clearer and easier to read, that is more complex.

"...recent scholarship demonstrates that the majority of manuscripts, as seen in the traditional Greek *Textus Receptus* and its translation, the *King James Version*, represent the earliest, broadest (numerically and geographically) and most consistent edition of the New Testament. On the other hand the new versions and their underlying unsettled Nestle's-Aland type eclectic text, use later readings, representing a narrow 'fraction of 1%' of the extant manuscripts, from one locale." (Ibid., p. 503)

The information in this chapter is by no means complete in its scope. We only want to demonstrate that an evil, dangerous problem has been created by many modern translators and that we must be very careful in our choice of translations of God's Word. Personally we will use only the KJV and the Amplified Bible from this point on.

For extensive information about the problem of modern versions of the Bible we would suggest that you read the book, *New Age Bible Versions*, written by G.A. Riplinger. If your bookstore does not carry it, you can write to A.V. Publications, Box 388, Munroe Falls, Ohio 44262 for instructions on how to purchase it.

QUESTION: "What are subliminal messages / are they dangerous?"

Any message you don't hear or understand that is fed in to your mind has a potential for problems. The growing interest in subliminal messages by the world's system is evident in the growing popularity of mind control. They promote their wares by telling people they can lose weight, stop smoking, become successful in business and have better health.

But there is an even greater danger than these seemingly harmless messages they are promoting. Satan is trying to use every means possible to invade our minds. He wants to "initiate" as many as he can into mind-control so he will have a common ground to communicate with humanity. What better way to get people tuned into messages they aren't aware of, but are willing to listen to anyway! Satan uses hypnosis, mind altering drugs, subliminal message tapes, TM, spiritism and every other means he can to entrap them before his time runs out.

Satan knows that faith comes by hearing God's Word so he seeks to turn peoples minds away from God's Word by building strongholds in their minds that restructure their thinking. These mind control methods limit people to earthly and demonic knowledge. The New-Age entices people into becoming receptive to the "higher levels of understanding" through various methods.

As a result, the great majority of people today are looking for health, wealth and wisdom by occultic means. Even some Christians convince themselves that God is looking the other way and doesn't notice them. But this stuff brings them into occultic bondage because God will not tolerate such foolishness. These "Christians" may still go through the forms and activities of serving God, but their headship has changed hands.

We are admonished in the Bible not to seek counsel of the ungodly. When we need wisdom we ask the *real* source of all wisdom— the Holy Spirit and God's Word. We show we are of God by the way we talk and the activities we are involved in. Magic, spirit guides, new-age music, etc. are all smoke screens to entice the victims, but only God really satisfies. Don't settle for second class passage into eternity because second class doesn't have the same destination as first class on this ride.

Cut off all the practices of these new "enchantments" of the New Agers and get back to the Way, the Truth, and the Life!

QUESTION: "What is New Age Music?"

New age music is a lilting melody that runs up and down the harmonic scales without the distraction of words. The music doesn't follow any particular beat, it just flows along, making the person feel like they are floating in a sea of pleasant sound waves. This music is promoted as a method of relaxation for listeners and hidden in the music are deadly subliminal messages to entrap the mind. Leave it alone! A number of people have called us who were snared by the enemy after listening to these musical strains. One lady said that the first time she listened to New Age cassettes, she experienced a sharp pain in her brain and from that moment on the pain moved from place to place in her body. She was constantly under attack from demonic entities, had terrible dreams and constant delusions. She said voices threatened her about many things.

Isaiah 28:12 tells us that the Holy Spirit has given us a prayer language to refresh us and cause the weary to rest and be refreshed. *"Thou will keep him in perfect peace, whose mind is stayed on thee; because he trusteth in thee.* (Isaiah 26:3)

If you have listened to or been involved with subliminal messages or New Age music, repent and ask God to forgive you. Renew Jesus as the Lord of your life and command the devil to take his hands off your mind. You can have the mind of Christ that Paul mentioned in I Corinthians 2:16.

QUESTION: "What is the Luciferian initiation that the New

Agers use to entrap people?"

The New Age Movement is trapping people by using visualizations and other esoteric (spiritual) experiences. People love to delve into the unknown. Reincarnation is as old as Babylon itself. Astrology is nothing new—the Chaldeans were very good at it thousands of years ago. These activities became the birthing parents of the Hindu religion, Voodoo practices and almost every other religion that leaves out Jesus Christ's redemption by faith. There seems to be a constant push to "go where no man has gone before..." and yet it has all been done before in one shape or another over the centuries.

Many people, Christian included, enter into the Luciferian initiation by using visualizations and other forms of occultic practices that are so common. People control others by using "prophecies" and "words of knowledge" that are anything but the genuine gifts of the Holy Spirit. Believers must try the spirits and know when the Spirit of God is speaking and when it is an imitation.

The New Age is nothing more than a satanic revival of the age-old occult practices that are aimed at destroying the Church. Lucifer said in Isaiah 14, "I will exalt my throne above the stars of God:" He also promised Eve in the garden that if she ate of the fruit of the tree of knowledge of good and evil that she would become as a god. *"...that in the day ye eat thereof, then your eyes shall be opened, and ye shall be as gods, knowing good and evil."* (Genesis 3:5) He continues to use the same tattered line of reasoning with each succeeding generation with great success. If he can't get people openly or secretly involved with evil, then he tries using the earthly, carnal knowledge to solve the world's problems by suggesting things like socialistic governments, welfare states, euthanasia and abortion to control the population.

A few years ago we had dinner with some people in Florida who had been involved in the New Age Movement. They outlined some of the ways the New Agers have successfully introduced their deception. They shared that stress management is one of the prime ways people are seduced into such things as transcendental meditation and visualization activities. They said that many stress management people are actually New Age gurus who have adapted a certain amount of "christianese" so they can speak the language of church people. Scriptures are added to their programs and their literature is repackaged to infiltrate churches. During their sessions of inner healing they substitute the image of Jesus instead of a wise man for the visualization. No one questions this. Directions are blindly followed. These sessions result in more victims being added to the initiation rites and more people becoming dependent on spirit-guide masters (demons).

When these infiltrators seduce and deceive people into participating in a Luciferian initiation through these methods, they have caused them to set up another god in their lives. They have pledged their allegiance to "the god of this world," Satan. If you have been involved in any of these activities, or anything similar, repent and renounce them. Don't argue or put it off another day, reconfirm your faith in Jesus Christ as your only Lord and Savior and follow God's Word specifically.

QUESTION: "What is the worship of the goddess 'Sophia?'"

It is amazing what is taking place these days, under the heading of "Christianity." A feminist conference held in Minneapolis, MN in November, 1993 spotlighted this new/old concept.

"In a feminist liturgy, the Reimaging conference of about 2,200 women shared in a communion of milk and honey.

"'Our maker Sophia, we are women in your image,' the Sunday worship liturgy said. 'With nectar between our thighs we invite a lover, we birth a child; with our warm body fluids we remind the world of its pleasures and sensations.

"The conference, organized mostly by the Minneapolis Council of Churches, marked the mid-point of the 'Ecumenical Decade of the Churches in Solidarity With Women' observed by the World Council of Churches and National Council of Churches.

"Other accounts emphasized that keynote speakers said such feminist revisions aimed to be a 'second Reformation' in Christian churches. A liturgy celebrating lesbians also was held.

"Some Re-imaging conference speakers rejected traditional notions of Christ's death to atone for sin because 'in light of social experience, such as slavery and female sexual abuse, understandings of sacrifice, atonement, and martyrdom are being re-examined,' it said.

"Participants at the three-day conference included 405 Presbyterians, 391 Methodists, 313 Lutherans, 234 Roman Catholics and representatives of many other Protestant groups." (*Churches in an uproar over worship of "Sophia"*,Larry Witham, The Washington Times, National Weekly Edition, June 13-19, 1994.)

Deception is so strong that God's Word seems to mean nothing to these blinded followers.

Spirit of Death 30

QUESTION: "How can I keep from being afraid of death and dying?"

Just as we must learn to live by faith, we have to learn how to **die** by faith also.

There is a brainwashing process that goes on in this world's society which we must recognize and resist. We are children of God and joint heirs with Christ Jesus (Romans 8:16,17) and therefore we are not subject to the same kinds of things which sinners have to put up with in this life. Jesus has set us free from the bondage of the devil which includes, among other things, sin, disease, fear, poverty and death.

As far as death is concerned, we are now on God's timetable instead of the devil's, provided we prepare for this transition part of our life by filling our heart with faith and not fear. *"Forasmuch then as the children are partakers of flesh and blood, he (Jesus)also himself likewise took part of the same; that through death he might destroy him that had the power of death, that is, the devil; and **deliver them who through fear of death were all their lifetime subject to bondage**."* (Hebrews 2:14,15)

Jesus has freed us from bondage so we have the right to resist any fear and particularly, in this case, the fear of death. Whenever it sticks up its ugly head we must take authority over it and bind it in the Name of Jesus and then loose or allow the faith of God to flood our spirit. Don't allow thoughts to linger in your mind of how you may die or what death will feel like physically or any of the other tricks the devil uses to get us out of faith and into fear. Cast them out of your mind as II Corinthians 10:3-5 tells us and think about what God tell us death will be like for His children. Throughout the New Testament

239

death is referred to as going to sleep and waking up in Heaven. That sounds wonderful and that's exactly what it is! It is part of our inheritance as a child of God **IF** we will receive it by faith, just as we do anything else God has promised us in His Word.

I always thought I would eventually have to die of a disease or an accident like everyone else if the Lord didn't return for His Church during my lifetime. In fact, the devil had convinced me that I would die young. I had to reverse that in the Name of Jesus when I came into the knowledge of what God's Word says about it.

I remember one day when Richard Jeffery, the evangelist who taught us how to have open-air crusades in Latin America, and I were doing some work at the crusade lot in Managua, Nicaragua. While he was working on a step-ladder, he slipped slightly and jabbed his rib-cage on the top part of the ladder. It was painful and I noticed that he immediately rebuked the devil in the Name of Jesus. I was concerned that he had damaged his heart or something and I asked if He was alright. After a couple of minutes he was just fine.

He must have noticed that I was looking at him more than I would have normally and he told me something I don't remember ever having heard in my life. He said, "Jerry, I am believing God not to die of a disease. I am believing by faith that when my time comes to die, I will just take a breath and be gone from this world and enter into the Presence of Jesus." And he went on to explain that there is no place in the Bible that says we have to die of a disease. We don't have to live like sinners and we shouldn't have to die like them either.

I asked him rather naively, "Is it possible to do that?" And he said that it was and explained what I have been talking about here. Then he told me about his brother-in-law who had died exactly as he had just described.

Wow, I thought! And I said out loud, "I claim that for myself in the Name of Jesus." From that time, the fear of death has been a thing of the past in my life. After all, what is there to fear if there is just a breath between earth and Heaven?

To start with, God has promised us at least 70 years of life and 80 years if things are going well and we desire to remain here on earth instead of going to be with the Lord. *"The days of our years are threescore years and ten, or even if by reason of strength fourscore years..."* (Psalms 90:10) So unless the Lord tells us something different and we are absolutely sure it is the Lord and not the devil trying to trick us into an early departure, we can stand against anything that would try to take us out early in the Name of Jesus. To a certain extent God leaves up to us how long we want to continue living in this cesspool of a world. As long as we are able to contribute to the kingdom of God, He needs everyone He can get down here on earth to accomplish what needs to be done.

We have a friend in Portland, Oregon who told us that she was able to tell the spirit of death to take a hike when it came to her prematurely. She suffered a stroke at an age that was considerably younger than 70 years. Shortly after that she saw a dark-robed figure coming down the stairs toward her and she knew it was the spirit of death. She rebuked it in the Name of Jesus and told it to go. Immediately it turned and left and has never come back!

When we understand that we can live by faith in God's Word and know without a shadow of doubt that no one or no thing can take us out ahead of God's schedule for our life, it removes all the fear that surrounds death. People who have died, gone to heaven and come back from the dead say that death is actually a pleasurable experience. If they were in pain, the pain instantly disappeared and they felt more alive than they had ever felt in their life. So what is there to fear? **It is just a trick of the devil to rob us of the last victory we will ever have over the him in this life.**

If Jesus tarries, I want my death to be an uplifting experience for everyone that I leave behind and a testimony of the Power of God to the sinners.

Unfortunately, most Christians do not know they have the right to believe for such a death. It doesn't mean that they don't go to heaven—they just go there in a way that isn't necessary or uplifting for those who are left behind.

Goodbye World Goodbye

A friend of ours, Rev. Reuben J. Carlson, provided a perfect example of how to die . He was the pastor of the church we attended while attending Bible College and later became the top official of our denomination in that area of the U.S. In his later years we were able to visit with him from time to time and I always appreciated his positive attitude and encouragement. He always complimented me on the articles that I had written for different magazines and he told me that he had followed our progress as missionaries through the years.

After one of our missionary services while on itineration, he took the time to write out a detailed chart of the multiplying power of numbers. It showed that if one person would win another person to the Lord, who would win another and each one who is won to Christ would win another, that the world could be won to Christ in just a few years.

He was asked to play the piano and sing a couple of songs for the 74th Annual Session of the Northwest District Council of the denomination we belong to—his 60th consecutive District Council. One of the songs he chose to sing was, "Good-bye World, Good-bye." It tells of the fact that this world isn't our home because we are headed for a land in the sky. The author tells people not to weep for him when he leaves for heaven and that the Lord will be with him as he flies through the sky to heaven. The last phrase of the song says, "Heaven is near and I can't stay here. Good-bye World, Good-bye!"

After he finished singing and playing, he went back to his seat and within a few moments, at the age of 80, was actually doing what he had just sung about—arriving in the presence of the Lord. **Now that's the way to die!** The most repeated comment in the District Council after that was, "What a way to go!"

Of course the ultimate would be to go up in the Rapture when Jesus returns for His Church and not even have to use the door of death. According to all the signs in God's Word, that event should happen very soon. What a joy it will be to enter the presence of our Lord and Savior and know that we will be with Him forever more!

God's Time-Table

More people than we realize are advised by the Holy Spirit that death is about to take place in their life. Few people recognize the name of Len L. Legters, the co-founder of Wycliffe Bible Translators. Together with Cameron Townsend, he saw the need to translate the Bible into the language of the indigenous peoples of the earth and did something about it. He was an unpredictable kind of person and he often shocked people when speaking in churches. He thought nothing of walking up and down the aisle and directing his words to individuals seated in the pews. But he was very successful in getting the ear of the Christian public during his time so that he could gather recruits for Bible translation.

Cameron Townsend tells of the summer when he asked Len, "Could you give us a little more time next year?"

"I'd like to, Cameron," Legters replied, "but the Lord has not given me liberty to take appointments beyond next May. I don't know why. Maybe He'll promote me to glory by then."

In May, 1940 Legters died suddenly of a heart attack. Leonard Livingston Legters went home to glory to claim the victor's crown. (In Other Words, March, 1992, page 6)

I believe that if we are walking step by step with the Lord, He will indicate to us that our time in this life is coming to an end before we reach the final step so that we can be prepared for the last step. Why would He withhold this information from us if He has faithfully revealed His will to us step by step throughout our entire Christian life? And remember that He will reveal this to us in our spirit or heart, not our head, because that is where the Holy Spirit communicates with us. (John 4:24)

Martin Luther King

"Correta Scott King recalls the chilling prophecy her husband made after seeing reports of John F. Kennedy's assassination in Dallas in 1963."

"He said, 'That's exactly what's going to happen to me,' says King...He didn't expect to survive the revolution—the non-violent revolution that he was leading." (USA Today, January 9, 1989, page 8A)

"Pistol" Pete Maravich

"Pistol" Pete Maravich was a fantastic basketball player who played for the Atlanta Hawks professional basketball team for ten years. He was the type of player who passed or dribbled the ball behind his back with the same ease as other players did it normally and scored points at a record pace throughout his high school, college and pro career.

While doing an interview with sportswriter, Andy Nuzzo, for the Beaver County Times in Beaver, PA, he made the comment, "I don't want to play 10 years in the NBA, and die of a heart attack at age 40."

After retiring he stayed in great shape, working out regularly. But one day he fell to the floor during a pick-up basketball game and died of a heart attack—at the age of 40 after he had played 10 years in the National Basketball Association! (USA Today, January 7, 1988, page 2C)

Listen To What Jesus Is Preparing For Us

Heaven and the New Jerusalem will be so wonderful that we really can't grasp the full scope of it with our human minds at this time. It is probably just as well because if we could, we would want to go there immediately.

Carl Johnson, a Missionary-Evangelist and a dear friend who ministered in our crusades when 2500 new converts received the Baptist of the Holy Spirit in San Jose, Costa Rica, had the privilege of seeing this awesome sight.

He had just returned from the mission field after holding crusades that had left him exhausted. He lay down to get some rest one day and fell into a deep sleep. When he woke up, but before he opened his eyes, the Holy Spirit spoke to him in his heart and said, "This is the New Jerusalem."

When he opened his eyes he saw right through the ceiling of the bedroom and the roof of the house as though they didn't exist and in the sky was the most beautiful sight he had ever seen in his life. A huge city was descending down from heaven toward him. It looked like a translucent, blue-green jewel and as it got closer he could distinguish the spires and large buildings that rose in breathtaking beauty above the walls of the city. The Glory and Light of God shone out of it and he felt an unusual anointing of the Holy Spirit settle down upon him. Just like the Bible says, the walls were made of sparkling, precious stones and the streets were made of pure, transparent gold. He could actually feel the peacefulness, purity and power emanating from the city.

Then the Voice of God asked him, "Do you think it is worth it to live for Me in this life so you can go to this city in the next life?"

Carl answered, "Oh yes Lord!"

As he was viewing the details of this beautiful Holy City, the New Jerusalem, he heard the doorbell ring and realized a couple who needed counseling had arrived for their appointment. He was so disturbed because the vision faded away that it took all the grace he could muster to be decent to them when he answered the door.

An interesting result of the vision was that he didn't want to continue living any more—he wanted to die and go to that wonderful place. It took days for the vision to fade from his mind enough so that he could start living a normal life again.

But he said, "Now I know what is waiting for us on the other side! It will truly be worth it all because the most important thing, in addition to all that I saw, is that Jesus will be there too, and we'll be with Him forever!"

That, my friend, is the bottom line!

About the Robesons

Drs. Jerry and Carol Robeson were missionaries to Latin America for twenty years. They ministered in Nicaragua, Costa Rica, Paraguay, Jamaica, Mexico, and Chile. They specialized in open-air crusades that were held every night in an area of the city where a new church was needed. One crusade church in Costa Rica, for example, has more than ten thousand people in attendance.

The Robesons maintained an active television and radio ministry. They produced and directed more than twelve hundred Christian television programs in Latin America and the United States, and many hundreds of radio broadcasts. They also appeared as guests on television programs all over the United States.

Jerry and Carol graduated from Northwest College in Kirkland, WA, and Vision International University in San Diego, CA, where they each earned a Ph.D. in Theology in 1996.

Jerry died September 18, 1999, leaving his wife, Carol, with two married daughters and four grandchildren. Until 1999, the Robesons were both very active in teaching seminars in the United States and Latin America. Carol continues on with this ministry of seminars and retreats.

Carol is the owner of Shiloh Publishing House, located in Keizer, Oregon. She has authored *God's Royal Road to Success, Mighty Warriors Jr. Activity and Coloring Book,* and *Dynamic Faith of the Believer.* With her husband she co-authored *Strongman's His Name...What's His Game?* and *Strongman's His Name...II.*

For information, contact:
Dr. Carol Robeson
P.O. Box 100
Woodburn, OR 97071
1.800.607.6195

OTHER BOOKS AND MATERIALS BY
DRS. JERRY AND CAROL ROBESON

Books:
➤ Trust God, He Really Does Love You
➤ Suddenly…One Was Taken! (a novel)
➤ La Guerra Espiritual (Spanish)
➤ Le Combat Spiritual (French)
➤ Dynamic Faith of the Believer
➤ Knee-Deep in the Soup (for teens)
➤ Faith in Eruption
➤ Mighty Warriors, Jr. Activity and Coloring Book
➤ Strongman Study Guide

Video Teaching:
➤ Riding in the Chariot to Victory (1 hr.)
➤ Strongman's His Name (8-hr. series)

Teaching on Cassette:
Singles
➤ Verses of Praise from the Psalms
➤ Can Satan Understand Tongues or Read Your Mind?
➤ Conquering the Giants of Your Life
➤ God's Royal Road to Success
➤ How to Receive Your Prayer Language
➤ Rise and Be Healed!
➤ Run to Win!
➤ What's Wrong with Rock Music?
➤ Spirit, Soul, & Body
➤ The Holy Spirit in Esther
➤ The Mystery of Job
➤ False Prophecy Unmasked

2-Cassette Series
➤ Victory over Fear
➤ Good Things Come from God!

4-Cassette Albums
➤ Seven Ministry Gifts to Success
➤ The Nine Gifts of the Holy Spirit
➤ The Fruit of the Spirit
➤ Strongman's His Name (6-hour live seminar)

6-Cassette Album
➤ Strongman audio book with study guide booklet

12-Cassette Series
➤ Strongman audio book, The Nine Gifts of the Holy Spirit, Victory over Fear, and two booklets
➤ Deluxe Gift Set: The Nine Gifts of the Holy Spirit, Seven Ministry Gifts to Success, and The Fruit of the Spirit, plus one study guide